Workshop on Language Generation and Summarisation 2009

(UCNLG+Sum 2009)

Held at ACL-IJCNLP 2009

Singapore
6 August 2009

ISBN: 978-1-61738-449-3

Printed from e-media with permission by:

Curran Associates, Inc.
57 Morehouse Lane
Red Hook, NY 12571

CURRAN ASSOCIATES INC. proceedings.com

Some format issues inherent in the e-media version may also appear in this print version.

Printed by Curran Associates, Inc. (2010)

Association for Computational Linguistics
209 N. Eighth Street
Stroudsburg, Pennsylvania 18360

Phone: 1-570-476-8006
Fax: 1-570-476-0860

acl@aclweb.org

Additional copies of this publication are available from:

Curran Associates, Inc.
57 Morehouse Lane
Red Hook, NY 12571 USA
Phone: 845-758-0400
Fax: 845-758-2634
Email: curran@proceedings.com
Web: www.proceedings.com

Preface

The Workshop on Language Generation and Summarisation (UCNLG+MT) took place in Singapore on 6th August 2009, as part of ACL-IJCNLP'09. It was the third of the UCNLG workshops which have the general aims

1. to provide a forum for reporting and discussing corpus-oriented methods for generating language;
2. to foster cross-fertilisation between NLG and related fields by looking for common ground through corpus-oriented approaches; and
3. to promote the sharing of data and methods in all language generation research.

Each of these workshops has a special theme: at the first workshop (at Corpus Linguistics in 2005) it was the use of corpora in NLG, at the second (at MT Summit in 2007) it was Language Generation and Machine Translation. The special theme of this third UCNLG workshop was Language Generation and Text Summarisation. The core aim was to provide a forum for NLG and summarisation researchers to examine the similarities and differences between their current approaches to generating language, and to explore the potential for cross-fertilisation and the extent to which resources and techniques can be shared between the NLG and summarisation fields.

The call for papers issued at the end of January 2009 elicited a good number of high-quality submissions, each of which was peer-reviewed by three members of the programme committee. The interest in the workshop from leading researchers in both fields and the quality of submissions was high, so we aimed to be as inclusive as possible within the practical constraints of the workshop. In the end we accepted six submissions as long papers and four as short papers.

The resulting workshop programme packed a lot of exciting content into one day. We were delighted to start the workshop with a keynote presentation from Prof Kathy McKeown, one of the most eminent researchers in NLG and its application to summarisation. Our technical programme included papers on structuring abstracts (Saggion), selecting content for summaries (Cheung, Carenini and Ng), sentence compression (Xu and Grishman; Cordiero, Dias and Brazdil), sentence revision for summarisation (Tanaka et al.), evaluating summaries (Owczarzak and Dang), corpus-based generation of directions (Schuldes et al.), reducing redundancy in summarisation (Hendrickx et al.), generation of narrative content (Caropreso et al.) and summarisation of non-textual content (Kumar et al.). The programme also included a session reporting the results of the Generation of Referring Expressions in Context (GREC) shared task evaluations (part of the Generation Challenges 2009 initiative), and still had space for a general discussion on synergies between NLG and summarisation.

We would like to thank all the people who have contributed to the organisation and delivery of this workshop: the authors who submitted such high quality papers; the programme committee for their prompt and effective reviewing; our keynote speaker, Kathy McKeown; our panelists (at the time of writing), Ed Hovy, Kathy McKeown and Donia Scott; the ACL-IJCNLP 2009 Organising Committee, especially the workshop chairs, Jimmy Lin and Yuji Matsumoto, and Jing-Shin Chang; all the particpants in the workshop and future readers of these proceedings for your shared interest in this exciting area of research.

August 2009 Anja Belz, Roger Evans and Sebastian Varges

Workshop Organisers: Anja Belz, University of Brighton, UK
Roger Evans, University of Brighton, UK
Sebastian Varges, University of Trento, Italy

Programme Committee: Enrique Alfonseca, Google Zurich, Switzerland
Srinivas Bangalore, AT&T, USA
Robert Dale, Macquarie University, Australia
Daniel Marcu, ISI, University of Southern California, USA
Chris Mellish, Universiy of Aberdeen, UK
Ani Nenkova, University of Pennsylvania, USA
Amanda Stent, SUNY, USA
Michael Strube, EML Research, Germany
Stephen Wan, Macquarie University, Australia
Mike White, Ohio State University, USA
Jianguo Xiao, Peking University, China

Invited Speaker: Kathy McKeown, Columbia University, USA

Panelists: Ed Hovy, ISI, University of Southern California, USA
Kathy McKeown, Columbia University, USA
Donia Scott, Open University, UK
(at time of writing)

Table of Contents

Invited Paper

Long Papers

Short Papers

GREC'09 Papers

Workshop Program

6 August, 2009

Morning Session 1: Sentence Compression and Revision

08:30–09:00 *Unsupervised Induction of Sentence Compression Rules*
Joao Cordeiro, Gael Dias and Pavel Brazdil

09:00–09:30 *A Parse-and-Trim Approach with Information Significance for Chinese Sentence Compression*
Wei Xu and Ralph Grishman

09:30–10:00 *Syntax-Driven Sentence Revision for Broadcast News Summarization*
Hideki Tanaka, Akinori Kinoshita, Takeshi Kobayakawa, Tadashi Kumano and Naoto Katoh

10:00–10.30 Coffee Break

Morning Session 2: Invited Talk / Content Selection

10:30–11:30 *Query-focused Summarization Using Text-to-Text Generation: When Information Comes from Multilingual Sources*
Kathy McKeown

11:30–12:00 *A Classification Algorithm for Predicting the Structure of Summaries*
Horacio Saggion

12:00–12:30 *Optimization-based Content Selection for Opinion Summarization*
Jackie Chi Kit Cheung, Giuseppe Carenini and Raymond T. Ng

12:30–13:50 Lunch

6 August, 2009 (continued)

Afternoon Session 1: Evaluation

13:50–15:00 GREC 2009 Shared Task Evaluation results session

The GREC Main Subject Reference Generation Challenge 2009: Overview and Evaluation Results
Anja Belz, Eric Kow, Jette Viethen and Albert Gatt

The GREC Named Entity Generation Challenge 2009: Overview and Evaluation Results
Anja Belz, Eric Kow and Jette Viethen

ICSI-CRF: The Generation of References to the Main Subject and Named Entities Using Conditional Random Fields
Benoit Favre and Bernd Bohnet

UDel: Generating Referring Expressions Guided by Psycholinguistc Findings
Charles Greenbacker and Kathleen McCoy

JUNLG-MSR: A Machine Learning Approach of Main Subject Reference Selection with Rule Based Improvement
Samir Gupta and Sivaji Bandopadhyay

UDel: Extending Reference Generation to Multiple Entities
Charles Greenbacker and Kathleen McCoy

WLV: A Confidence-based Machine Learning Method for the GREC-NEG'09 Task
Constatin Orasan and Iustin Dornescu

15:00–15:30 *Evaluation of Automatic Summaries: Metrics under Varying Data Conditions*
Karolina Owkzarzak and Hoa Trang Dang

15:30–16:00 Coffee Break

Afternoon Session 2: Short Papers/Discussion

16:00–16:20 *Visual Development Process for Automatic Generation of Digital Games Narrative Content*
Maria Fernanda Caropreso, Diana Inkpen, Shahzad Khan and Fazel Keshtkar

16:20–16:40 *Reducing Redundancy in Multi-document Summarization Using Lexical Semantic Similarity*
Iris Hendrickx, Walter Daelemans, Erwin Marsi and Emiel Krahmer

16:40–17:00 *Non-textual Event Summarization by Applying Machine Learning to Template-based Language Generation*
Mohit Kumar, Dipanjan Das, Sachin Agarwal and Alexander Rudnicky

17:00–17:20 *Creating an Annotated Corpus for Generating Walking Directions*
Stephanie Schuldes, Michael Roth, Anette Frank and Michael Strube

17:20–18:00 Panel-led discussion on synergies between summarisation and NLG, including shared tasks

Invited paper

Query-focused Summarization Using Text-to-Text Generation: When Information Comes from Multilingual Sources

Kathleen McKeown
Department of Computer Science
Columbia University
kathy@cs.columbia.edu

Abstract

The past five years have seen the emergence of robust, scalable natural language processing systems that can summarize and answer questions about online material. One key to the success of such systems is that they re-use text that appeared in the documents rather than generating new sentences from scratch. Re-using text is absolutely essential for the development of robust systems; full semantic interpretation of unrestricted text is beyond the state of the art. Better summaries and answers can be produced, however, if systems can generate new sentences from the input text, fusing relevant phrases and discarding irrelevant ones. When the underlying sources for summarization come from multiple languages, the need for text-to-text generation is even more pronounced.

In this invited talk I present research on query-focused summarization over a variety of sources, including news, broadcast news, talks shows and blogs. Our research combines approaches from summarization and information extraction to answer open-ended questions. Because our sources include informal genres as well as formal genres and draw from English, Arabic and Chinese, text-to-text generation is critical for improving the intelligibility of responses. In our systems, we exploit information available at question answering time to edit sentences, removing redundant and irrelevant information and correcting errors in translated sentences.

Proceedings of the 2009 Workshop on Language Generation and Summarisation, ACL-IJCNLP 2009, page 3,
Suntec, Singapore, 6 August 2009.

Long Papers

Optimization-based Content Selection for Opinion Summarization

Jackie Chi Kit Cheung
Department of Computer Science
University of Toronto
Toronto, ON, M5S 3G4, Canada
jcheung@cs.toronto.edu

Giuseppe Carenini and **Raymond T. Ng**
Department of Computer Science
University of British Columbia
Vancouver, BC, V6T 1Z4, Canada
{carenini,rng}@cs.ubc.ca

Abstract

We introduce a content selection method for opinion summarization based on a well-studied, formal mathematical model, the p-median clustering problem from facility location theory. Our method replaces a series of local, myopic steps to content selection with a global solution, and is designed to allow content and realization decisions to be naturally integrated. We evaluate and compare our method against an existing heuristic-based method on content selection, using human selections as a gold standard. We find that the algorithms perform similarly, suggesting that our content selection method is robust enough to support integration with other aspects of summarization.

1 Introduction

It is now possible to find a large amount of information on people's opinions on almost every subject online. The ability to analyze such information is critical in complex, high-stakes decision making processes. At the individual level, someone wishing to buy a laptop may read customer reviews from others who have purchased and used the product. At the corporate level, customer feedback on a newly launched product may help to identify weaknesses and features that are in need of improvement (Dellarocas et al., 2004).

Effective summarization systems are thus needed to convey people's opinions to users. A challenging problem in implementing this approach in a particular domain is to devise a content selection strategy that identifies what key information should be presented. In general, content selection is a critical task at the core of both summarization and NLG and it represents a promising area for cross-fertilization.

Existing NLG systems tend to approach content selection by defining a heuristic based on several relevant factors, and maximizing this heuristic function. ILEX (Intelligent Labelling Explorer) is a system for generating labels for sets of objects defined in a database, such as for museum artifacts (O'Donnell et al., 2001). Its content selection strategy involves computing a heuristic relevance score for knowledge elements, and returning the items with the highest scores.

In GEA (Generator of Evaluative Arguments), evaluative arguments are generated to describe an entity as positive or negative (Carenini and Moore, 2006). An entity is decomposed into a hierarchy of features, and a relevance score is independently calculated for each feature, based on the preferences of the user and the value of that feature for the product. Content selection involves selecting the most relevant features for the current user.

There is also work in sentiment analysis relying on optimization or clustering-based approaches. Pang and Lee (2004) frame the problem of detecting subjective sentences as finding the minimum cut in a graph representation of the sentences. They produce compressed versions of movie reviews using just the subjective sentences, which retain the polarity information of the review. Gamon et al. (2005) use a heuristic approach to cluster sentences drawn from car reviews, grouping sentences that share common terms, especially those salient in the domain such as 'drive' or 'handling'. The resulting clusters are displayed by a Treemap visualization.

Our work is most similar to the content selection method of the multimedia conversation system RIA (Responsive Information Architect) (Zhou and Aggarwal, 2004). In RIA, content selection involves selecting dimensions (such as *price* in the real estate domain) in response to a query such that the desirability of the dimensions selected for the query is maximized while respect-

Proceedings of the 2009 Workshop on Language Generation and Summarisation, ACL-IJCNLP 2009, pages 7–14,
Suntec, Singapore, 6 August 2009.

ing time and space constraints. The maximization of desirability is implemented as an optimization problem similar to a knapsack problem. RIA's content selection method performs similarly to expert human designers, but the evaluation is limited in scale (two designers, each annotating two series of queries to the system), and no heuristic alternative is compared against it. Our work also frames content selection as a formal optimization problem, but we apply this model to the domain of opinion summarization.

A key advantage of formulating a content selection strategy as a p-median optimization problem is that the resulting framework can be extended to select other characteristics of the summary at the same time as the information content, such as the realization strategy with which the content is expressed. The p-median clustering works as a module separate from its interpretation as the solution to a content selection problem, so we can freely modify the conversion process from the selection problem to the clustering problem. Work in NLG and summarization has shown that content and realization decisions (including media allocation) are often dependent on each other, which should be reflected in the summarization process. For example, in multi-modal summarization, complex information can be more effectively conveyed by combining graphics and text (Tufte et al., 1998). While graphics can present large amounts of data compactly and support the discovery of trends and relationships, text is much more effective at explaining key points about the data. In another case specific to opinion summarization, the *controversiality* of the opinions in a corpus was found to correlate with the type of text summary, with abstractive summarization being preferred when the controversiality is high (Carenini and Cheung, 2008).

We first test whether our optimization-based approach can achieve reasonable performance on content selection alone. As a contribution of this paper, we compare our optimization-based approach to a previously proposed heuristic method. Because our approach replaces a set of myopic decisions with an extensively studied procedure (the p-median problem) that is able to find a global solution, we hypothesized our approach would produce better selections. The results of our study indicate that our optimization-based content selection strategy performs about as well as the heuristic method. These results suggest that our framework is robust enough for integrating other aspects of summarization with content selection.

2 Previous Heuristic Approach

2.1 Assumed Input Information

We now define the expected input into the summarization process, then describe a previous greedy heuristic method. The first phase of the summarization process is to extract opinions about an entity from free text or some other source, such as surveys. and express the extracted information in a structured format for further processing. We adopt the approach to opinion extraction described by Carenini et al. (2006), which we summarize here.

Given a corpus of documents expressing opinions about an entity, the system extracts a set of evaluations on aspects or features of the product. An evaluation consists of a polarity, a score for the strength of the opinion, and the feature being evaluated. The polarity expresses whether the opinion is positive or negative, and the strength expresses the degree of the sentiment, which is represented as an integer from 1 to 3. Possible polarity/strength (P/S) scores are thus [-3,-2,-1,+1,+2,+3], with +3 being the most positive evaluation, and -3 the most negative. For example, using a DVD player as the entity, the comment "Excellent picture quality—on par with my Pioneer, Panasonic, and JVC players." contains an opinion on the *picture quality*, and is a very positive evaluation (+3).

The features and their associated opinions are organized into a hierarchy of *user-defined features* (UDFs), so named because they can be defined by a user according to the user's needs or interests.[1] The outcome of the process of opinion extraction and structuring is a UDF hierarchy in which each node is annotated with all the evaluations it received in the corpus (See Figure 1 for an example).

2.2 Heuristic Content Selection Strategy

Using the input information described above, content selection is framed as the process of selecting a subset of those features that are deemed more

[1]Actually, the system first extracts a set of surface-level *crude features* (CFs) on which opinions were expressed, using methods described by Hu and Liu (2004). Next, the CFs are mapped onto the UDFs using term similarity scores. The process of mapping CFs to UDFs groups together semantically similar CFs and reduces redundancy. Our study abstracts away from this mapping process, as well as the process of creating the UDF structure. We leave the explanation of the details to the original papers.

Camera
    Lens [+1,+1,+3,-2,+2]
        Digital Zoom
        Optical Zoom
        ...
    Editing/Viewing [+1,+1]
    Viewfinder [-2,-2,-1]
    ...
        Flash [+1,+1,+3,+2,+2]
    ...

Image
    Image Type
        TIFF
        JPEG
        ...
    Resolution
        Effective Pixels
        Aspect Ratio
    ...

Figure 1: Partial view of assumed input information (UDF hierarchy annotated with user evaluations) for a digital camera.

important and relevant to the user. This is done using an importance measure defined on the available features (UDFs). This measure is calculated from the P/S scores of the evaluations associated to each UDF. Let $PS(u)$ be the set of P/S scores that UDF u receives. Then, a measure of importance is defined as some function of the P/S scores. Previous work considered only summing the squares of the scores. In this work, we also consider summing the absolute value of the scores. So, the importance measure is defined as

$$dir\_moi(u) = \sum_{ps \epsilon PS(u)} ps^2 \text{ or } \sum_{ps \epsilon PS(u)} |ps|$$

where the term 'direct' means the importance is derived only from that feature and not from its descendant features. The basic premises of these metrics are that a feature's importance should be proportional to the number of evaluations of that feature in the corpus, and that stronger evaluations should be given more weight. The two versions implement the latter differently, using the sum of squares or the absolute values respectively. Notice that each non-leaf node in the feature hierarchy effectively serves a dual purpose. It is both a feature upon which a user might comment, as well as a category for grouping its sub-features. Thus, a non-leaf node should be important if either its descendants are important or the node itself is important. To this end, a total measure of importance $moi(u)$ is defined as

$$moi(u) = \begin{cases} dir\_moi(u) & \text{if } CH(u) = \emptyset \\ [\alpha\ dir\_moi(u) + \\ (1-\alpha)\times \\ \sum_{v \in CH(u)} moi(v)] & \text{otherwise} \end{cases}$$

where $CH(u)$ refers to the children of u in the hierarchy and α is some real parameter in the range $[0.5, 1]$ that adjusts the relative weights of the parent and children. We found in our experimentation that the parameter setting does not substantially change the performance of the system, so we select the value 0.9 for α, following previous work. As a result, the total importance of a node is a combination of its direct importance and of the importance of its children.

The selection procedure proceeds as follows. First, the most obvious simple greedy selection strategy was considered–sort the nodes in the UDF by the measure of importance and select the most important node until a desired number of features is included. However, since a node derives part of its 'importance' from its children, it is possible for a node's importance to be dominated by one or more of its children. Including both the child and parent node would be redundant because most of the information is contained in the child. Thus, a dynamic greedy selection algorithm was devised in which the importance of each node was recalculated after each round of selection, with all previously selected nodes removed from the tree. In this way, if a node that dominates its parent's importance is selected, its parent's importance will be reduced during later rounds of selection. Notice, however, that this greedy selection consists of a series of myopic steps to decide which features to include in the summary next, based on what has been selected already and what remains to be selected at this step. Although this series of local decisions may be locally optimal, it may result in a suboptimal choice of contents overall.

3 Clustering-Based Optimization Strategy

To address the limitation of local optimality of this initial strategy, we explore if the content selection problem for opinion summarization can be naturally and effectively solved by a global optimization-based approach. Our approach assumes the same input information as the previous approach, and we also use the direct measure of importance defined above. Our framework is UDF-based in the following senses. First, a UDF is the basic unit of content that is selected for inclusion in the summary. Also, the information content that needs to be "covered" by the summary is the sum of the information content in all of the UDFs in the UDF hierarchy.

To reduce content selection to a clustering problem, we need the following components. First, we need a cost function to quantify how well a UDF (if selected) can express the information content in another UDF. We call this measure the *information coverage cost*. To define this cost function, we need to define the semantic relatedness between the selected content and the covered content, which is domain-dependent. For example, we can rely on similarity metrics such as ones based on WordNet similarity scores (Fellbaum and others, 1998). In the consumer product domain in which we test our method, we use the UDF hierarchy of the entity being summarized.

Second, we need a clustering paradigm that defines the quality of a proposed clustering; that is, a way to globally quantify how well all the information content is represented by the set of UDFs that we select. The clustering paradigm that we found to most naturally fit our task is the p-median problem (also known as the k-median problem), from facility location theory. In its original interpretation, p-median is used to find optimal locations for opening facilities which provide services to customers, such that the cost of serving all of the customers with these facilities is minimized. This matches our intuition that the quality of a summary of opinions depends on how well it represents all of the opinions to be summarized. Formally, given a set F of m potential locations for facilities, a set U of n customers, a cost function $d : F \times U \longrightarrow \Re$ representing the cost of serving a customer $u \in U$ with a facility $f \in F$, and a constant $p \leq m$, an optimal solution to the p-median problem is a subset S of F, such that the expression

$$\sum_{u \in U} \min_{f \in S} d(f, u)$$

is minimized, and $|S| = p$. The subset S is exactly the set of UDFs that we would include in the summary, and the parameter p can be set to determine the summary length.

Although solving the p-median problem is NP-hard in general (Kariv and Hakimi, 1979), viable approximation methods do exist. We use POPSTAR, an implementation of an approximate solution (Resende and Werneck, 2004) which has an average error rate of less than 0.4% on all the problem classes it was tested on in terms of the p-median problem value. As an independent test of the program's efficacy, we compare the program's output to solutions which we obtained by brute-force search on 12 of the 36 datasets we worked with which are small enough such that an exact solution can be feasibly found. POPSTAR returned the exact solution in all 12 instances.

We now reinterpret the p-median problem for summarization content selection by specifying the sets U, F, and the information coverage cost d in terms of properties of the summarization process. We define the basic unit of the summarization process to be UDFs, so the sets U and F correspond to the set of UDFs describing the product. The constant p is a parameter to the p-median problem, determining the summary size in terms of the number of features.

The cost function is $d(u, v)$, where u is a UDF that is being considered for inclusion in the summary, and v is the UDF to be "covered" by u. To specify this cost, we need to consider both the total amount of information in v as well as the semantic relationship between the two features. We use the importance measure defined earlier, based on the number and strength of evaluations of the covered feature to quantify the former. The raw importance score is modified by multipliers which depend on the relationship between u and v. One is the semantic relatedness between the two features, which is modelled by the UDF tree hierarchy. We hypothesize that it is easier for a more general feature to cover information about a more specific feature than the reverse, and that features that are not in a ancestor-descendant relationship cannot cover information about each other because of the tenuous semantic connection between them. For example, knowing that a camera is well-liked in general provides stronger evidence that its durability is also well-liked than the reverse. Based on these assumptions, we define a multiplier for the above measure of importance based on the UDF tree structure, $T(u, v)$, as follows.

$$T(u,v) = \begin{cases} T_{up} \times k, & \text{if } u \text{ is a descendant of } v \\ k, & \text{if } u \text{ is an ancestor of } v \\ \infty, & \text{otherwise} \end{cases}$$

k is the length of the path from u to v in the UDF

hierarchy. T_{up} is a parameter specifying the relative difficulty of covering information in a feature that is an ancestor in the UDF hierarchy. Mirroring our experience with the heuristic method, the value of the parameter does not affect performance very much. In our experiments and the example to follow, we pick the values $T_{up} = 3$, meaning that covering information in an ancestor node is three times more difficult than covering information in a descendant node.

Another multiplier to the opinion domain is the distribution of evaluations of the features. Coverage is expected to be less if the features are evaluated differently; for example, if users rated a *camera* well overall but the feature *zoom* poorly, a sentence about how well the camera is rated in general does not provide much evidence that the zoom is not well liked, and vice versa. Since evaluations are labelled with P/S ratings in our data, it is natural to define this multiplier based on the distributions of ratings for the features. Given these P/S ratings between -3 and +3, we first aggregate the positive and negative evaluations. As before, we test both summing absolute values and squared values. Define:

$$imp\_pos(u) = \sum_{ps \in PS(u) \wedge ps > 0} ps^2 \text{ or } |ps|$$

$$imp\_neg(u) = \sum_{ps \in PS(u) \wedge ps < 0} ps^2 \text{ or } |ps|$$

Then, we calculate the parameter to the Bernoulli distribution corresponding to the ratio of the importance of the two polarities. That is, Bernoulli with parameter

$$\theta(u) = imp\_pos(u)/(imp\_pos(u) + imp\_neg(u))$$

The distribution-based multiplier $E(u, v)$ is the Jensen-Shannon divergence from $Ber(\theta(u))$ to $Ber(\theta(v))$, plus one for multiplicative identity when the divergence is zero.

$$E(u, v) = JS(\theta(u), \theta(v)) + 1$$

The final formula for the information coverage cost is thus

$$d(u, v) = dir\_moi(v) \times T(u, v) \times E(u, v)$$

Consider the following example consisting of four-node UDF tree and importance scores.

i.		*Covered*				*ii.* Solutions		
		A	B	C	D	p	*Selected*	*Val.*
Covering	A	0	50	30	240	1	A	320
	B	165	0	∞	120	2	A,D	80
	C	165	∞	0	∞	3	A,B,D	30
	D	330	150	∞	0	4	A,B,C,D	0

Table 1: *i.* Information coverage cost scores for the worked example. Rows represent the covering feature, while columns represent the covered feature. *ii.* Optimal solution to p-median problem in the worked example at different numbers of features selected.

A $dir\_moi(A) = 55$

↙↘

B C $dir\_moi(B) = 50, dir\_moi(C) = 30$

↓

D $dir\_moi(D) = 120$

With parameter $T_{up} = 3$ and setting the distribution-based multiplier E to 1 to simplify calculations (or for example, if the features received the same distributions of evaluations), this tree yields the information coverage cost scores found in Table 1*i*. Running p-median on these values produces the optimal results found in Table 1*ii*. This method trades off selecting centrally located nodes near the root of the UDF tree and the importance of the individual nodes. In this example, D is selected after the root node A even though D has a greater importance value.

4 Comparative Evaluation

4.1 Stochastic Data Generation

In our experiments we wanted to compare the two content selection strategies (heuristic vs. p-median optimization) on datasets that were both realistic and diverse. Despite the widespread adoption of user reviews in online websites, there is to our knowledge no publicly available corpus of customer reviews of sufficient size which is annotated with features arranged in a hierarchy. While small-scale corpora do exist for a small number of products, the size of the corpora is too small to be representative of all possible distributions of evaluations and feature hierarchies of products, which limits our ability to draw any meaningful conclusion from the dataset.[2] Thus, we stochastically

[2]Using a constructed dataset based on real data where no resources or agreed-upon evaluation methodology yet exists has been done in other NLP tasks such as topic boundary detection (Reynar, 1994) and local coherence modelling (Barzilay and Lapata, 2005). We are encouraged, however, that subsequent to our experiment, more resources for opinion anal-

	mean	*std.*
# Features	55.3889	8.5547
# Evaluated Features	21.6667	5.9722
# Children (depth 0)	11.3056	0.7753
# Children (depth 1 fertile)	5.5495	1.7724

Table 2: Statistics on the 36 generated data sets. At depth 1, 134 of the 407 features in total across the trees were barren. The generated tree hierarchies were quite flat, with a maximum depth of 2.

generated the data for the products to mimic real product feature hierarchies and evaluations. We did this by gathering statistics from existing corpora of customer reviews about electronics products (Hu and Liu, 2004), which contain UDF hierarchies and evaluations that have been defined and annotated. Using these statistics, we created distributions over the characteristics of the data, such as the number of nodes in a UDF hierarchy, and sampled from these distributions to generate new UDF hierarchies and evaluations. In total, we generated 36 sets of data, which covered a realistic set of possible scenarios in term of feature hierarchy structures as well as in term of distribution of evaluations for each feature. Table 2 presents some statistics on the generated data sets.

4.2 Building a Human Performance Model

We adopt the evaluation approach that a good content selection strategy should perform similarly to humans, which is the view taken by existing summarization evaluation schemes such as ROUGE (Lin, 2004) and the Pyramid method (Nenkova et al., 2007). For evaluating our content selection strategy, we conducted a user study asking human participants to perform a selection task to create "gold standard" selections. Participants viewed and selected UDF features using a Treemap information visualization. See Figure 2 for an example.

We recruited 25 university students or graduates, who were each presented with 19 to 20 of the cases we generated as described above. Each case represented a different hypothetical product, which was represented by a UDF hierarchy, as well as P/S evaluations from -3 to +3. These were displayed to the participants by a Treemap visualization (Shneiderman, 1992), which is able to give an overview of the feature hierarchy and the evaluations that each feature received. Treemaps have been shown to be a generally successful tool for visualizing data in the customer review domain, even for novice users (Carenini et al., 2006). In a Treemap, the feature hierarchy is represented by nested rectangles, with parent features being larger rectangles, and children features being smaller rectangles contained within its parent rectangle. The size of the rectangles depends on the number of evaluations that this feature received directly, as well as indirectly through its children features. Each evaluation is also shown as a small rectangle, coloured according to its P/S rating, with -3 being bright red, and +3 being bright green.

Participants received 30 minutes of interactive training in using Treemaps, and were presented with a scenario in which they were told to take the role of a friend giving advice on the purchase of an electronics product based on existing customer reviews. They were then shown 22 to 23 scenarios corresponding to different products and evaluations, and asked to select features which they think would be important to include in a summary to send to a friend. We discarded the first three selections that participants made to allow them to become further accustomed to the visualization.

The number of features that participants were asked to select from each tree was 18% of the number of selectable features. A feature is considered selectable if it appears in the Treemap visualization; that is, the feature receives at least one evaluation, or one of its descendant features does. This proportion was the average proportion at which the selections made by the heuristic greedy strategy and p-median diverged the most when we were initially testing the algorithms. Because each tree contained a different number of features, the actual number of features selected ranged from two to seven. Features were given generic labels like *Feature 34*, so that participants cannot rely on preexisting knowledge about that

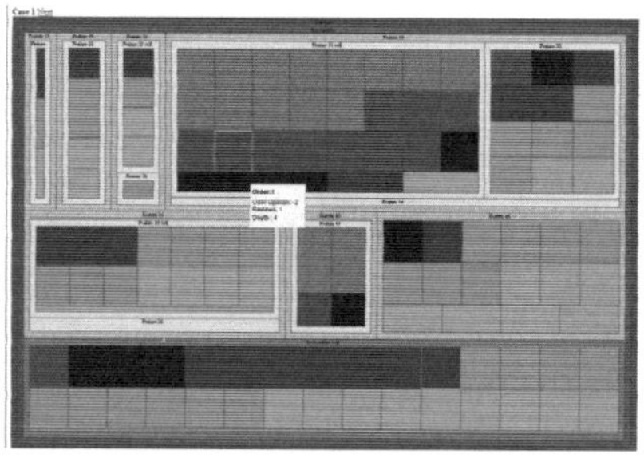

Figure 2: A sample Treemap visualization of the customer review data sets shown to participants.

ysis such as a user review corpus by Constant et al. (2008) have been released, as an anonymous reviewer pointed out.

Selection method	*Cohen's Kappa*
heuristic, squared moi	0.4839
heuristic, abs moi	0.4841
p-median, squared moi	0.4679
p-median, abs moi	0.4821

Table 3: Cohen's kappa for heuristic greedy and p-median methods against human selections. Two versions of the measure of importance were tested, one using squared P/S scores, the other using absolute values.

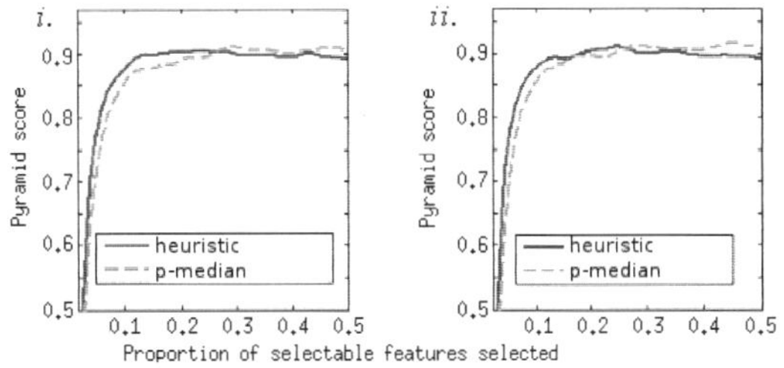

Figure 3: Pyramid scores for the two selection approaches at different numbers of features *i.* using the squared importance measure, *ii.* using the absolute value importance measure.

kind of product in their selections.

4.3 Evaluation Metrics

Using this human gold standard, we can now compare the greedy heuristic and the p-median strategies. We report the agreement between the human and machine selections in terms of kappa and a version of the Pyramid method. The Pyramid method is a summarization evaluation scheme built upon the observation that human summaries can be equally informative despite being divergent in content (Nenkova et al., 2007). In the Pyramid method, Summary Content Units (SCUs) in a set of human-written model summaries are manually identified and annotated. These SCUs are placed into a pyramid with different tiers, corresponding to the number of model (i.e. human) summaries in which each SCU appears. A summary to be evaluated is similarly annotated by SCUs and is scored by the scores of its SCUs, which are the tier of the pyramid in which the SCU appears. The Pyramid score is defined as the sum of the weights of the SCUs in the evaluated summary divided by the maximum score achievable with this number of SCUs, if we were to take SCUs starting from the highest tier of the pyramid. Thus, a summary scores highly if its SCUs are found in many of the model summaries. We use UDFs rather than text passages as SCUs, since UDFs are the basic units of content in our selections. Moderate inter-annotator agreement between human feature selections shows that our data fits the assumption of the Pyramid method (i.e. diversity of human annotations); the Fleiss' kappa (1971) scores for the human selections ranged from 0.2984 to 0.6151, with a mean of 0.4456 among all 33 sets which were evaluated. A kappa value above 0.6 is generally taken to indicate substantial agreement (Landis and Koch, 1977).

4.4 Results

The greedy heuristic method and p-median perform similarly at the number of features that the human participants were asked to select. The difference is not statistically significant by a two-tailed t-test. Table 3 shows that using absolute values of P/S scores in the importance measure is better than using squares. Squaring seems to give too much weight to extreme evaluations over more neutral evaluations. P-median is particularly affected, which is not surprising as it uses the measure of importance both in the raw importance score and in the distribution-based multiplier.

The Pyramid method allows us to compare the algorithms at different numbers of features. Figure 3 shows the average pyramid score for the two methods over the proportion of features that are selected. Overall, both algorithms perform well, and reach a score of about 0.9 at 10% of features selected. The heuristic method performs slightly better when the proportion is below 25%, but slightly worse above that proportion.

We consider several possible explanations for the surprising result that the heuristic greedy method and p-median methods perform similarly. One possibility is that the approximate p-median solution we adopted (POPSTAR) is error-prone on this task, but this is unlikely as the approximate method has been rigorously tested both externally on much larger problems and internally on a subset of our data. Another possibility is that the automatic methods have reached a ceiling in performance by these evaluation metrics.

Nevertheless, these results are encouraging in showing that our optimization-based method is a viable alternative to a heuristic strategy for content selection, and validate that incorporating other summarization decisions into content selection is an option worth exploring.

5 Conclusions and Future Work

We have proposed a formal optimization-based method for summarization content selection based on the p-median clustering paradigm, in which content selection is viewed as selecting clusters of related information. We applied the framework to opinion summarization of customer reviews. An experiment evaluating our p-median algorithm found that it performed about as well as a comparable existing heuristic approach designed for the opinion domain in terms of similarity to human selections. These results suggest that the optimization-based approach is a good starting point for integration with other parts of the summarization/NLG process, which is a promising avenue of research.

6 Acknowledgements

We would like to thank Lucas Rizoli, Gabriel Murray and the anonymous reviewers for their comments and suggestions.

References

R. Barzilay and M. Lapata. 2005. Modeling Local Coherence: An Entity-based Approach. In *Proc. 43rd ACL*, pages 141–148.

G. Carenini and J.C.K. Cheung. 2008. Extractive vs. NLG-based abstractive summarization of evaluative text: The effect of corpus controversiality. In *Proc. 5th INLG*.

G. Carenini and J.D. Moore. 2006. Generating and evaluating evaluative arguments. *Artificial Intelligence*, 170(11):925–952.

G. Carenini, R.T. Ng, and A. Pauls. 2006. Interactive multimedia summaries of evaluative text. In *Proc. 11th Conference on Intelligent User Interfaces*, pages 124–131.

N. Constant, C. Davis, C. Potts, and F. Schwarz. 2008. The pragmatics of expressive content: Evidence from large corpora. *Sprache und Datenverarbeitung*.

C. Dellarocas, N. Awad, and X. Zhang. 2004. Exploring the Value of Online Reviews to Organizations: Implications for Revenue Forecasting and Planning. In *Proc. 24th International Conference on Information Systems*.

C. Fellbaum et al. 1998. *WordNet: an electronic lexical database*. Cambridge, Mass: MIT Press.

J.L. Fleiss et al. 1971. Measuring nominal scale agreement among many raters. *Psychological Bulletin*, 76(5):378–382.

M. Gamon, A. Aue, S. Corston-Oliver, and E. Ringger. 2005. Pulse: Mining customer opinions from free text. *Lecture Notes in Computer Science*, 3646:121–132.

M. Hu and B. Liu. 2004. Mining and summarizing customer reviews. In *Proc. 2004 ACM SIGKDD International Conference on Knowledge Discovery and Data Mining*, pages 168–177. ACM Press New York, NY, USA.

O. Kariv and S.L. Hakimi. 1979. An algorithmic approach to network location problems. II: the p-medians. *SIAM Journal on Applied Mathematics*, 37(3):539–560.

J.R. Landis and G.G. Koch. 1977. The measurement of observer agreement for categorical data. *Biometrics*, 33(1):159–174.

C.Y. Lin. 2004. ROUGE: A Package for Automatic Evaluation of Summaries. In *Proc. Workshop on Text Summarization Branches Out*, pages 74–81.

A. Nenkova, R. Passonneau, and K. McKeown. 2007. The Pyramid Method: Incorporating human content selection variation in summarization evaluation. *ACM Transactions on Speech and Language Processing (TSLP)*, 4(2).

M. O'Donnell, C. Mellish, J. Oberlander, and A. Knott. 2001. ILEX: an architecture for a dynamic hypertext generation system. *Natural Language Engineering*, 7(03):225–250.

B. Pang and L. Lee. 2004. A sentimental education: Sentiment analysis using subjectivity summarization based on minimum cuts. In *Proc. 42nd ACL*, pages 271–278.

M.G.C. Resende and R.F. Werneck. 2004. A Hybrid Heuristic for the p-Median Problem. *Journal of Heuristics*, 10(1):59–88.

J.C. Reynar. 1994. An automatic method of finding topic boundaries. In *Proc. 32nd ACL*, pages 331–333.

B. Shneiderman. 1992. Tree visualization with tree-maps: 2-d space-filling approach. *ACM Transactions on Graphics (TOG)*, 11(1):92–99.

E.R. Tufte, S.R. McKay, W. Christian, and J.R Matey. 1998. Visual Explanations: Images and Quantities, Evidence and Narrative. *Computers in Physics*, 12(2):146–148.

M.X. Zhou and V. Aggarwal. 2004. An optimization-based approach to dynamic data content selection in intelligent multimedia interfaces. In *Proc. 17th annual ACM symposium on User interface software and technology*, pages 227–236. ACM Press New York, NY, USA.

Unsupervised Induction of Sentence Compression Rules

João Cordeiro
CLT and Bioinformatics
University of Beira Interior
Covilhã, Portugal
jpaulo@di.ubi.pt

Gaël Dias
CLT and Bioinformatics
University of Beira Interior
Covilhã, Portugal
ddg@di.ubi.pt

Pavel Brazdil
LIAAD
University of Porto
Porto, Portugal
pbrazdil@liaad.up.pt

Abstract

In this paper, we propose a new unsupervised approach to sentence compression based on shallow linguistic processing. For that purpose, paraphrase extraction and alignment is performed over web news stories extracted automatically from the web on a daily basis to provide structured data examples to the learning process. Compression rules are then learned through the application of Inductive Logic Programming techniques. Qualitative and quantitative evaluations suggests that this is a worth following approach, which might be even improved in the future.

1 Introduction

Sentence compression, simplification or summarization has been an active research subject during this decade. A set of approaches involving machine learning algorithms and statistical models have been experimented and documented in the literature and several of these are described next.

1.1 Related Work

In (Knight & Marcu, 2002) two methods were proposed, one is a probabilistic model - the noisy channel model - where the probabilities for sentence reduction ($P\{S_{compress}|S)\}$ [1]) are estimated from a training set of 1035 $(Sentence, Sentence_{compress})$ pairs, manually crafted, while considering lexical and syntactical features. The other approach learns syntactic tree rewriting rules, defined through four operators: SHIFT, REDUCE DROP and ASSIGN. Sequences of these operators are learned from the training set, and each sequence defines a complete transformation from an original sentence to the compressed version.

In the work of (Le Nguyen & Ho, 2004) two sentence reduction algorithms were also proposed. The first one is based on *template-translation learning*, a method inherited from the *machine translation* field, which learns lexical transformation rules[2], by observing a set of 1500 $(Sentence, Sentence_{reduced})$ pair, selected from a news agency and manually tuned to obtain the training data. Due to complexity difficulties found for the application of this big lexical ruleset, they proposed an improvement where a stochastic *Hidden Markov Model* is trained to help in the decision of which sequence of possible lexical reduction rules should be applied to a specific case.

An unsupervised approach was included in the work of (Turner & Charniak, 2005), where training data are automatically extracted from the Penn Treebank corpus, to fit a noisy channel model, similar to the one used by (Knight & Marcu, 2002). Although it seems an interesting approach to provide new training instances, it still be dependent upon data manually labeled.

More recently, the work of (Clarke & Lapata, 2006) devise a different and quite curious approach, where the sentence compression task is defined as an *optimization* goal, from an *Integer Programming* problem. Several constraints are defined, according to language models, linguistic, and syntactical features. Although this is an unsupervised approach, without using any paralel corpus, it is completely knowledge driven, like a set of crafted rules and heuristics incorporated into a system to solve a certain problem.

1.2 Our Proposal

In this paper, we propose a new approach to this research field, which follows an unsupervised methodology to learn sentence compression rules

[1] In the original paper the $P(t|s)$ notation is used, where t is the sentence in the target language and s the original sentence in the source language.

[2] Those rules are named there as *template-reduction rules*.

Proceedings of the 2009 Workshop on Language Generation and Summarisation, ACL-IJCNLP 2009, pages 15–22,
Suntec, Singapore, 6 August 2009. ©2009 ACL and AFNLP

based on shallow linguistic processing. We designed a system composed of four main steps working in pipeline, where the first three are responsible for data extraction and preparation and in the last one the induction process takes place. The first step gathers web news stories from related news events collected on a daily basis from which paraphrases are extracted. In the second step, word alignment between two sentences of a paraphrase is processed. In the third step, special regions from these aligned paraphrases, called *bubbles*, are extracted and conveniently preprocessed to feed the induction process. The whole sequence is schematized in figure 1.

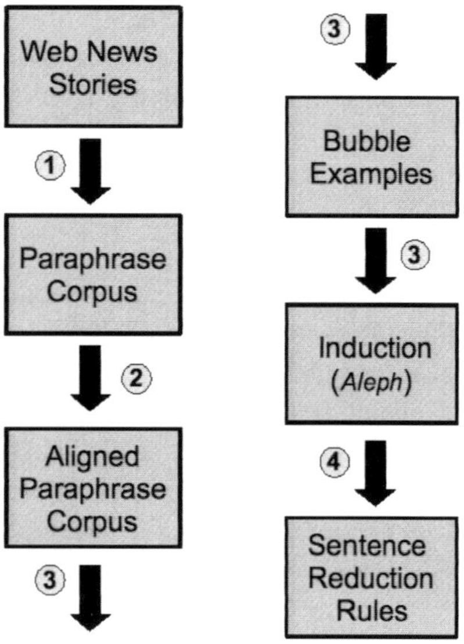

Figure 1: The Pipeline Architecture.

The induction process generates sentence reduction rules which have the following general structure: $L_{cond} \wedge X_{cond} \wedge R_{cond} \Rightarrow suppress(X)$. This means that the sentence segment X will be eliminated if certain conditions hold over left (L), middle (X) and right (R) segments[3]. In Figure 2, we present seven different rules which have been automatically induced from our architecture. These rules are formed by the conjunction of several literals, and they define constraints under which certain sentence subparts may be deleted, therefore compressing or simplifying the sentence. The X symbol stands for the segment

[3]For the sake of simplicity and compact representation, we will omit the rule consequent, which is always the same ("$\Rightarrow suppress(X)$"), whenever a rule is presented.

$$Z_{(X)} = 1 \wedge L_c = NP \wedge X_1 = JJ \wedge R_1 = IN \quad (1)$$
$$Z_{(X)} = 1 \wedge L_c = NP \wedge X_1 = RB \wedge R_1 = IN \quad (2)$$

$$Z_{(X)} = 2 \wedge L_1 = and \wedge X_1 = the \wedge R_1 = JJ \quad (3)$$
$$Z_{(X)} = 2 \wedge L_1 = the \wedge X_2 = of \wedge R_1 = NN \quad (4)$$
$$Z_{(X)} = 2 \wedge L_1 = the \wedge X_c = NP \wedge R_1 = NN \quad (5)$$

$$Z_{(X)} = 3 \wedge L_c = PP \wedge X_1 = the \wedge R_c = NP \quad (6)$$
$$Z_{(X)} = 3 \wedge L_c = NP \wedge X_1 = and \wedge R_2 = VB \quad (7)$$

Figure 2: Learned Sentence Compression Rules.

to be dropped, $L_{(\star)}$ and $R_{(\star)}$ are conditions over the left and right contexts respectively. The numeric subscripts indicate the positions[4] where a segment constraint holds and the c subscript stands for a syntactic chunk type. The $Z_{(\bullet)}$ function computes the length of a given segment, by counting the number of words it contains. For instance, the first rule means that a word[5] will be eliminated if we have a NP (Noun Phrase) chunk in the left context, and a preposition or subordinating conjunction, in the right context ($R_1 = IN$). The rule also requires that the elimination word must be an adjective, as we have $X_1 = JJ$.

This rule would be applied to the following segment[6]

```
[NP mutual/jj funds/nns information/nn]
[ADJP available/jj] [PP on/in] [NP
reuters.com/nn]
```

and would delete the word `available` giving rise to the simplified segment:

```
[NP mutual/jj funds/nns information/nn]
[PP on/in] [NP reuters.com/nn].
```

Comparatively to all existing works, we propose in this paper a framework capable to extract compression rules in a real world environment. Moreover, it is fully unsupervised as, at any step of the process, examples do not need to be labeled.

In the remaining of the paper, we will present the overall architecture which achieves precision

[4]The position starts with 1 and is counted from left to right, on the word segments, except for the left context, where it is counted reversely.

[5]As we have $Z_{(X)} = 1$, the candidate segment size to eliminate is equal to one.

[6]The segment is marked with part-of-speech tags (POS) and chunked with a shallow parser. Both transformations were made with the OpenNLP toolkit.

values up to 85.72%, correctness up to 4.03 in 5 and utility up to 85.72%.

2 Data Preparation

Creating relevant training sets, with some thousands examples is a difficult task, as well as is the migration of such a system to process other languages. Therefore, we propose an unsupervised methodology to automatically create a training set of aligned paraphrases, from electronically available texts on the web. This step is done through step one and step two of Figure 1, and the details are described in the next two subsections.

2.1 Paraphrase Extraction

Our system collects web news stories on a daily basis, and organized them into clusters, which are exclusively related to different and unique events, happening each day: "a company acquisition", "a presidential speech", "a bomb attack", etc. Usually, such clusters contain near 30 small or medium news articles, collected from different media sources. This environment proves to be very fruitful for paraphrase extraction, since we have many sentences conveying similar information yet written in a different form.

A few unsupervised metrics have been applied to automatic paraphrase identification and extraction (Barzilay & Lee, 2003; Dolan et al., 2004). However, these unsupervised methodologies show a major drawback by extracting quasi-exact or even exact match pairs of sentences as they rely on classical string similarity measures such as the *Edit Distance* in the case of (Dolan et al., 2004) and *Word N-gram Overlap* for (Barzilay & Lee, 2003). Such pairs are useless for our purpose, since we aim to identify asymmetrical paraphrase pairs to be used for sentence compression rule induction, as explained in (Cordeiro et al., Oct 2007). There we proposed a new metric, the *Sumo-Metric*, specially designed for asymmetrical entailed pairs identification, and proved better performance over previous established metrics, even in the specific case when tested with the Microsoft Paraphrase Research Corpus (Dolan et al., 2004), which contains mainly symmetrical cases. For a given sentence pair, having each sentence x and y words, and with λ exclusive links between the sentences, the Sumo-Metric is defined in Equation 8 and 9.

$$S(S_a, S_b) = \begin{cases} S(x,y,\lambda) & if\ S(x,y,\lambda) < 1.0 \\ 0 & if\ \lambda = 0 \\ e^{-k*S(x,y,\lambda)} & otherwise \end{cases} \quad (8)$$

where

$$S(x,y,\lambda) = \alpha \log_2(\frac{x}{\lambda}) + \beta \log_2(\frac{y}{\lambda}) \quad (9)$$

with $\alpha, \beta \in [0,1]$ and $\alpha + \beta = 1$.

We have shown (Cordeiro et al., Oct 2007) that *Sumo-Metric* outperforms all state-of-the-art metrics over all tested corpora and allows to identifying similar sentences with high probability to be paraphrases. In Figure 3, we provide the reader with an example of an extracted paraphrase.

```
(1) To the horror of their fans, Miss Ball
    and Arnaz were divorced in 1960.

(2) Ball and Arnaz divorced in 1960.
```

Figure 3: An Assymetrical Paraphrase

2.2 Paraphrase Alignment

From a corpus of asymmetrical paraphrases, we then use biology-based gene alignment algorithms to align the words contained in each of the two sentences within each paraphrase. For that purpose, we implemented two well established algorithms, one identifying local alignments (Smith & Waterman, 1981) and the other one computing global alignments (Needleman & Wunsch, 1970). We also proposed a convenient dynamic strategy (Cordeiro et al., 2007), which chooses the best alignment algorithm to be applied to a specific case at runtime.

The difference between local and global sequence alignments is illustrated below, where we use letters, instead of words, to better fit our paper space constraints. Suppose that we have the following two sequences: `[D,H,M,S,T,P,R,Q,I,S]` and `[T,P,Q,I,S,D,H,S]` a global alignment would produce the following pair.

```
D H M S T P R Q I S _ _ _
_ _ _ _ T P _ Q I S D H S
```

For the same two sequences, a local alignment strategy could generate two or more aligned subsequences as follows.

```
|D H M S|        |T P R Q I S|
|D H _ S|        |T P _ Q I S|
```

Hence, at this stage of the process, we end with a corpus of aligned[7] asymmetrical paraphrases. In Figure 4, we present the alignment of the paraphrase of Figure 3.

```
(1) To the horror of their fans ,
(2) __ ___ ______ __ _____ ____ _

(1) Miss Ball and Arnaz were divorced in 1960.
(2) ____ Ball and Arnaz ____ divorced in 1960.
```

Figure 4: An Aligned Paraphrase

The next section describes how we use this structured data to extract instances which are going to feed a learning system.

3 Bubble Extraction

In order to learn rewriting rules, we have focus our experiences on a special kind of data, selected from the corpus of aligned sentences, and we named this data as *Bubbles*[8]. Given two word aligned sentences, a bubble is a non-empty segment aligned with an empty segment of the other sentence of the paraphrase, sharing a "strong" context. In Figure 5, we show different examples of bubbles.

```
the situation here in chicago with the workers
the situation ____ in chicago with the workers

obama talks exclusively with tom brokaw on meet
obama talks ___________ with tom brokaw on meet

Ball and Arnaz were divorced in 1960
Ball and Arnaz ____ divorced in 1960

america is in the exact same seat as sweigert and
america is in ___ _____ same seat as sweigert and

after a while at the regents park gym, the president
after a while at ___ _______ ____ gym, the president
```

Figure 5: Examples of Bubbles

To extract a bubble, left and right contexts of equally aligned words must occur, and the probability of such extraction depends on the contexts size as well as the size of the region aligned with the empty space. The main idea is to eliminate cases where the bubble middle sequence is too large when compared to the size of left and right contexts. More precisely, we use the condition in Equation 10 to decide whether a bubble should be extracted or not.

$$Z_{(L)} - Z_{(X)} + Z_{(R)} \geq 0 \qquad (10)$$

where L and R stand for the left and right contexts, respectively, and X is the middle region. The $Z_{(\bullet)}$ function computes the length of a given segment, in terms of number of words. For example, in the first and last examples of Figure 5, we have: $2 - 1 + 5 = 6 \geq 0$ and $4 - 3 + 4 = 5 \geq 0$. In this case, both bubbles will be extracted. This condition is defined to prevent from extracting eccentric cases, as the ones shown in the examples shown in Figure 6, where the conditions respectively fail: $0 - 8 + 3 = -5 < 0$ and $1 - 7 + 2 = -4 < 0$.

```
To the horror of their fans , Miss Ball and Arnaz
__ ___ ______ __ _____ ____ _ ____ Ball and Arnaz

will vote __ ___ _______ ____ __ _____ __ friday .
____ vote on the amended bill as early as friday .
```

Figure 6: Examples of Rejected Bubbles

Indeed, we favor examples with high common contexts and few deleted words to enhance the induction process.

So far, we only consider bubbles where the middle region is aligned with a void segment ($X \stackrel{transf}{\longrightarrow} \emptyset$). However, more general transformations will be investigated in the future. Indeed, any transformation $X \stackrel{transf}{\longrightarrow} Y$, where $Y \neq \emptyset$, having $Z_{(X)} > Z_{(Y)}$, may be a relevant compression example.

Following this methodology, we obtain a huge set of examples, where relevant sentence transformations occur. To have an idea about the amount of data we are working with, from a set of 30 days web news stories (133.5 MB of raw text), we identified and extracted 596678 aligned paraphrases, from which 143761 bubbles were obtained.

In the next section, we show how we explore Inductive Logic Programming (ILP) techniques to generalize regularities and find conditions to compress sentence segments.

4 The Induction of Compression Rules

Many different algorithms exist to induce knowledge from data. In this paper, we use Inductive Logic Programming (ILP) (Muggleton, 1991) and it was a choice based on a set of relevant features like: the capacity to generate symbolic and

[7] By "aligned" we mean, from now on, word alignment between paraphrase sentence pairs.

[8] There are other possible regions to explore, but due to the complexity of this task, we decided to initially work only with bubbles

relational knowledge; the possibility to securely avoid negative instances; the ability to mix different types of attribute and to have more control over the theory search process.

Unlike (Clarke & Lapata, 2006), we aim at inducing human understandable knowledge, also known as symbolic knowledge. For that purpose, ILP satisfies perfectly this goal by producing clauses based on *first order logic*. Moreover, most of the learning algorithms require a complete definition and characterization of the feature set, prior to the learning process, where any attribute must be specified. This is a conceptual bottleneck to many learning problems such as ours, since we need to combine different types of attributes i.e. lexical, morpho-syntactic and syntactical. With ILP, we only need to define a set of possible features and the induction process will search throughout this set.

4.1 The Aleph System

The *Aleph* system(Srinivasan, 2000) is an empirical ILP system, initially designed to be a prototype for exploring ILP ideas. It has become a quite mature ILP implementation, used in many research projects, ranging form Biology to NLP. In fact, Aleph is the successor of several and "more primitive" ILP systems, like: Progol (Muggleton, 1999), FOIL (Quinlan, 1990), and Indlog (Camacho, 1994), among others, and may be appropriately parametrized to emulate any of those older systems.

One interesting advantage in *Aleph* is the possibility to learn exclusively from positive instances, contrarily to what is required by most learning systems. Moreover, there is theoretical research work (Muggleton, 1996) demonstrating that the increase in the learning error tend to be negligible with the absence of negative examples, as the number of learning instances increases. This is a relevant issue, for many learning domains, and specially ours, where negative examples are not available.

4.2 Learning Instances

In our problem, we define predicates that characterize possible features to be considered during the induction process. Regarding the structure of our learning instances (bubbles), we define predicates which restrict left and right context sequences as well as the aligned middle sequence. In particular, we limit the size of our context sequences to a maximum of three words and, so far, only use bubbles in which the middle sequence has a maximum length of three[9] words. The notion of contexts from bubbles is clarified with the next example.

```
L2  L1  X1 X2 X3  R1  R2  R3  R4
L2  L1  __ __ __  R1  R2  R3  R4
```

For such a case, we consider `[L1, L2]` as the left context, `[R1, R2, R3]` as the right context, and `[X1, X2, X3]` as the aligned middle sequence. Such an example is represented with a Prolog term with arity 5 (`bub/5`) in the following manner:

```
bub(ID, t(3,0), [L1,L2],
    [X1,X2,X3]--->[],
    [R1,R2,R3]).
```

The `ID` is the identifier of the sequence instance, `t/2` defines the "transformation dimension", in this case from 3 words to 0. The third and fifth arguments are lists with the left and right contexts, respectively, and the fourth argument contains the list with the elements deleted from the middle sequence. It is important to point out that every L_i, X_i and R_i are structures with 3 elements such as `word/POS/Chunk`. For example, the word `president` would be represented by the expanded structure `president/nn/np`.

4.3 Feature Space

As mentioned previously, with an ILP system, and in particular with *Aleph*, the set of attributes is defined through a set of conditions, expressed in the form of predicates. These predicates are the building blocks that will be employed to construct rules, during the induction process. Hence, our attribute search space is defined using Prolog predicates, which define the complete set of possibilities for rule body construction. In our problem, we let the induction engine seek generalization conditions for the bubble main regions (left, middle, and right). Each condition may be from one of the four types: dimensional, lexical, POS, and chunk. Dimensional conditions simply express the aligned sequence transformation dimensionality. Lexical conditions impose a fixed position to match a given word. The POS condition is similar to the lexical one, but more general, as the position must match a specific part-of-speech tag. Likely, chunk conditions bind a region to be equal to a particular chunk type. For example, by looking

[9]They represent 83.47% from the total number of extracted bubbles.

at Figure 2, the attentive reader may have noticed that these three conditions are present in rule 7. In terms of *Aleph* declaration mode, these conditions are defined as follows.

```
:- modeh(1,rule(+bub)).

:- modeb(1,transfdim(+bub,n(#nat,#nat))).
:- modeb(3,chunk(+bub,#side,#chk)).
:- modeb(*,inx(+bub,#side,#k,#tword)).

:- determination(rule/1,transfdim/2).
:- determination(rule/1,chunk/3).
:- determination(rule/1,inx/4).
```

The `inx/4` predicate defines lexical and POS type conditions, the `chunk/3` predicate defines chunking conditions and the `transfdim/2` predicate defines the transformation dimensionality, which is in the form `transfdim(N,0)` with `N>0`, according to the kind of bubbles we are working with.

4.4 The Rule Value Function

The *Aleph* system implements many different evaluation[10] functions which guide the theory search process, allowing the basic procedure for theory construction to be altered. In order to better fit to our problem, we define a new evaluation function calculated as the geometrical mean between the coverage percentage and the rule size value, as shown in Equation 11 where R is the candidate rule and $Cov(R)$ is the proportion of positive instances covered by R and the $LV(\bullet)$ function defines the rule value in terms of its length, returning a value in the $[0, 1]$ interval.

$$Value(R) = \sqrt{Cov(R) \times LV(R)} \qquad (11)$$

The $Value(\bullet)$ function guides the induction process, by preferring not too general rules having maximum possible coverage value. As shown in Figure 7, the $Value(\bullet)$ function gives preferences to rules with 3, 4 and 5 literals.

5 Results

The automatic evaluation of a system is always the best way to do it, due to its objectivity and scalability. However, in many cases it is unfeasible for several practical reasons, like the unavailability of data or the difficulty to prepare an appropriate

[10]In the *Aleph* terminology, this function is named as the "cost" function, despite the fact that it really computes the value in the sense that the grater the value, the more likely it is to be chosen.

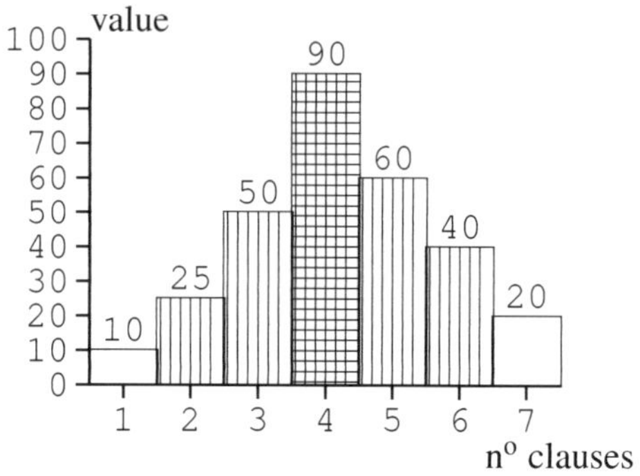

Figure 7: Rule length value function

dataset. Some supervised learning approach use manually labeled test sets to evaluated their systems. However, these are small test sets, for example, (Knight & Marcu, 2002) use a set of 1035 sentences to train the system and only 32 sentences to test it, which is a quite small test set. As a consequence, it is also important to propose more through evaluation. In order to assess as clearly as possible the performance of our methodology on large datasets, we propose a set of qualitative and quantitative evaluations based on three different measures: Utility, Ngram simplification and Correctness.

5.1 Evaluation

A relevant issue, not very commonly discussed, is the *Utility* of a learned theory. In real life problems, people may be more interested in the volume of data processed than the quality of the results. Maybe, between a system which is 90% precise and processes only 10% of data, and a system with 70% precision, processing 50% of data, the user would prefer the last one. The Utility may be a stronger than the Recall measure, used for the evaluation of supervised learning systems, because the later measures how many instances were well identified or processed from the test set only, and the former takes into account the whole universe. For example, in a sentence compression system, it is important to know how many sentences would be compressed, from the whole possible set of sentences encountered in electronic news papers, or in classical literature books, or both. This is what we mean here by Utility.

The *Ngram-Simplification* methodology is an automatic extrinsic test, performed to perceive how much a given sentence reduction ruleset would simplify sentences in terms of syntactical complexity. The answer is not obvious at first sight, because even smaller sentences can contain more improbable syntactical subsequences than their uncompressed versions. To evaluate the syntactical complexity of a sentence, we use a $4-gram$ model and compute a relative[11] sequence probability as defined in Equation 12 where $\vec{W} = [t_1, t_2, ..., t_m]$ is the sequence of part-of-speech tags for a given sentence with size m.

$$P\{\vec{W}\} = \Big(\prod_{k=n}^{m-n} P\{t_k \mid t_{k-1}, ..., t_{k-n}\}\Big)^{\frac{1}{m}} \qquad (12)$$

The third evaluation is qualitative. We measure the quality of the learned rules when applied to sentence reduction. The objective is to assess how correct is the application of the reduction rules. This evaluation was made through manual annotation for a statistically representative random sample of compressed sentences. A human judged the adequacy and *Correctness* of each compression rule to a given sentence segment, in a scale from 1 to 5, where 1 means that it is absolutely incorrect and inadequate, and 5 that the compression rule fits perfectly to the situation (sentence) being analyzed.

To perform our evaluation, a sample of 300 sentences were randomly extracted, where at least one compression rule had been applied. This evaluation set may be subdivided into three subsets, where 100 instances came from rules with $Z_{(X)} = 1$ (**BD1**), 100 from rules with $Z_{(X)} = 2$ (**BD2**), and the other 100 from rules with $Z_{(X)} = 3$ (**BD3**). Another random sample, also with 100 cases has been extracted to evaluate our base-line (**BL**) which consists in the direct application of the bubble set to make compressions. This means that no learning process is performed. Instead, we store the complete bubble set as if they were rules by themselves (in the same manner as (Le Nguyen & Ho, 2004) do).

Table 1 compiles the comparative results for Correctness, Precision, Utility and Ngram-simplification for all datasets. In particular, Ngram-simplification in percentage is the proportion of test cases where $P\{reduced(\vec{W})\} \geq P\{\vec{W}\}$.

Table 1 provides evidence of the improvement achieved with the induction rules, in comparison with the base line, on each test parameter: Correctness, Utility and Ngram-simplification. Considering the three experiences, **BD1**, **BD2**, and **BD3**, as a unique evaluation run, we obtained a mean Correctness quality of 3.867 (i.e. 77.33% Precision), a mean Utility of 48.45%, and a mean Ngram-simplification equal to 89.53%, which are significantly better than the base line.

Parameter	BL	BD1	BD2	BD3
Correctness:	2.93	3.56	4.03	4.01
Precision:	58.60%	71.20%	80.60%	80.20%
Utility:	8.65%	32.67%	85.72%	26.86%
NG-Simpl:	47.39%	89.33%	90.03%	89.23%

Table 1: Results with Four Evaluation Parameters.

Moreover, best results overall are obtained for **BD2** with 80.6% Precision, 85.72% Utility and 90.03% Ngram-simplification which means that we can expect a reduction of two words with high quality for a great number of sentences. In particular, Figure 2 shows examples of learned rules.

5.2 Time Complexity

In the earlier[12] days of ILP, the computation time spent by their systems was a serious difficult obstacle, disabling its implementation for real life problems. However, nowadays these time efficiency issues have been overcome, opening a wide range of application possibilities, for many problems, from Biology to Natural Language Processing. The graph in figure 8, shows that even with considerable big datasets, our learning system (based on *Aleph*) evidences acceptable feasible computation time.

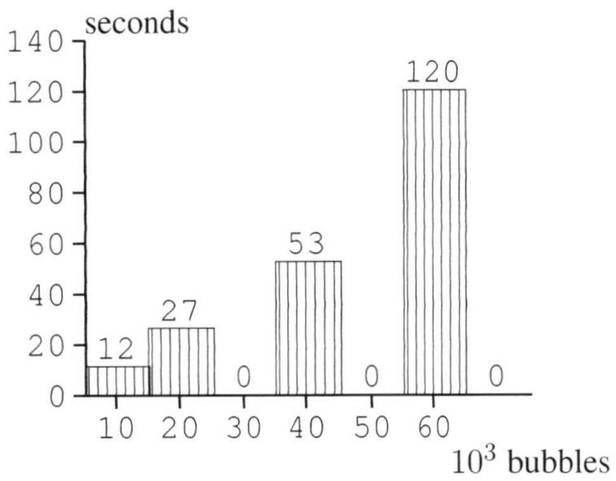

Figure 8: Time spent during the induction process, for datasets with size expressed in thousands of bubbles.

To give an idea about the size of an induced rule set, and taking as an example the learned rules

[11] Because it is raised to the inverse power of m, which is the number of words in the sentence.

[12] In the 1990-2000 decade.

with $Z_{(X)} = 2$, these were learned from a dataset containing 37271 $t(2, 0)$ bubbles, and in the final 5806 sentence reduction rules were produced.

6 Conclusion and Future Directions

Sentence Compression is an active research topic, where several relevant contributions have recently been proposed. However, we believe that many milestones still need to be reached. In this paper, we propose a new framework in the form of a pipeline, which processes huge sets of web news articles and retrieves compression rules in an unsupervised way. For that purpose, we extract and align paraphrases, explore and select specific text characteristics called bubbles and finally induce a set of logical rules for sentence reduction in a real-world environment. Although we have only considered bubbles having $Z_{(X)} \leq 3$, a sentence may have a compression length greater than this value, since several compression rules may be applied to a single sentence.

Our results evidence good practical applicability, both in terms of Utility, Precision and Ngram-simplification. In particular, we assess results up to 80.6% Precision, 85.72% Utility and 90.03% Ngram-simplification for reduction rules of two word length. Moreover, results were compared to a base line set of rules produced without learning and the difference reaches a maximum improvement using Inductive Logic Programming of 22%.

Acknowledgments

This work was supported by the VIPACCESS project - *Ubiquitous Web Access for Visually Impaired People*. Funding Agency: *Fundação para a Ciência e a Tecnologia* (Portugal). Reference: PTDC/PLP/72142/2006.

References

Barzilay R. and Lee L.. 2003. Learning to paraphrase: An unsupervised approach using multiple-sequence alignment. In *HLT-NAACL 2003: Main Proceedings*, pages 16–23.

Camacho R. 1994. Learning stage transition rules with Indlog. *Gesellschaft für Mathematik und Datenverarbeitung MBH.*, Volume 237 of GMD- Studien, pp. 273-290.

Clarke J., and Lapata M. 2006. Constraint-based Sentence Compression: An Integer Programming Approach. *21st International Conference on Computational Linguistics and 44th Annual Meeting of the Association for Computational Linguistics.*

Cordeiro J. and Dias G. and Cleuziou G. 2007. Biology Based Alignments of Paraphrases for Sentence Compression. *In Proceedings of the Workshop on Textual Entailment and Paraphrasing* (ACL-PASCAL / ACL2007), Prague, Czech Republic.

Cordeiro J. and Dias G. and Brazdir P. October 2007. New Functions for Unsupervised Asymmetrical Paraphrase Detection. *In Journal of Software.*, Volume:2, Issue:4, Page(s): 12-23. Academy Publisher. Finland. ISSN: 1796-217X.

Dolan W.B. and Quirck C. and Brockett C. 2004. Unsupervised construction of large paraphrase corpora: Exploiting massively parallel news sources. In *Proceedings of 20th International Conference on Computational Linguistics (COLING 2004).*

Knight K. and Marcu D. 2002. Summarization beyond sentence extraction: A probabilistic approach to sentence compression. *Artificial Intelligence*, 139(1):91-107.

Muggleton S. 1991. *Inductive Logic Programming. New Generation Computing*, 8 (4):295-318.

Muggleton S. 1996. *Learning from positive data. Proceedings of the Sixth International Workshop on Inductive Logic Programming (ILP-96), LNAI 1314*, Berlin, 1996. Springer-Verlag.

Muggleton S. 1999. *Inductive logic programming: Issues, results and the challenge of learning language in logic. Artificial Intelligence*, 114 (1-2), 283?296.

Le Nguyen M., Horiguchi S., A. S., and Ho B. T. 2004. Example-based sentence reduction using the hidden markov model. *ACM Transactions on Asian Language Information Processing (TALIP)*, 3(2):146-158.

Needleman SB, Wunsch CD. 1970. A general method applicable to the search for similarities in the amino acid sequence of two proteins. *Journal of Molecular Biology*, 48 (3): 443–53.

Quinlan J. R. 1990. *Learning Logical Deinitions from Relations. Machine Learning.*, 5 (3), 239-266. 33, 39, 41.

Smith TF, Waterman MS. 1981. Identification of Common Molecular Subsequences. *Journal of Molecular Biology*, 147: 195–197.

Srinivasan A. 2000. *The Aleph Manual*, Technical Report. Computing Laboratory, Oxford University, UK.

Turner J, Charniak E. 2005. Supervised and Unsupervised Learning for Sentence Compression. Proceedings of the 43rd Annual Meeting of the ACL, pages 290-297.

Evaluation of automatic summaries: Metrics under varying data conditions

Karolina Owczarzak and **Hoa Trang Dang**
Information Access Division
National Institute of Standards and Technology
Gaithersburg, MD 20899
karolina.owczarzak@nist.gov hoa.dang@nist.gov

Abstract

In evaluation of automatic summaries, it is necessary to employ multiple topics and human-produced models in order for the assessment to be stable and reliable. However, providing multiple topics and models is costly and time-consuming. This paper examines the relation between the number of available models and topics and the correlations with human judgment obtained by automatic metrics ROUGE and BE, as well as the manual Pyramid method. Testing all these methods on the same data set, taken from the TAC 2008 Summarization track, allows us to compare and contrast the methods under different conditions.

1 Introduction

Appropriate evaluation of results is an important aspect of any research. In areas such as automatic summarization, the problem is especially complex because of the inherent subjectivity in the task itself and its evaluation. There is no single objective standard for a good quality summary; rather, its value depends on the summary's purpose, focus, and particular requirements of the reader (Spärck Jones, 2007). While the purpose and focus can be set as constant for a specific task, the variability of human judgment is more difficult to control. Therefore, in attempts to produce stable evaluations, it has become standard to use multiple judges, not necessarily for parallel evaluation, but in such a way that each judge evaluates a different subset of the many summaries on which the final system assessment is based. The incorporation of multiple points of view is also reflected in automatic evaluation, where it takes the form of employing multiple model summaries to which a candidate summary is compared.

Since these measures to neutralize judgment variation involve the production of multiple model summaries, as well as multiple topics, evaluation can become quite costly. Therefore, it is interesting to examine how many models and topics are necessary to obtain a relatively stable evaluation, and whether this number is different for manual and automatic metrics. In their examination of summary evaluations, van Halteren and Teufel (2003) suggest that it is necessary to use at least 30 to 40 model summaries for a stable evaluation; however, Harman and Over (2004) argue that a stable evaluation can be conducted even with a single model, as long as there is an adequate number of topics. This view is supported by Lin (2004a), who concludes that "correlations to human judgments were increased by using multiple references but using single reference summary with enough number of samples was a valid alternative". Interestingly, similar conclusions were also reached in the area of Machine Translation evaluation; in their experiments, Zhang and Vogel (2004) show that adding an additional reference translation compensates the effects of removing 10–15% of the testing data, and state that, therefore, "it seems more cost effective to have more test sentences but fewer reference translations".

In this paper, we look at how various metrics behave with respect to a variable number of topics and models used in the evaluation. This lets us determine the stability of individual metrics, and helps to illuminate the trade-offs inherent in designing a good evaluation. For our experiments, we used data from the Summarization track at the Text Analysis Conference (TAC) 2008, where participating systems were assessed on their summarization of 48 topics, and the automatic metrics ROUGE and BE, as well as the manual Pyramid evaluation method, had access to 4 human models. TAC 2008 was the first task of the TAC/DUC (Document Understanding Conference) series in which the Pyramid method was used on all evaluated data, making it possible to conduct a full com-

Proceedings of the 2009 Workshop on Language Generation and Summarisation, ACL-IJCNLP 2009, pages 23–30,
Suntec, Singapore, 6 August 2009.

parison among the manual and automatic methods. Despite the lack of full Pyramid evaluation in DUC 2007, we look at the remaining metrics applied that year (ROUGE, BE, and Content Responsiveness), in order to see whether they confirm the insights gained from the TAC 2008 data.

2 Summary evaluation

The main evaluation at TAC 2008 was performed manually, assessing the automatic candidate summaries with respect to Overall Responsiveness, Overall Readability, and content coverage according to the Pyramid framework (Nenkova and Passonneau, 2004; Passonneau et al., 2005). Task participants were asked to produce two summaries for each of the 48 topics; the first (initial summary) was a straightforward summary of 10 documents in response to a topic statement, which is a request for information about a subject or event; the second was an update summary, generated on the basis of another set of 10 documents, which followed the first set in temporal order and described further developments in the given topic. The idea behind the update summary was to avoid repeating all the information included in the first set of documents, on the assumption that the reader is familiar with that information already.

The participating teams submitted up to three runs each; however, only the first and second runs were evaluated manually due to limited resources. For each summary under evaluation, assessors rated the summary from 1 (very poor) to 5 (very good) in terms of Overall Responsiveness, which measures how well the summary responds to the need for information expressed in the topic statement and whether its linguistic quality is adequate. Linguistic qualities such as grammaticality, coreference, and focus were also evaluated as Overall Readability, also on the scale from 1 to 5. Content coverage of each summary was evaluated using the Pyramid framework, where assessors create a list of information nuggets (called Summary Content Units, or SCUs) from the set of human-produced summaries on a given topic, then decide whether any of these nuggets are present in the candidate summary. All submitted runs were evaluated with the automatic metrics: ROUGE (Lin, 2004b), which calculates the proportion of *n*-grams shared between the candidate summary and the reference summaries, and Basic Elements (Hovy et al., 2005), which compares the candidate to the models in terms of head-modifier pairs.

2.1 Manual metrics

Evaluating Overall Responsiveness and Overall Readability is a rather straightforward procedure, as most of the complex work is done in the mind of the human assessor. Each candidate summary is given a single score, and the final score for the summarization system is the average of all its summary-level scores. The only economic factor here is the number of topics, i.e. summaries per system, that need to be judged in order to neutralize both intra- and inter-annotator variability and obtain a reliable assessment of the summarization system.

When it comes to the Pyramid method, which measures content coverage of candidate summaries, the need for multiple topics is accompanied by the need for multiple human model summaries. First, independent human assessors produce summaries for each topic, guided by the topic statement. Next, in the Pyramid creation stage, an assessor reads all human-produced summaries for a given topic and extracts all "information nuggets", called Summary Content Units (SCUs), which are short, atomic statements of facts contained in the text. Each SCU has a weight which is directly proportional to the number of model summaries in which it appears, on the assumption that the fact's importance is reflected in how many human summarizers decide to include it as relevant in their summary. Once all SCUs have been harvested from the model summaries, an assessor then examines each candidate summary to see how many of the SCUs from the list it contains. The final Pyramid score for a candidate summary is its total SCU weight divided by the maximum SCU weight available to a summary of average length (where the average length is determined by the mean SCU count of the model summaries for this topic). The final score for a summarization system is the average score of all its summaries. In TAC 2008, the evaluation was conducted with 48 topics and 4 human models for each topic.

We examined to what extent the number of models and topics used in the evaluation can influence the Pyramid score and its stability. The stability, similarly to the method employed by Voorhees and Buckley (2002) for Information Retrieval, is determined by how well a system ranking based on a small number of models/topics cor-

Models	Pyramid	ROUGE-2	ROUGE-SU4	BE
1	0.8839	0.8032	0.7842	0.7680
2	0.8943	0.8200	0.7957	0.7983
3	0.8974*	0.8258	0.7999*	0.8098
4 (bootstr)	0.8972*	0.8310	0.8023*	0.8152
4 (actual)	0.8997	0.8302	0.8033	0.8171

Table 1: Mean correlations of Responsiveness and other metrics using 1, 2, 3, or 4 models for TAC 2008 initial summaries. Values in each row are significantly different from each other at 95% level.

Models	Pyramid	ROUGE-2	ROUGE-SU4	BE
1	0.9315	0.8861	0.8874	0.8716
2	0.9432	0.9013	0.8961	0.8978
3	0.9474*	0.9068*	0.8994	0.9076
4 (bootstr)	0.9481*	0.9079*	0.9023	0.9114
4 (actual)	0.9492	0.9103	0.9020	0.9132

Table 2: Mean correlations of Responsiveness and other metrics using 1, 2, 3, or 4 models for TAC 2008 update summaries. Values in each row are significantly different from each other at 95% level except ROUGE-2 and ROUGE-SU4 in 1-model category.

Models	ROUGE-2	ROUGE-SU4	BE
1	0.8789	0.8671	0.8553
2	0.8972	0.8803	0.8917
3	0.9036	0.8845	0.9048
4 (bootstr)	0.9082	0.8874	0.9107
4 (actual)	0.9077	0.8877	0.9123

Table 3: Mean correlations of 4-model Pyramid score and other metrics using 1, 2, 3, or 4 models for TAC 2008 initial summaries. Values in each row are significantly different from each other at 95% level except ROUGE-2 and BE in 4-model category.

Models	ROUGE-2	ROUGE-SU4	BE
1	0.9179	0.9110	0.9016
2	0.9336	0.9199	0.9284
3	0.9392	0.9233	0.9383
4 (bootstr)	0.9443	0.9277	0.9436
4 (actual)	0.9429	0.9263	0.9446

Table 4: Mean correlations of 4-model Pyramid score and other metrics using 1, 2, 3, or 4 models for TAC 2008 update summaries. Values in each row are significantly different from each other at 95% level except ROUGE-2 and BE in 4-model category.

relates with the ranking based on another set of models/topics, where the two sets are randomly selected and mutually exclusive. This methodology allows us to check the correlations based on up to half of the actual number of models/topics only (because of the non-overlap requirement), but it gives an indication of the general tendency. We also look at the correlation between the Pyramid score and Overall Responsiveness. We don't expect a perfect correlation between Pyramid and Responsiveness in the best of times, because Pyramid measures content *identity* between the candidate and the model, and Responsiveness measures content *relevance* to topic as well as linguistic quality. However, the degree of variation between the two scores depending on the number of models/topics used for the Pyramid will give us a certain indication of the amount of information lost.

2.2 Automatic metrics

Similarly to the Pyramid method, ROUGE (Lin, 2004b) and Basic Elements (Hovy et al., 2005) require multiple topics and model summaries to produce optimal results. ROUGE is a collection of automatic n-gram matching metrics, ranging from unigram to four-gram. It also includes measurements of the longest common subsequence, weighted or unweighted, and the option to compare stemmed versions of words and omit stopwords. There is also the possibility of accepting skip-n-grams, that is, counting n-grams as matching even if there are some intervening non-matching words. The skip-n-grams together with stemming are the only ways ROUGE can accomodate alternative forms of expression and match concepts even though they might differ in terms of their syntactic or lexical form.

These methods are necessarily limited, and so ROUGE relies on using multiple parallel model summaries which serve as a source of lexical/syntactic variation in the comparison process. The fewer models there are, the less reliable the score. Our question here is not only what this relation looks like (as it was examined on the basis of Document Understanding Conference data in Lin (2004a)), but also how it compares to the reliability of other metrics.

Basic Elements (BE), on the other hand, goes beyond simple string matching and parses the syntactic structure of the candidate and model to obtain a set of head-modifier pairs for each, and then compares the sets. A head-modifier pair consist of the head of a syntactic unit (e.g. the noun in a noun phrase), and the word which modifes the head (i.e. a determiner in a noun phrase). It is also possible to include the name of the relation which connects them (i.e. *subject*, *object*, etc.). Since BEs reflect thematic relations in a sentence rather than surface word order, it should be possible to accommodate certain differences of expression that might appear between a candidate summary and a reference, especially as the words can be stemmed. This could, in theory, allow us to use fewer models for the evaluation. In practice, however, it fails to account for the total possible variety, and, what is more, the additional step of parsing the text can introduce noise into the comparison.

TAC 2008 and DUC 2007 evaluations used ROUGE-2 and ROUGE-SU4, which refer to the recall of bigram and skip-bigram (with up to 4 intervening words) matches on stemmed words, respectively, as well as a BE score calculated on the basis of stemmed head-modifier pairs without relation labels. Therefore, these are the versions we use in our comparisons.

3 Number of models

Since Responsiveness score does not depend on the number of models, it serves as a reference against which we compare the remaining metrics, while we calculate their score with only 1, 2, 3, or all 4 models. Given 48 topics in TAC 2008, and 4-model summaries for each topic, there are 4^{48} possible combinations to derive the final score in the single-model category, so to keep the experiments simple we only selected 1000 random samples from that space. For 1000 repetitions, each time we selected a random combination of model summaries (only one model out of 4 available per topic), against which we evaluated the candidate summaries. Then, for each of the 1000 samples, we calculated the correlation between the resulting score and Responsiveness. We then took the 1000 correlations produced in this manner, and computed their mean. In the same way, we calculated the scores based on 2 and 3 model summaries, randomly selected from the 4 available for each topic. The correlation means for all metrics and categories are given in Table 1 for initial summaries and Table 2 for update summaries. We also ran a one-way analysis of variance (ANOVA) on these correlations to determine whether the correlation means were significantly different from each other. For the 4-model category there was only one possible sample for each metric, so in order to perform ANOVA we bootstrapped this sample to produce 1000 samples. The actual value of the 4-model correlation is given in the tables as **4 (actual)**, and the mean value of the bootstrapped 1000 correlations is given as **4 (bootstr)**.

Values for initial summaries are significantly different from their counterparts for update summaries at the 95% level. Pairwise testing of values for statistically significant differences is shown with symbols: in each column, the first value marked with a particular symbol is not significantly different from any subsequent value marked with the same symbol.

We also examined the correlations of the metrics with the 4-model Pyramid score. Table 3 presents the correlation means for the initial summaries, and Table 4 shows the correlation means for the update summaries.

Since the Pyramid, contrary to Responsiveness, makes use of multiple model summaries, we examine its stability given a decreased number of models to rely on. For this purpose, we correlated the Pyramid score based on randomly selected 2 models (half of the model pool) for each topic with the score based on the remaining 2 models, and repeated this 1000 times. We also looked at the 1-model category, where the Pyramid score calculated on the basis of one model per topic was correlated with the Pyramid score calculated on the basis on another randomly selected model. In both case we witness a very high mean correlation: 0.994 and 0.995 for the 2-model category, 0.982 and 0.985 for the 1-model category for TAC initial and update summaries, respectively. As an illustration, Figure1 shows the variance of correlations for the initial summaries.

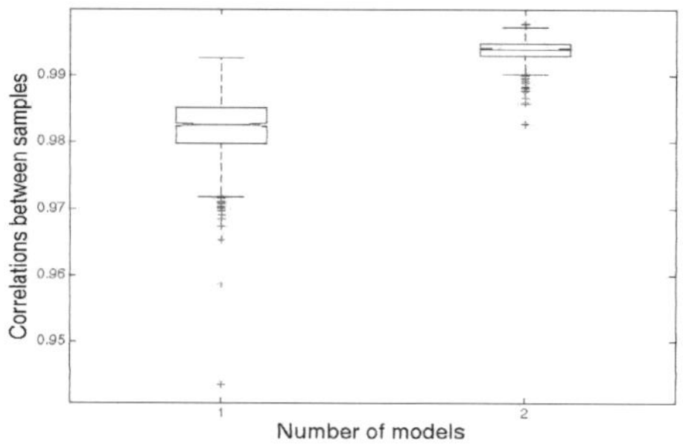

Figure 1: Correlations between Pyramid scores based on 1 or 2 model summaries for TAC 2008 initial summaries.

The variation in correlation levels between other metrics and Pyramid and Responsiveness, presented in Tables 3–4, is more visible in the graph form. Figures 2-3 illustrate the mean correlation values for TAC 2008 initial summaries. While all the metrics record the steepest increase in correlation values with the addition of the second model, adding the third and fourth model provides the metrics with smaller but steady improvement, with the exception of Pyramid-Responsiveness correlation in Figure 2. The increase in correlation mean is most dramatic for BE, which in all cases starts as the lowest-correlating metric in the single-model category, but by the 4-model point it outperforms one or both versions of ROUGE. The Pyramid metric achieves significantly higher correlations than any other metric, independent of the number of models, which is perhaps unsurprising given that it is a manual evaluation method. Of the two ROUGE versions, ROUGE-2 seems consistently a better predictor of both Responsiveness and the "full" 4-model Pyramid score than ROUGE-SU4.

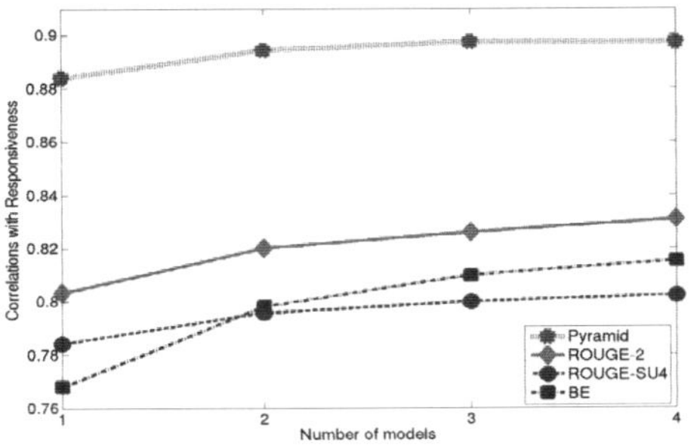

Figure 2: Responsiveness vs. other metrics with 1, 2, 3, or 4 models for TAC 2008 initial summaries.

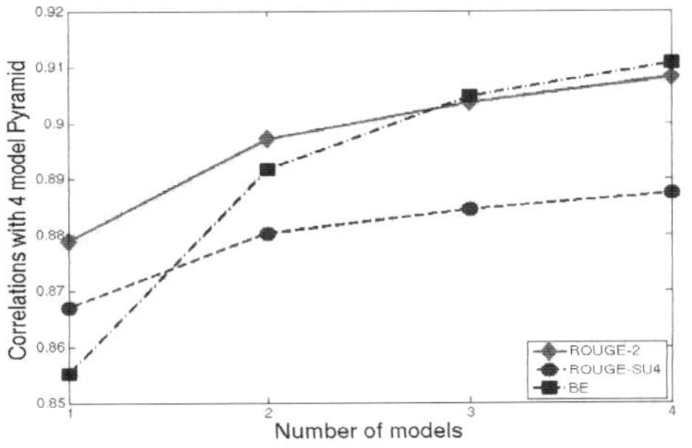

Figure 3: 4-model Pyramid vs. other metrics with 1, 2, 3, or 4 models for TAC 2008 initial summaries.

Similar patterns appear in DUC 2007 data (Table 5), despite the fact that the Overall Responsiveness of TAC 2008 is replaced with Content Responsiveness (ignoring linguistic quality), against which we calculate all the correlations. Although the increase in correlation means from 1- to 4-models for the three automatic metrics is smaller than for TAC 2008, the clearest rise occurs with the addition of a second model, especially for BE, and the subsequent additions change little. As in the case of initial summaries 2008, ROUGE-2 outperforms the remaining two metrics independently of the number of models. However, most of the increases are too small to be significant.

This comparison suggests diminishing returns

Models	ROUGE-2	ROUGE-SU4	BE
1	0.8681	0.8254	0.8486
2	0.8747*	0.8291*	0.8577*
3	0.8766*†	0.8299*†	0.8599*
4 (bootstr)	0.8761*†	0.8305*†	0.8633
4 (actual)	0.8795	0.8301	0.8609

Table 5: Mean correlations of Content Responsiveness and other metrics using 1, 2, 3, or 4 models for DUC 2007 summaries. Values in each row are significantly different from each other at 95% level.

with the addition of more models, as well as different reactions among the metrics to the presence or absence of additional models. When correlating with Responsiveness, the manual Pyramid metric benefits very little from the fourth model, but automatic BE benefits most from almost every addition. ROUGE is situated somewhere between the two, noting small but often significant increases. On the whole, the use of multiple models (at least two) seems supported, especially if we use automatic metrics in our evaluation.

4 Number of topics

For the second set of experiments we kept all four models, but varied the number of topics which went into the final average system score. To determine the stability of Responsiveness and Pyramid we looked at the correlations between the scores based on smaller sets of topics. For 1000 repetitions, we calculated Pyramid/Responsiveness score based on a set of 1, 3, 6, 12, or 24 topics randomly chosen from the pool of 48, and compared the system ranking thus created with the ranking based on another, equally sized set, such that the sets did not contain common topics. Table 6 shows the mean correlation for each case. Although such comparison was only possible up to 24 topics (half of the whole available topic pool), the numbers suggest that at the level of 48 topics both Responsiveness and Pyramid are stable enough to serve as reference for the automatic metrics.

	Responsiveness		Pyramid	
Topics	Initial	Update	Initial	Update
1	0.182	0.196	0.333	0.267
3	0.405	0.404	0.439	0.520
6	0.581	0.586	0.608	0.690
12	0.738	0.738	0.761	0.816
24	0.849	0.866	0.851	0.901

Table 6: Mean correlations between Responsiveness/Pyramid scores based on 1, 3, 6, 12, and 24 topic samples for TAC 2008 initial and update summaries.

In a process which mirrored that described in Section 3, we created 1000 random samples in each of the n-topics category: 1, 3, 6, 12, 24, 36,

Topics	Pyramid	ROUGE-2	ROUGE-SU4	BE
1	0.4219	0.4276	0.4375	0.3506
3	0.6204	0.5980	0.9016	0.5108
6	0.7274	0.6901	0.6836	0.6233
12	0.8159	0.7618	0.7456	0.7117
24	0.8679	0.8040	0.7809	0.7762
36	0.8890*	0.8208*	0.7951*	0.8017*
39	0.8927*†	0.8231*†	0.7967*†	0.8063*†
42	0.8954*†‡	0.8258*†‡	0.7958*†‡	0.8102*†‡
45	0.8977*†‡§	0.8274*†‡§	0.8008*†‡§	0.8132†‡§
48 (bootstr)	0.8972*†‡§	0.8302*†‡§	0.8046†‡§	0.8138†‡§
48 (actual)	0.8997	0.8302	0.8033	0.8171

Table 7: Mean correlations of 48 topic Responsiveness and other metrics using from 1 to 48 topics for TAC 2008 initial summaries. Values in each row are significantly different from each other at 95% level except: ROUGE-2, ROUGE-SU4 and BE in 1-topic category, ROUGE-2 and ROUGE-SU4 in 3- and 6-topic category.

Topics	Pyramid	ROUGE-2	ROUGE-SU4	BE
1	0.5005	0.4882	0.5609	0.4011
3	0.7053	0.6862	0.7340	0.6097
6	0.8080	0.7850	0.8114	0.7274
12	0.8812	0.8498	0.8596	0.8188
24	0.9250	0.8882	0.8859	0.8774
36	0.9408*	0.9023*	0.8960*	0.8999*
39	0.9433*†	0.9045*†	0.8973*†	0.9037*†
42	0.9455*†‡	0.9061*†‡	0.8987*†‡	0.9068*†‡
45	0.9474†‡§	0.9078*†‡§	0.8996*‡‡§	0.9094†‡§
48 (bootstr)	0.9481†‡§	0.9101†‡§	0.9015*†‡§	0.9111†‡§
48 (actual)	0.9492	0.9103	0.9020	0.9132

Table 8: Mean correlations of 48 topic Responsiveness and other metrics using from 1 to 48 topics for TAC 2008 update summaries. Values in each row are significantly different from each other at 95% level except: Pyramid and ROUGE-2 in 1-topic category, Pyramid and ROUGE-SU4 in 6-topic category, ROUGE-2 and BE in 39-, 42-, and 48-topic category.

Topics	ROUGE-2	ROUGE-SU4	BE
1	0.4693	0.4856	0.3888
3	0.6575	0.6684	0.5732
6	0.7577	0.7584	0.6960
12	0.8332	0.8245	0.7938
24	0.8805	0.8642	0.8684
36	0.8980*	0.8792*	0.8966*
39	0.9008*†	0.8812*†	0.9017*†
42	0.9033*†‡	0.8839*†‡	0.9058†‡
45	0.9052*†‡§	0.8853*†‡§	0.9093†‡§
48 (bootstr)	0.9074†‡§	0.8877†‡§	0.9107†‡§
48 (actual)	0.9077	0.8877	0.9123

Table 9: Mean correlations of 48 topic Pyramid score and other metrics using from 1 to 48 topics for TAC 2008 initial summaries. Values in each row are significantly different from each other at 95% level except: ROUGE-2 and ROUGE-SU4 in the 6-topic category, ROUGE-2 and BE in 39- and 48-topic category.

Topics	ROUGE-2	ROUGE-SU4	BE
1	0.5026	0.5729	0.4094
3	0.7106	0.7532	0.6276
6	0.8130	0.8335	0.7512
12	0.8806	0.8834	0.8475
24	0.9196	0.9092	0.9063
36	0.9343*	0.9198*	0.9301*
39	0.9367*†	0.9213*†	0.9341*†
42	0.9386*†‡	0.9227*†‡	0.9376*†‡
45	0.9402*†‡§	0.9236*†‡§	0.9402†‡§
48 (bootstr)	0.9430†‡§	0.9280§	0.9444‡§
48 (actual)	0.9429	0.9263	0.9446

Table 10: Mean correlations of 48 topic Pyramid score and other metrics using from 1 to 48 topics for TAC 2008 update summaries. Values in each row are significantly different from each other at 95% level except: ROUGE-2 and ROUGE-SU4 in 12-topic category, ROUGE-2 and BE in 45-topic category.

39, 42, or 45. Within each of these categories, for a thousand repetitions, we calculated the score for automatic summarizers by averaging over n topics randomly selected from the pool of 48 topics available in the evaluation. Again, we examined the correlations between the metrics and the "full" 48-topic Responsiveness and Pyramid. As previously, we then used ANOVA to determine whether the correlation means differed significantly. Because there was only one possible sample with all 48 topics for each metric, we bootstrapped this sample to provide 1000 new samples in the 48-topic category, in order to perfom the ANOVA comparison of variance. Tables 7 and 8, as well as Figures 4 and 5, show the metrics' changing correlations with Responsiveness. Tables 9 and 10, and Figures 6 and 7, show the correlations with the 48-topic Pyramid score. Values for initial summaries are significantly different from their counterparts for update summaries at the 95% level.

In all cases, it becomes clear that the curves flatten out and the correlations stop increasing almost completely beyond the 36-topic mark. This means that the scores for the automatic summarization systems based on 36 topics will be on average practically indistiguishable from the scores based on all 48 topics, showing that beyond a certain minimally necessary number of topics adding or removing a few (or even ten) topics will not influence the system scores much. (However, we cannot conclude that a further considerable increase in the number of topics – well beyond 48 – would not bring more improvement in the correlations, perhaps increasing the stable "correlation window" as well.)

Topics	ROUGE-2	ROUGE-SU4	BE
1	0.6157	0.6378	0.5756
3	0.7597	0.7511	0.7323
6	0.8168	0.7904	0.7957
12	0.8493	0.8123	0.8306
24	0.8690	0.8249*	0.8517*
36	0.8751*	0.8287*†	0.8580*†
39	0.8761*†	0.8295*†‡	0.8592†‡
42	0.8768*†‡	0.8299*†‡§	0.8602†‡§
45 (bootstr)	0.8761*†‡	0.8305†‡§	0.8627†‡§
45 (actual)	0.8795	0.8301	0.8609

Table 11: Mean correlations of 45 topic Content Responsiveness and other metrics using from 1 to 45 topics for DUC 2007 summaries. Values in each row are significantly different from each other at 95% level.

An interesting observation is that if we produce such limited-topic scores for the manual metrics, Responsiveness and Pyramid, and correlate them with their own "full" versions based on

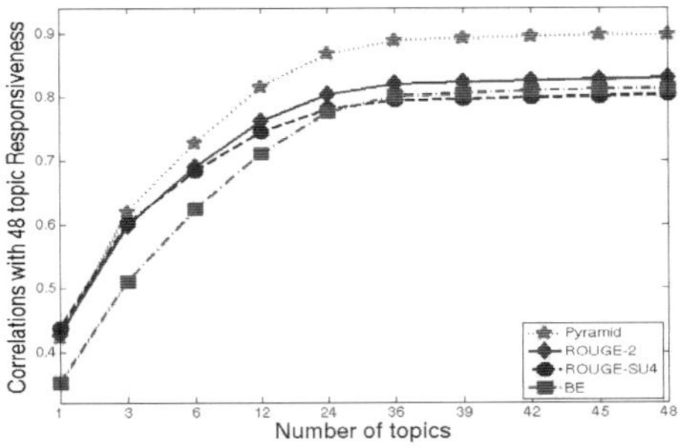

Figure 4: Responsiveness vs. other metrics with 1 to 48 topics for TAC 2008 initial summaries.

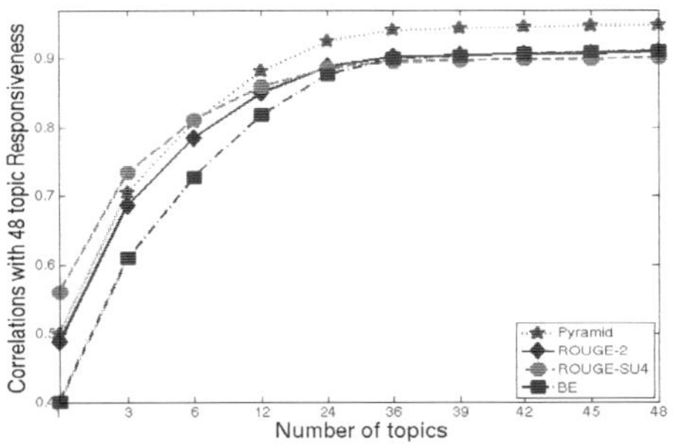

Figure 5: Responsiveness vs. other metrics with 1 to 48 topics for TAC 2008 update summaries.

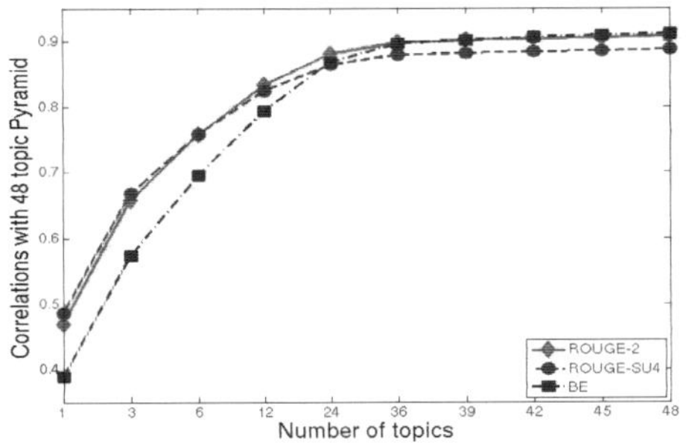

Figure 6: 48-topic Pyramid vs. other metrics with 1 to 48 topics for TAC 2008 initial summaries.

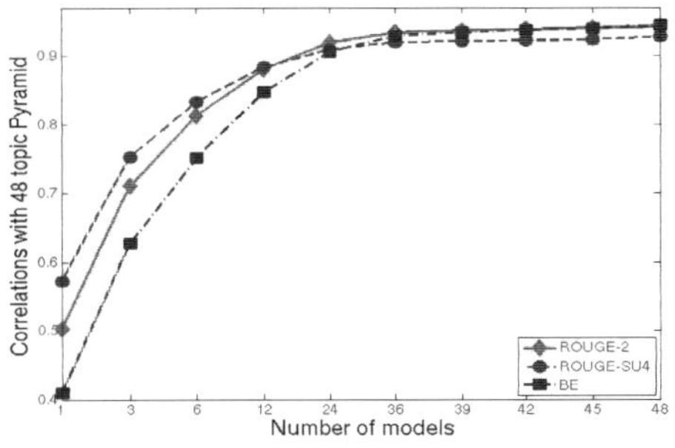

Figure 7: 48-topic Pyramid vs. other metrics with 1 to 48 topics for TAC 2008 update summaries.

all 48 topics, it appears that they are less stable than the automatic metrics, i.e. there is a larger gap between the worst and best correlations they achieve.[1] The mean correlation between the "full" Responsiveness and that based on 1 topic is 0.443 and 0.448 for the initial and update summaries, respectively; for that based on 3 topics, 0.664 and 0.667. Pyramid based on 1 topic achieves 0.467 for initial and 0.525 for update summaries; Pyramid based on 3 topics obtains 0.690 and 0.742, respectively. Some of these values, especially for update summaries, are even lower than those obtained by ROUGE in the same category, despite the fact that 1- and 3-topic Responsiveness or Pyramid is a proper subset of the 48-topic Responsiveness/Pyramid. On the other hand, ROUGE achieves considerably worse correlations with Responsiveness than Pyramid when there are many topics available. ROUGE-SU4 seems to be more stable than ROUGE-2; in all cases ROUGE-2 starts with lower correlations than ROUGE-SU4, but by the 12-topic mark its correlations increase above it.

Additionally, despite being an automatic metric, BE seems to follow the same pattern as the manual metrics. It is seriously affected by the decreasing number of topics; in fact, if the number of topics drops below 24, BE is the least reliable indicator of either Responsiveness or Pyramid. However, by the 48-topic mark it rises to levels comparable with ROUGE-2.

As in the case of models, DUC 2007 data shows mostly the same pattern as TAC 2008. Again, in this data set, the increase in the correlation mean with the addition of topics for each metric are smaller than for either initial or update summaries in TAC 2008, but the relative rate of increase remains the same: BE gains most from additional topics (+0.28 in DUC vs. +0.47 and +0.51 in TAC), ROUGE-SU4 again shows the smallest increase (+0.19 in DUC vs. +0.36 and +0.34 in TAC), which means it is the most stable of the metrics across the variable number of topics.[2]

[1] For reasons of space, these values are not included in the tables, as they offer little insight besides what is mentioned here.

[2] The smaller total increase might be due to the smaller number of available topics (45 in DUC vs. 48 in TAC), but we have seen the same effect in Section 3 while discussing models, so it might just be an accidental property of a given data set.

5 Discussion and conclusions

As the popularity of shared tasks increases, task organizers face an ever growing problem of providing an adequate evaluation to all participating teams. Often, evaluation of multiple runs from the same team is required, as a way to foster research and development. With more and more system submissions to judge, and the simultaneous need for multiple topics and models in order to provide a stable assessment, difficult decisions of cutting costs and effort might sometimes be necessary. It would be useful then to know where such decisions will have the smallest negative impact, or at least, what might be the trade-offs inherent in such decisions.

From our experiments, it appears that manual metrics such as Pyramid gain less from the addition of more model summaries than the automatic metrics. A Pyramid score based on any two models correlates very highly with the score based on any other two models. For the automatic metrics, the largest gain is recorded with adding the second model; afterwards the returns diminish. BE seems to be the most sensitive metric to changes in the number of models and topics; ROUGE-SU4, on the other hand, is the least sensitive to such changes and the most stable, but it does not obtain the highest correlations when many models and topics are available.

Whatever the number of models, manual Pyramid considerably outperforms automatic metrics, as can be expected, since human understanding is not hampered by the possible differences in surface expression between a candidate and a model. But when it comes to decreased number of topics, the inherent variability of human judgment shows strongly, to the extent that, in extreme cases of very few topics, it might be more prudent to use ROUGE-SU4 than Pyramid or Responsiveness.

Lastly, we observe that, as with models, adding one or two topics to the evaluation plays a great role only if we have very few topics to start with. Our experiments suggest that, as the number of topics available for evaluation increases, so does the number of additional topics necessary to make a difference in the system ranking produced by a metric. It seems that in the case of evaluation based on 48 topics, as in the TAC Summarization track, it would be possible to decrease the number to about 36 without sacrificing much stability.

References

Donna Harman and Paul Over. 2004. The effects of human variation in DUC summarization evaluation. In *Proceedings of the ACL-04 Workshop: Text Summarization Branches Out*, pages 10–17, Barcelona, Spain.

Eduard Hovy, Chin-Yew Lin, and Liang Zhou. 2005. Evaluating DUC 2005 using Basic Elements. In *Proceedings of the 5th Document Understanding Conference (DUC)*.

Chin-Yew Lin. 2004a. Looking for a few good metrics: Automatic summarization evaluation - how many samples are enough? In *Proceedings of NTCIR Workshop 4*, Tokyo, Japan.

Chin-Yew Lin. 2004b. ROUGE: A package for automatic evaluation of summaries. In *Proceedings of the ACL 2004 Workshop: Text Summarization Branches Out*, pages 74–81.

Ani Nenkova and Rebecca J. Passonneau. 2004. Evaluating content selection in summarization: The Pyramid method. In *Proceedings of the Human Language Technology Conference of the North American Chapter of the Association for Computational Linguistics*, pages 145–152, Boston, MA.

Rebecca J. Passonneau, Ani Nenkova, Kathleen McKeown, and Sergey Sigelman. 2005. Applying the Pyramid method in DUC 2005. In *Proceedings of the 5th Document Understanding Conference (DUC)*, Vancouver, Canada.

Karen Spärck Jones. 2007. Automatic summarising: The state of the art. *Information Processing and Management*, 43(6):1449–1481.

Hans van Halteren and Simone Teufel. 2003. Examining the consensus between human summaries: Initial experiments with factoid analysis. In *Proceedings of the HLT-NAACL DUC Workshop 2003*, pages 57–64, Edmonton, Canada.

Ellen M. Voorhees and Chris Buckley. 2002. Effect of topic set size on retrieval experiment error. In *Proceedings of the 25th Annual International ACM SIGIR conference on Research and Development in Information Retrieval*, pages 317–323, Tampere, Finland.

Ying Zhang and Stephan Vogel. 2004. Measuring confidence intervals for the Machine Translation evaluation metrics. In *Proceedings of the 10th Conference on Theoretical and Methodological Issues in Machine Translation*, pages 85–94, Baltimore, MD.

A Classification Algorithm for Predicting the Structure of Summaries

Horacio Saggion
University of Sheffield
211 Portobello Street
Sheffield - S1 4DP
United Kingdom
http://www.dcs.shef.ac.uk/~saggion
H.Saggion@dcs.shef.ac.uk

Abstract

We investigate the problem of generating the structure of short domain independent abstracts. We apply a supervised machine learning approach trained over a set of abstracts collected from abstracting services and automatically annotated with a text analysis tool. We design a set of features for learning inspired from past research in content selection, information ordering, and rhetorical analysis for training an algorithm which then predicts the discourse structure of unseen abstracts. The proposed approach to the problem which combines local and contextual features is able to predict the local structure of the abstracts in just over 60% of the cases.

1 Introduction

Mani (2001) defines an abstract as "a summary at least some of whose material is not present in the input". In a study of professional abstracting, Endres-Niggemeyer (2000) concluded that professional abstractors produce abstracts by "cut-and-paste" operations, and that *standard sentence patterns* are used in their production. Examples of abstracts produced by a professional abstractor are shown in Figures 1 and 2. They contain fragments "copied" from the input documents together with phrases (underlined in the figures) inserted by the professional abstractors. In a recent study in human abstracting (restricted to the amendment of authors abstracts) Montesi and Owen (2007) noted that professional abstractors prepend third person singular verbs in present tense and without subject to the author abstract, a phenomenon related – yet different – from the problem we are investigating in this paper.

Note that the phrases or predicates prepended to the selected *sentence fragments* copied from the input document have a communicative function: they inform or alert the reader about the content of the abstracted document by explicitly marking what the author *says or mentions*, *presents or introduces*, *concludes*, or *includes*, in her paper. Montesi and Owen (2007) observe that the revision of abstracts is carried out to improve comprehensibility and style and to make the abstract objective.

> Presents a model instructional session that was prepared and taught by librarians to introduce college students, faculty, and staff to the Internet by teaching them how to join listservs and topic- centered discussion groups. Describes the sessions' audience, learning objectives, facility, and course design. Presents a checklist for preparing an Internet instruction session.

Figure 1: Professional Abstracts with Inserted Predicates from LISA Abstracting Service

> Talks about Newsblaster, an experimental software tool that scans and summarizes electronic news stories, developed by Columbia University's Natural Language Processing Group. Reports that Newsblaster is a cross between a search engine and ... Explains that Newsblaster publishes the summaries in a Web page that divides the day summaries into .... Mentions that Newsblaster is considered an aid to those who have to quickly canvas large amounts of information from many sources.

Figure 2: Professional Abstract with Inserted Predicates from Internet & Personal Computing Abstracts

We investigate how to create the discourse structure of the abstracts: more specifically we are interested in predicting the inserted predicates or phrases and at which positions in the abstract they should be prepended.

Abstractive techniques in text summarization include sentence compression (Cohn and Lapata, 2008), headline generation (Soricut and Marcu, 2007), and canned-based generation (Oakes and Paice, 2001). Close to the problem studied here is Jing and McKeown's (Jing and McKeown, 2000) cut-and-paste method founded on Endres-Niggemeyer's observations. The cut-and-paste

Proceedings of the 2009 Workshop on Language Generation and Summarisation, ACL-IJCNLP 2009, pages 31–38,
Suntec, Singapore, 6 August 2009.

method includes such operations as sentence truncation, aggregation, specialization/generalization, reference adjustment and rewording. None of these operations account for the transformations observed in the abstracts of Figures 1 and 2. The formulaic expressions or predicates inserted in the abstract "glue" together the extracted fragments, thus creating the abstract's discourse structure.

To the best of our knowledge, and with the exception of Saggion and Lapalme (2002) indicative generation approach which included operations to add extra linguistic material to generate an indicative abstract, the work presented here is the first to investigate this relevant operation in the field of text abstracting and to propose a robust computational method for its simulation.

In this paper we are interested in the process of generating the structure of the abstract by automatic means. In order to study this problem, we have collected a corpus of abstracts written by abstractors; we have designed an algorithm for predicting the structure; implemented the algorithm; and evaluated the structure predicted by the automatic system against the true structure.

2 Problem Specification, Data Collection, and Annotation

The abstracts we study in this research follow the pattern:

$$\text{Abstract} \equiv \bigoplus_{i=1}^{n} \text{Pred}_i \oplus \beta_i$$

where Pred_i is a phrase used to introduce the "content" β_i of sentence i, n is the number of sentences in the abstract, $\bigoplus$ indicates multiple concatenation, and $X \oplus Y$ indicates the concatenation of X and Y. In this paper we concentrate only on this "linear" structure, we plan to study more complex (e.g., tree-like representations) in future work.

The problem we are interested in solving is the following: given sentence fragments β_i extracted from the document, how to create the Abstract. Note that if N is the number of different phrases (Pred_i) used in the model, then *a priori* there are N^n possible discourse structures to select from for the abstract, generating all possibilities and selecting the most appropriate would be impractical. We present an algorithm that decides which predicate or phrase is most suitable for each sentence, doing this by considering the sentence content and the abstract generated so far. For the experiments to be reported in this paper, the discourse structure of the abstracts is created using predicates or expressions learned from a corpus a subset of which is shown in Table 1.

We have collected abstracts from various databases including LISA, ERIC, and Internet & Personal Computing Abstracts, using our institutional library's facilities and the abstracts' providers' keyword search facilities. Electronic copies of the abstracted documents can also be accessed through our institution following a link, thus allowing us to check abstracts against abstracted document (additional information on the abstracts is given in the Appendix).

2.1 Document Processing and Annotation

Each electronic version of the abstract was processed using the freely available GATE text analysis software (Cunningham et al., 2002). First each abstract was analyzed by a text structure analysis program to identify meta-data such as title, author, source document, the text of the abstract, etc. Each sentence in the abstract was stripped from the predicate or phrase inserted by the abstractor (e.g., "Mentions that", "Concludes with") and a normalised version of the expression was used to annotate the sentence, in a way similar to the abstracts in Figures 1 and 2. After this each abstract and document title was tokenised, sentence splitted, part-of-speech tagged, and morphologically analyzed. A rule-based system was used to carry out partial, robust syntactic and semantic analysis of the abstracts (Gaizauskas et al., 2005) producing predicate-argument representations where predicates which are used to represent entities are created from the morphological roots of nouns or verbs in the text (unary predicates) and predicates with are used to represent binary relations are a closed set of names representing grammatical relations such as the verb logical object, or the verb logical subject or a prepositional attachment, etc. This predicate-argument structure representation was further analysed in order to extract "semantic" triples which are used in the experiments reported here. Output of this analysis is shown in Figure 3. Note that the representation also contains the tokens of the text, their parts of speech, lemmas, noun phrases, verb phrases, etc.

3 Proposed Solution

Our algorithm (see Algorithm 1) takes as input an ordered list of sentence fragments obtained from the source document and decides how to "paste" the fragments together into an abstract;

to address; to add; to advise; to assert; to claim; to comment; to compare; to conclude; to define; to describe; to discuss; to evaluate; to examine; to explain; to focus; to give; to highlight; to include; to indicate; to note; to observe; to overview; to point out; to present; to recommend; to report; to say; to show; to suggest; ...
to report + to indicate + to note + to declare + to include; to provide + to explain + to indicate + to mention; to point out + to report + to mention + to include; to discuss + to list + to suggest + to conclude; to present + to say + to add + to conclude + to contain; to discuss + to explain + to recommend; to discuss + to cite + to say; ...

Table 1: Subset of predicates or expressions used by professional abstractors and some of the discourse structures used.

> **Sentence**: *Features a listing of ten family-oriented programs, including vendor information, registration fees, and a short review of each.*
> **Representation**: listing-det-a; listing-of-program; family-oriented-adj-program; fee-qual-registration; information-qual-vendor; listing-apposed-information; ...

Figure 3: Sentence Representation (partial)

Algorithm 1 Discourse Structure Prediction Algorithm

Given: a list of n sorted text fragments β_i
begin
Abstract ← "";
Context ← START;
for all $i : 0 \leq i \leq n-1$; **do**
  Pred ← PredictPredicate(Context, β_i);
  Abstract ← Abstract ⊕ Pred ⊕ β_i ⊕ ".";
  Context ← ExtractContext(Abstract);
end for
return Abstract
end

at each iteration the algorithm selects the "best" available phrase or predicate to prepend to the current fragment from a finite vocabulary (induced from the analysed corpus) based on local and contextual information. One could rely on existing trainable sentence selection (Kupiec et al., 1995) or even phrase selection (Banko et al., 2000) strategies to pick up appropriate β_i's from the document to be abstracted and rely on recent information ordering techniques to sort the β_i fragments (Lapata, 2003). This is the reason why we only address here the discourse structure generation problem.

3.1 Predicting Discourse Structure as Classification

There are various possible ways of predicting what expression to insert at each point in the generation process (i.e., the *PredictPredicate* function in Algorithm 1). In the experiments reported here we use a classification algorithm based on lexical, syntactic, and discursive features, which decides which of the N possible available phrases is most suitable. The algorithm is trained over the annotated abstracts and used to predict the structure of unseen test abstracts.

Where the classification algorithm is concerned, we have decided to use Support Vector Machines which have recently been used in different tasks in natural language processing, they have been shown particularly suitable for text categorization (Joachims, 1998). We have tried other machine learning algorithms such as Decision Trees, Naive Bayes Classification, and Nearest Neighbor from the Weka toolkit (Witten and Frank, 1999), but the support vector machines gave us the best classification accuracy (a comparison with Naive Bayes will be presented in Section 4).

The features used for the experiments reported here are inspired by previous work in text summarization on content selection (Kupiec et al., 1995), rhetorical classification (Teufel and Moens, 2002), and information ordering (Lapata, 2003). The features are extracted from the analyzed abstracts with specialized programs. In particular we use positional features (position of the predicate to be generated in the structure), length features (number of words in the sentence), title features (e.g., presence of title words in sentence), content features computed as the syntactic head of noun and verb phrases, semantic features computed as the

to add; to conclude; to contain; to describe; to discuss; to explain; to feature; to include; to indicate; to mention; to note; to point out; to present; to provide; to report; to say

Table 2: Predicates in the reduced corpus

arguments of "semantic" triples (Section 2.1) extracted from the parsed abstracts. Features occurring less than 4 times in the corpus were removed for the experiments. For each sentence, a cohesion feature is also computed as the number of nouns in common with the previous sentence fragment (or title if first sentence). Cohesion information has been used in rhetorical-based parsing for summarization (Marcu, 1997) in order to decide between "list" or "elaboration" relations and also in content selection for summarization (Barzilay and Elhadad, 1997). For some experiments we also use word-level information (lemmas) and part-of-speech tags. For some of the experiments reported here the variable *Context* at iteration i in Algorithm 1 is instantiated with the predicates predicted at iterations $i-1$ and $i-2$.

4 Experiments and Results

The experiments reported here correspond to the use of different features as input for the classifier. In these experiments we have used a subset of the collected abstracts, they contain predicates which appeared at least 5 times in the corpus. With this restriction in place the original set of predicates used to create the discourse structure is reduced to sixteen (See Table 2), however, the number of possible structures in the reduced corpus is still considerable with a total of 179 different structures.

In the experiments we compare several classifiers:

- Random Generation selects a predicate at random at each iteration of the algorithm;
- Predicate-based Generation is a SVM classifier which uses the two previous predicates to generate the current predicate ignoring sentence content;
- Position-based Generation is a SVM classifier which also ignores sentence content but uses as features for classification the absolute position of the sentence to be generated;

Configuration	**Avg.Acc**
Random Generation	10%
Predicate-based Generation	35%
Position-based Generation	38%
tf*idf-based Generation	55%
Summarization-based Generation	60%

Table 3: Average accuracy of different classification configurations.

- *tf*idf*-based Generation is a SVM classifier which uses lemmas of the sentence fragment to be generated to pick up one predicate (note that position features and predicates were added to the mix without improving the classifier);
- Summarization-based Generation is a SVM which uses the summarization and discourse features discussed in the previous section including contextual information ($Pred_{i-2}$ and $Pred_{i-1}$ – with special values when $i=0$ and $i=1$).

We measure the performance of each instance of the algorithm by comparing the predicted structure against the true structure. We compute two metrics: (i) accuracy at the sentence level (as in classification), which is the proportion of predicates which were correctly generated; and (ii) accuracy at the textual level, which is the proportion of abstracts correctly generated. For the latter we compute the proportion of abstracts with zero errors, less than two errors, and less than three errors.

For every instance of the algorithm we perform a cross-validation experiment, selecting for each experiment 20 abstracts for testing and the rest of the abstracts for training. Accuracy measures at sentence and text levels are averages of the cross-validation experiments.

Results of the algorithms are presented in Tables 3 and 4. Random generation has very poor performance with only 10% local accuracy and less than 1% of full correct structures. Knowledge of the predicates selected for previous sentences improves performance over the random system (35% local accuracy and 5% of full correct structures predicted). As in previous summarization studies, position proved to contribute to the task: the positional classifier predicts individual predicates with a 38% accuracy; however only 8% of the structures are recalled. Differences between the accuracies of the two algorithms (predicate-based and position-based) are significant at 95% confidence level (a *t-test* was used). As it is usually the case in text classification experiments, the use of word level information (lemmas in our case) achieves good performance: 55% classification accuracy at sentence level, and 18% of full structures correctly predicted. The use of lexical (noun and verb heads, arguments), syntactic (parts of speech information), and discourse (predicted predicates, position, cohesion) features has the better performance with 60% classification accuracy at sentence level predicting 21% of all structures with 73% of the structures containing less than 3 errors. The differences in accuracy between the word-based classifier and the summarization-based classifier are statistically significant at 95% confidence level (a *t-test* was used). A Naive Bayes classifier which uses the summarization features achieves 50% classification accuracy.

Conf.	**0 errs**	$<$ **2 errrs**	$<$ **3 errs**
Random	0.3%	4%	20%
Predicate-based	5%	24%	48%
Position-based	8%	33%	50%
tf*idf-based	18%	42%	67%
Summ-based	21%	55%	73%

Table 4: Percent of correct and partially correct structures predicted. Averaged over all runs.

Table 5 shows a partial confusion table for predicates "to add", "to conclude", "to explain", and "to present" while and Table 6 reports individual classification accuracy. All these results are based on averages of the summarization-based classifier.

5 Discussion

We have presented here a problem which has not been investigated before in the field of text summarization: the addition of extra linguistic material (i.e., not present in the source document) to the abstract "informational content" in order to create the structure of the abstract. We have proposed an algorithm which uses a classification component at each iteration to predict predicates or phrases to be prepended to fragments extracted from a document. We have shown that this classifier based on summarization features including linguistic, semantic, positional, cohesive, and discursive information can predict the local discourse structures in over 60% of the cases. There is a mixed picture on the prediction of individual predicates, with most predicates correctly classified in most of the cases except for predicates such as "to describe", "to note", and "to report" which are confused with other phrases. Predicates such as "to present" and "to include" have the tendency of appearing towards the very beginning or the very end of the abstract been therefore predicted by position-based features (Edmundson, 1969; Lin and Hovy, 1997). Note that in this work we have decided to evaluate the predicted structure against the true structure (a hard evaluation measure), in future work we will assess the abstracts with a set of quality questions similar to those put forward by the Document Understanding Conference Evaluations (also in a way similar to (Kan and McKeown, 2002) who evaluated their abstracts in a retrieval environment). We expect to obtain a reasonable evaluation result given that it appears that some of the predicates or phrases are "interchangeable" (e.g., "to contain" and "to include").

Actual Pred.	**Predicted Pred.**	**Conf.Freq.**
to add	to add	32%
	to explain	16%
	to say	10%
to conclude	to conclude	35%
	to say	29%
	to add	7%
to explain	to explain	35%
	to say	15%
	to add	11%
to present	to present	86%
	to discuss	7%
	to provide	1%

Table 5: Classification Confusion Table for a Subset of Predicates in the Corpus (Average Frequency).

6 Related Work

Liddy (1991) produced a formal model of the informational or conceptual structure of abstracts of empirical research. This structure was elicited from abstractors of two organizations ERIC and PsycINFO through a series of tasks. Lexical clues which predict the components of the structure were latter induced by corpus analysis. In the domain of indicative summarization, Kan and McK-

Predicate	Avg. Accuracy
to add	31.40
to conclude	34.78
to contain	10.96
to describe	15.69
to discuss	54.55
to explain	35.63
to feature	34.38
to include	85.86
to indicate	20.69
to mention	26.47
to note	6.78
to point out	91.67
to present	86.19
to provide	40.94
to report	1.59
to say	75.86

Table 6: Predicate Classification Accuracy

eown (2002) studied the problem of generating abstracts for bibliographical data which although in a restricted domain has some contact points with the work described here. As in their work we use the abstracts in our corpus to induce the model. They rely on a more or less fixed discourse structure to accommodate the generation process. In our approach the discourse structure is not fixed but predicted for each particular abstract. Related to our classification experiments is work on semantic or rhetorical classification of "structured" abstracts (Saggion, 2008) from the MEDLINE abstracting database where similar features to those presented here were used to identify in abstracts semantic categories such as objective, method, results, and conclusions. Related to this is the work by Teufel and Moens (2002) on rhetorical classification for content selection. In cut-and-paste summarization (Jing and McKeown, 2000), sentence combination operations were implemented manually following the study of a set of professionally written abstracts; however the particular "pasting" operation presented here was not implemented. Previous studies on text-to-text abstracting (Banko et al., 2000; Knight and Marcu, 2000) have studied problems such as sentence compression and sentence combination but not the "pasting" procedure presented here. The insertion in the abstract of linguistic material not present in the input document has been addressed in paraphrase generation (Barzilay and Lee, 2004) and canned-based summarization (Oakes and Paice, 2001) in limited domains. Saggion and Lapalme (2002) have studied and implemented a rule-based "verb selection" operation in their SumUM system which has been applied to introduce document topics during indicative summary generation.

Our discourse structure generation procedure is in principle generic but depends on the availability of a corpus for training.

7 Conclusions

In text summarization research, most attention has been paid to the problem of what information to select for a summary. Here, we have focused on the problem of how to combine the selected content with extra linguistic information in order to create the structure of the summary.

There are several contributions of this work:

- First, we have presented the problem of generating the discourse structures of an abstract and proposed a meta algorithm for predicting it. This problem has not been investigated before.
- Second, we have proposed – based on previous summarization research – a number of features to be used for solving this problem; and
- Finally, we have propose several instantiations of the algorithm to solve the problem and achieved a reasonable accuracy using the designed features;

There is however much space for improvement even though the algorithm recalls some "partial structures", many "full structures" can not be generated. We are currently investigating the use of induced rules to address the problem and will compare a rule-based approach with our classifier. Less superficial cohesion features are being investigated and will be tested in this classification framework.

Acknowledgements

We would like to thank three anonymous reviewers for their suggestions and comments. We thank Adam Funk who helped us improve the quality of our paper. Part of this research was carried out while the author was working for the EU-funded MUSING project (IST-2004-027097).

References

Michele Banko, Vibhu O. Mittal, and Michael J. Witbrock. 2000. Headline generation based on statistical translation. In *ACL '00: Proceedings of the 38th Annual Meeting on Association for Computational Linguistics*, pages 318–325, Morristown, NJ, USA. Association for Computational Linguistics.

Regina Barzilay and Michael Elhadad. 1997. Using Lexical Chains for Text Summarization. In *Proceedings of the ACL/EACL'97 Workshop on Intelligent Scalable Text Summarization*, pages 10–17, Madrid, Spain, July.

R. Barzilay and L. Lee. 2004. Catching the Drift: Probabilistic Content Models, with Applications to Generation and Summarization. In *Proceedings of HLT-NAACL 2004*.

T. Cohn and M. Lapata. 2008. Sentence compression beyond word deletion. In *Proceedings of COLING 2008*, Manchester.

H. Cunningham, D. Maynard, K. Bontcheva, and V. Tablan. 2002. GATE: A framework and graphical development environment for robust NLP tools and applications. In *ACL 2002*.

H.P. Edmundson. 1969. New Methods in Automatic Extracting. *Journal of the Association for Computing Machinery*, 16(2):264–285, April.

Brigitte Endres-Niggemeyer. 2000. SimSum: an empirically founded simulation of summarizing. *Information Processing & Management*, 36:659–682.

R. Gaizauskas, M. Hepple, H. Saggion, and M. Greenwood. 2005. SUPPLE: A Practical Parser for Natural Language Engineering Applications.

Hongyan Jing and Kathleen McKeown. 2000. Cut and Paste Based Text Summarization. In *Proceedings of the 1st Meeting of the North American Chapter of the Association for Computational Linguistics*, pages 178–185, Seattle, Washington, USA, April 29 - May 4.

T. Joachims. 1998. Text categorization with support vector machines: Learning with many relevant features. In *European Conference on Machine Learning (ECML)*, pages 137–142, Berlin. Springer.

Min-Yen Kan and Kathleen R.. McKeown. 2002. Corpus-trained text generation for summarization. In *Proceedings of the Second International Natural Language Generation Conference (INLG 2002)*, pages 1–8, Harriman, New York, USA.

Kevin Knight and Daniel Marcu. 2000. Statistics-based summarization - step one: Sentence compression. In *Proceedings of the 17th National Conference of the American Association for Artificial Intelligence*. AAAI, July 30 - August 3.

Julian Kupiec, Jan Pedersen, and Francine Chen. 1995. A Trainable Document Summarizer. In *Proc. of the 18th ACM-SIGIR Conference*, pages 68–73, Seattle, Washington, United States.

M. Lapata. 2003. Probabilistic Text Structuring: Experiments with Sentence Ordering. In *Proceedings of the 41st Meeting of the Association of Computational Linguistics*, pages 545–552, Sapporo, Japan.

Elizabeth D. Liddy. 1991. The Discourse-Level Structure of Empirical Abstracts: An Exploratory Study. *Information Processing & Management*, 27(1):55–81.

C. Lin and E. Hovy. 1997. Identifying Topics by Position. In *Fifth Conference on Applied Natural Language Processing*, pages 283–290. Association for Computational Linguistics, 31 March-3 April.

Inderjeet Mani. 2001. *Automatic Text Summarization*. John Benjamins Publishing Company.

D. Marcu. 1997. *The Rhetorical Parsing, Summarization, and Generation of Natural Language Texts*. Ph.D. thesis, Department of Computer Science, University of Toronto.

M. Montesi and J. M. Owen. 2007. Revision of author abstracts: how it is carried out by LISA editors. *Aslib Proceedings*, 59(1):26–45.

M.P. Oakes and C.D. Paice. 2001. Term extraction for automatic abstracting. In D. Bourigault, C. Jacquemin, and M-C. L'Homme, editors, *Recent Advances in Computational Terminology*, volume 2 of *Natural Language Processing*, chapter 17, pages 353–370. John Benjamins Publishing Company.

H. Saggion and G. Lapalme. 2002. Generating Indicative-Informative Summaries with SumUM. *Computational Linguistics*, 28(4):497–526.

H. Saggion. 2008. Automatic Summarization: An Overview. *Revue Française de Linguistique Appliquée* , XIII(1), Juin.

R. Soricut and D. Marcu. 2007. Abstractive headline generation using WIDL-expressions. *Inf. Process. Manage.*, 43(6):1536–1548.

S. Teufel and M. Moens. 2002. Summarizing Scientific Articles: Experiments with Relevance and Rhetorical Status. *Computational Linguistics*, 28(4):409–445.

Ian H. Witten and Eibe Frank. 1999. *Data Mining: Practical Machine Learning Tools and Techniques with Java Implementations*. Morgan Kaufmann, October.

Appendix I: Corpus Statistics and Examples

The corpus of abstracts following the specification given in Section 2 contains 693 abstracts, 10,423 sentences, and 305,105 tokens. The reduced corpus used for the experiments contains 300 abstracts.

Examples

Here we list one example of the use of each of the predicates in the reduced set of 300 abstracts used for the experiments.

Adds that it uses search commands and features that are similar to those of traditional online commercial database services, has the ability to do nested Boolean queries as well as truncation when needed, and provides detailed documentation that offers plenty of examples.

Concludes CNET is a network of sites, each dealing with a specialized aspect of computers that are accessible from the home page and elsewhere around the site.

Contains a step-by-step guide to using PGP.

Describes smallbizNet, the LEXIS-NEXIS Small Business Service, Small Business Administration, Small Business Advancement National Center, and other small business-related sites.

Discusses connections and links between differing electronic mail systems.

Explains DataStar was one of the first online hosts to offer a Web interface, and was upgraded in 1997.

Features tables showing the number of relevant, non-relevant, and use retrievals on both LEXIS and WIN for federal and for state court queries.

Includes an electronic organizer, an ergonomically correct keyboard, an online idle-disconnect, a video capture device, a color photo scanner, a real-time Web audio player, laptop speakers, a personal information manager (PIM), a mouse with built-in scrolling, and a voice fax-modem.

Indicates that the University of California, Berkeley, has the School of Information Management and Systems, the University of Washington has the Information School, and the University of Maryland has the College of Information Studies.

Mentions that overall, the interface is effective because the menus and sear screens permit very precise searches with no knowledge of searching or Dialog databases.

Notes that Magazine Index was originally offered on Lyle Priest's invention, a unique microfilm reader.

Points out the strong competition that the Internet has created for the traditional online information services, and the move of these services to the Internet.

Presents searching tips and techniques.

Provides summaries of African art; Allen Memorial Art Museum of Oberlin College; Art crimes; Asian arts; Da Vinci, Leonardo; Gallery Walk; and Native American Art Gallery.

Reports that Dialog has announced major enhancements to its alerting system on the DialogClassic, DialogClassic Web, and DialogWeb services.

Says that dads from all over the country share advice on raising children, educational resources, kids' software, and other related topics using their favorite online service provider.

Syntax-Driven Sentence Revision for Broadcast News Summarization

Hideki Tanaka, Akinori Kinoshita, Takeshi Kobayakawa,
Tadashi Kumano and Naoto Kato
NHK Science and Technology Research Labs.
1-10-11, Kinuta, Setagaya-ku, Tokyo, Japan
{tanaka.h-ja,kinoshita.a-ek,kobayakawa-t.ko,kumano.t-eq,kato.n-ga}@nhk.or.jp

Abstract

We propose a method of revising lead sentences in a news broadcast. Unlike many other methods proposed so far, this method does not use the coreference relation of noun phrases (NPs) but rather, insertion and substitution of the phrases modifying the same head chunk in lead and other sentences. The method borrows an idea from the sentence fusion methods and is more general than those using NP coreferencing as ours includes them. We show in experiments the method was able to find semantically appropriate revisions thus demonstrating its basic feasibility. We also show that that parsing errors mainly degraded the sentential completeness such as grammaticality and redundancy.

1 Introduction

We address the problem of revising the lead sentence in a broadcast news text to increase the amount of background information in the lead. This is one of the draft and revision approaches to summarization, which has received keen attention in the research community. Unlike many other methods that directly utilize noun phrase (NP) coreference (Nenkova 2008; Mani et al. 1999), we propose a method that employs insertion and substitution of phrases that modify the same chunk in the lead and other sentences. We also show its effectiveness in a revision experiment.

As is well known, the extractive summary that has been extensively studied from the early days of summarization history (Luhn, 1958) suffers from various drawbacks. These include the problems of a break in cohesion in the summary text such as dangling anaphora and a sudden shift in topic.

To ameliorate these problems, the idea of revising the extracted sentences was proposed in a single document summarization study. Jing and McKeown (1999; 2000) found that human summarization can be traced back to six cut-and-paste operations of a text and proposed a revision method consisting of sentence reduction and combination modules with a sentence extraction part. Mani and colleagues (1999) proposed a summarization system based on "draft and revision" together with sentence extraction. The revision part is achieved with the sentence aggregation and smoothing modules.

The cohesion break problem becomes particularly conspicuous in multi-document summarization. To ameliorate this, revision of the extracted sentences is also thought to be effective, and many ideas and methods have been proposed so far. For example, Otterbacher and colleagues (2002) analyzed manually revised extracts and factored out cohesion problems. Nenkova (2008) proposed a revision idea that utilizes noun coreference with linguistic quality improvements in mind.

Other than the break in cohesion, multi-document summarization faces the problem of information overlap particularly when the document set consists of similar sentences. Barzilay and McKeown (2005) proposed an idea called sentence fusion that integrates information in overlapping sentences to produce a non-overlapping summary sentence. Their algorithm firstly analyzes the sentences to obtain the dependency trees and sets a basis tree by finding the centroid of the dependency trees. It next augments the basis tree with the sub-trees in other sentences and finally prunes the predefined constituents. Their algorithm was further modified and applied to the German biographies by Filippova and Strube (2008).

Like the work of Jing and McKeown (2000) and Mani et al. (1999), our work was inspired by the summarization method used by human abstractors. Actually, our abstractors first extract important sentences, which is called lead identification, and then revise them, which is referred to as phrase elaboration or specification. In this paper, we concentrate on the revision part.

Our work can be viewed as an application of the sentence fusion method to the draft and revision

Proceedings of the 2009 Workshop on Language Generation and Summarisation, ACL-IJCNLP 2009, pages 39–47,
Suntec, Singapore, 6 August 2009.

approach to a single Japanese news document summarization. Actually, our dependency structure alignment is almost the same as that of Filippova and Strube (2008), and our lead sentence plays the role of a basis tree in the Barzilay and McKeown approach (2005). Though the idea of sentence fusion was developed mainly for suppressing the overlap in multi-document summarization, we consider this effective in augmenting the extracts in a single-document summarization task where we face less overlap among sentences.

Before explaining the method in detail, we will briefly introduce the Japanese dependency [1] structure on which our idea is based. The dependency structure is constructed based on the bunsetsu chunk, which we call "chunk" for simplicity. The chunk usually consists of one content-bearing word and a series of function words. All the chunks in a sentence except for the last one modify a chunk in the right direction. We call the modifying chunk the modifier and the modified chunk the head. We usually span a directed edge from a modifier chunk to the head chunk[2]. Our dependency tree has no syntactic information such as subject or object.

2 Broadcast news summarization

Tanaka et al. (2005) showed that most Japanese broadcast news texts are written with a three-part structure, i.e., the lead, body, and supplement. The most important information is succinctly mentioned in the lead, which is the opening sentence(s) of a news story, referred to as an "article" here. Proper names and details are sometimes avoided in favor of more abstract expressions such as "big insurance company." The lead is then detailed in the body by answering who, what, when, where, why, and how, and proper names only alluded to in the lead appear here. Necessary information that was not covered in the lead or the body is placed in the supplement.

The research also reports that professional news abstractors who are hired for digital text services summarize articles in a two-step approach. First, they identify the lead sentences and set it (them) as the starting point of the summary. As the average lead length is 95 characters and the allowed summary length is about 115 characters (or 150 characters depending on the screen design), they revise the lead sentences using expressions from the remainder of the story.

We see here that the extraction and revision strategy that has been extensively studied by many researchers for various reasons was actually applied by human abstractors, and therefore, the strategy can be used as a real summarization model. Inspired by this, we decided to study a news summarization system based on the above approach. To develop a complete summarization system, we have to solve three problems: 1) identifying the lead, body, and supplement structure in each article, 2) finding the lead revision candidates, and 3) generating a final summary by selecting and combining the candidates.

We have already studied problem 1) and showed that automatic recognition of three tags with a decision tree algorithm reached a precision over 92% (Tanaka et al. 2007). We then moved to problem 2), which we discuss extensively in the rest of this paper.

3 Manual lead revision experiment

To see how problem 2) in the previous section could be solved, we conducted a manual lead-revision experiment. We asked a native Japanese speaker to revise the lead sentences of 15 news articles using expressions from the body section of each article with cut-and-paste operations (insertion and substitution) of bunsetsu chunk sequences. We refer to chunk sequences as phrases. We also asked the reviser to find as many revisions as possible.

In the interview with her, we found that she took advantage of the syntactic structure to revise the lead sentences. Actually, she first searched for the "same" chunks in the lead and the body and checked whether the modifier phrases to these chunks could be used for revision. To see what makes these chunks the "same," we compared the syntactic head chunk of the lead and body phrases used for substitution and insertion.

Table 1 summarizes the results of the comparison in three categories: perfect match, partial match (content word match), and different.

The table indicates that nearly half of the head chunks were exactly the same, and the rest contained some differences. The second row shows the number where the syntactic heads had the same content words but not the same function words. The pair 会談し kaidan-shi 'talked' and 会談しました kaidan-shi-mashi-ta 'talked' is an

[1] This is the kakari-uke (modifier-modifiee) relation of Japanese, which differs from the conventional dependency relation. We use the term dependency for convenience in this paper.

[2] This is the other way around compared to the English dependency such as in Barzilay and McKeown (2005).

		Ins.	Sub.	Total
1)	Perfect	9	6	15
2)	Partial	6	6	12
3)	Different	1	6	7
	Total	16	18	34

Table 1. Degree of syntactic head agreement

example. These are the syntactic and aspectual variants of the same verb 会談する kaidan-suru 'talk.'

The third row represents cases where the syntactic heads had no common surface words. We found that even in this case, though, the syntactic heads were close in some way. In one example, there was accordance in the distant heads, for instance, in the pair 見つかった mitsuka-tta 'found' and 一部の ichibu-no 'part of.' In this case, we can find the chunk 見つかった mitsuka-tta 'found' at a short edge distance from 一部の ichibu-no 'part of.' Based on the findings, we devised a lead sentence revision algorithm.

4 Revision algorithm

4.1 Concept

We explain here the concept of our algorithm and show an example in Figure 1. We have a lead sentence and a body sentence, both of which have the "same" syntactic head chunk, 到着しました, touchaku-shima-shi-ta, 'arrived.'

The head chunk of the lead has two phrases (underlined with thick lines in Figure 1) that directly modify the head. We call such a phrase a *maximum phrase* of a head[3]. Like the lead sentence, the body sentence also has two maximum phrases. In the following part, we use the term phrase to refer to a maximum phrase for simplicity.

By comparing the phrases in Figure 1, we notice that the following operations can add useful information to the lead sentence; 1) inserting the first phrase of the body will supply the fact the visit was on the 4th, 2) substituting the first phrase of the lead with the second one in the body adds the detail of the IAEA team. This revision strategy was employed by the human reviser mentioned in section 2, and we consider this to be effective because our target document has a so-called inverse pyramid structure (Robin and McKeown 1996), in which the first sentence is elaborated by the following sentences.

[3] To be more precise, a maximum phrase is defined as the maximum chunk sequence on a dependency path of a head.

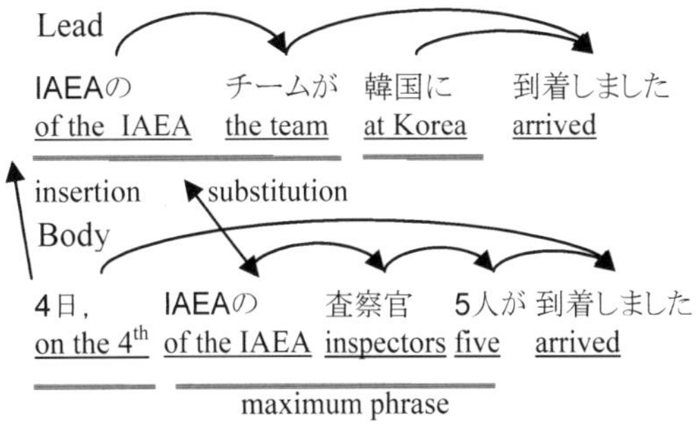

Figure 1. Concept of revision algorithm

Further analyzing the above fact, we devised the lead sentence revision algorithm below. We present the outline here and discuss the details in the next section. We suppose an input pair of a lead and a body sentence that are syntactically analyzed.

1) Trigger search
   We search for the "same" chunks in the lead and body sentences. We call the "same" chunks *triggers* as they give the starting point to the revision.
2) Phrase alignment
   We identify the maximum phrases of each trigger, and these phrases are aligned according to a similarity metric.
3) Substitution
   If a body phrase has a corresponding phrase in the lead, and the body phrase is richer in information, we substitute the body phrase for the lead phrase.
4) Insertion
   If a body phrase has no counterpart in the lead, that is, the phrase is floating, we insert it into the lead sentence.

Our method inserts and substitutes any type of phrase that modifies the trigger and therefore has no limitation in syntactic type. Although NP elaboration such as in (Nenkova 2008) is of great importance, there are other useful syntactic types for revision. An example is the adverbial phrase insertion of time and location. The insertion of the phrase 4日 yokka 'on the 4th' in figure 1 indeed adds useful information to the lead sentence.

4.2 Algorithm

The overall flow of the revision algorithm is shown in Algorithm 1. The inputs are a lead and a body sentence that are syntactically parsed, which are denoted by L and B respectively.

The whole algorithm starts with the all-trigger search in step 1. Revision candidates are then found for each trigger pair in the main loop from steps 2 to 6. The revision for each trigger pair is

Algorithm 1[4] (Left figures are the step numbers.)

1: find all trigger pairs between L and B and store them in T.
$T=\{(l, b)\ ;\ l \approx b,\ l \in L$ and $b \in B\}$
2: for all $(l, b) \in T$ do
find l's max phrases and store in P_l.
$P_l=\{p_l\ ;\ p_l \in$ max phrase of $l\}$
3: do the same for trigger b
$P_b=\{p_b\ ;\ p_b \in$ max phrase of $b\}$
4: align phrases in P_l and P_b and store result in A
$A=\{(p_l, p_b)\ ;\ p_l \leftrightarrow p_b,\ p_l \in P_l, p_b \in P_b\}$
5: for all $(p_l, p_b) \in A$ do
follow Table 2
end for
6: end for

		Body	
		$p_b = \emptyset$	$p_b \neq \emptyset$
Lead	$p_l = \emptyset$	4: no op.	1: insertion
	$p_l \neq \emptyset$	3: no op.	2: substitution

Table 2. Operations for step 5

found based on the idea in the previous section in steps 4 and 5. Now we explain the main parts.

- Step 1: trigger chunk pair search

We first detect the trigger pairs in step 1 that are the base of the revision process. What then can be a trigger pair that yields correct revisions? We roughly define trigger pairs as the "coreferential" chunk pairs of all parts of speech, i.e., the parts of speech that point to the same entity, event, action, change, and so on.

Notice that the term coreferential is used in an extended way as it is usually used to describe the phenomena in noun group pairs (Mitkov, 2002). The chunk 到着しました touchaku-shimashita 'arrived' and IAEA の IAEA-no 'of the IAEA' in Figure 1 are examples.

Identifying our coreferential chunks is even harder than the conventional coreference resolution, and we made a simplifying assumption as in Nenkova (2008) with some additional conditions that were obtained through our preliminary experiments.

(1) Assumption: Two chunks having the same surface forms are coreferential.
(2) Conditions for light verb (noun) chunks: Agreement of modifying verbal nous is further required for chunks whose content words consist only of light verbs such as ある aru 'be' and なる naru 'become': these chunks themselves have little lexical meaning. The agreement is checked with the hand-crafted rules. Similar checks are applied to chunks whose content words consist only of light nouns such as こと koto ('koto' makes the previous verb a noun) .
(3) Conditions for verb inflections: a chunk that contains a verb usually ends with a function word series that indicates a variety of information such as inflection type, dependency type, tense, aspect, and modality. Some information such as tense and aspect is vital to decide the coreference relation (exchanging the modifier phrases "arrive" and "will arrive" will likely bring about inconsistency in meaning), although some is not. We are in the process of categorizing function words that do not affect the coreference relation and temporally adopted the empirically obtained rule: the difference in verb inflection between the te-form (predicate modifying form) and dictionary form (sentence end form) can be ignored.

- Step 4: phrase alignment

We used the surface form agreement for similarity evaluation. We applied several metrics and explain them one by one.

1) Chunk similarity t, s
$t, s : x, y \in$ chunk $\rightarrow [0, 1]$.
Function t is the Dice coefficient between the set of content words in x and those in y. The same coefficient calculated with all words (function and content words) is denoted as s.

2) Phrase absorption ratio
$a : p_x, p_y \in$ phrases $\rightarrow [0, 1]$
This is the function that indicates how many chunks in phrase p_x is represented in p_y and is calculated with t as in,

$$a(p_x, p_y) := \frac{1}{|p_x|} \sum_{x \in p_x} \max_{y \in p_y}(t(x, y)).$$

3) Alignment quality
With the above two functions, the alignment quallity is evaluated by the function
$g : p_x, p_y \in$ phrases $\rightarrow [0, 1]$

$$g(p_x, p_y) := \alpha a(p_x, p_y) + (1-\alpha)s(x, y),$$

$$\alpha \in [0,1],$$

where the shorter phrase is set to p_x so that $|p_x| < |p_y|$. The variables x and y are the last

[4] The sign a $\approx$ b means the chunk "a" and "b" are triggers. The sign p $\leftrightarrow$ q means the phrases "p" and "q" are aligned.

chunks in p_x and p_y, respectively. Intuitively, the function evaluates how many chunks in the shorter phrase p_x are represented in p_y and how similar the last chunks are. The last chunk in a phrase, especially the function words in the chunk, determines the syntactic character of the phrase, and we measured this value with the second term of the alignment quality. The parameter α is decided empirically, which was set at 0.375 in this paper.

In alignment, we calculated the score for all possible phrase combinations and then greedily selected the pair with the highest score. We set the minimum alignment score at 0.185; those pairs with scores lower than this value were not aligned.

- Step 5 (Table 2, case 1): insertion

Step 5 starts either an insertion or substitution process, as in Table 2. If $p_b \neq \varnothing$ (body phrase is not null) and $p_l = \varnothing$ (lead phrase is null) in Table 2, the insertion process starts.

In this process, we check the following.

1) Redundancy check

Insertion may cause redundancy in information. As a matter of fact, redundancy often happens when there is an error in syntactic analysis. Suppose there are the same lead and body phrases that modify the same chunks in the lead and body sentences. If the lead phrase fails to modify the correct chunk because of an error, the body phrase loses the chance to be aligned to the lead phrase since they belong to different trigger chunks. As a result, the body phrase becomes a floating phrase and is inserted into the lead chunk, which duplicates the same phrase.

To prevent this, we evaluate the degree of duplication with the phrase absorption ratio a and allow phrase insertion when the score is below a predefined threshold θ: we allow insertion when

$a(p_b, L) < \theta, p_b \in \text{phrase}, L$: lead sentence,

is satisfied.

2) Discourse coherence check

Blind phrase insertion may invite a break in cohesion in a lead sentence. This frequently happens when the inserted phrase has words that require an antecedent. We then prepared a list of words that contain such context-requiring words and forbid phrase insertions that contain words that are on the list. This list contains the pronoun family such as この kono 'this' and special adjectives such as 違う chigau 'different.'

3) Insertion point decision

The body phrase should be inserted at the proper position in the lead sentence to maintain the syntactic consistency. Because we dealt with single-phrase insertion here, we employed a simple heuristics.

Since the Japanese dependency edge spans from left to right as we mentioned in section 1, we considered that the right phrase of the inserted phrase is important to keep the new dependency from the inserted phrase to the trigger chunk. Because we already know the phrase alignment status at this stage, we follow the next steps to determine the insertion position in the lead of the insertion phrase.

A) In the body sentence, find the nearest right substitution phrase p_r of the insertion phrase.
B) Find the p_r's aligned phrase in the lead p_r^L.
C) Insert the phrase to the left of the p_r^L.
D) If there is no p_r, insert the phrase to the left to the trigger.

- Step 5 (Table 2, case 2): substitution

If $p_b \neq \varnothing$ and $p_l \neq \varnothing$ in Table 2, the substitution process starts. This process first checks if each aligned phrase pair contains the same chunk other than the present trigger. If there is such a chunk, the substitution phrase is reduced to the subtree from the present trigger to the identical chunk. The newly found identical chunks are in trigger table T, and the remaining part will be evaluated later in the main loop. Owing to the phrase partitioning, we can avoid phrase substitutions which are in an inclusive relation.

The substitution candidate goes through three checks: information increase, redundancy, and discourse cohesion. As the latter two are almost the same as those in the insertion, we explain here the information increase. This involves checking whether the number of chunks in the body phrase is greater than that in the aligned lead phrase. This is based on the simple assumption that elaboration requires more words.

5 Revision experiments

5.1 Data and evaluation steps

- Purpose

We conducted a lead revision experiment with three purposes. The first one was to empirically evaluate the validity of our simplified assumptions: trigger identification and concreteness increase evaluation. For trigger identification, we basically viewed the identical chunks as triggers and added some amendments for light verbs (nouns) and verb inflections. For the check of an increase in concreteness, we assumed that phrases with more chunks were more concrete. However, these simplifications should be verified in experiments.

The second purpose was to check the validity of using the revision phrases only in body sentences and not in the supplemental sentences.

The last one was to determine how ineffective the result is if the syntactic parsing fails. With these purposes in mind, we designed our experiment as follows.

- Data

A total of 257 articles from news programs broadcast on 20 Jan., 20 Apr., and 20 July in 2004 were tagged with lead, body, and supplement tags by a native Japanese evaluator. The articles were morphologically analyzed by Mecab (Kudo et al., 2003) and syntactically parsed by Cabocha (Kudo and Matsumoto, 2002).

- Evaluator and evaluation detail

We prepared an evaluation interface that presents a lead with one revision point (insertion or substitution) that was obtained using the body and supplemental sentences to an evaluator.

A Japanese native speaker evaluated the results one by one with the above interface. We planned a linguistic evaluation like DUC2005 (Hoa Trang, 2005). Since their five-type evaluation is intended for multi-document summarization, whereas our task is single-document summarization, and we are interested in evaluating our questions mentioned above, we carried out the evaluation as follows. In future, we plan to increase the number of evaluation items and the number of evaluators.

Concreteness	Score
Decreased	0
Unchanged	1
Increased	2

Table 3. Evaluation of increased concreteness

Completeness	Required operations	Score
Poor	More than 2	0
Acceptable	One	1
Perfect	None	2

Table 4. Sentential completeness

E1) The evaluator judged if the revision was obtained from the lead and body sentences with or without parsing errors. Here, errors that did not affect the revision were not considered.

E2) Second, she checked whether the revision was semantically correct or revised information matching the fact described in the lead sentence. Here, she did not care about the grammaticality or the improvements in concreteness of the revision; if the revision was problematic but manually correctable, it was judged as OK. This step evaluated the correctness of the trigger selection; wrong triggers, i.e., those referring to different facts produce semantically inconsistent revisions as they mix up different facts.

The following evaluation was done for those judged correct in evaluation step E2, as we found that revisions that were semantically inconsistent with the lead's facts were often too difficult to evaluate further.

E3) Third, she evaluated the change in concreteness after revision with the revisions that passed evaluation E2. She judged whether or not the revision increased the concreteness of the lead in three categories (Table 3).
Notice that original lead sentences are supposed to have an average score of 1.

E4) Last, she checked the sentential completeness of the revision result that passed evaluation E2. They still contained problems such as grammatical errors and improper insertion position. Rather than evaluating these items separately, we measured them together for sentential completeness. At this time, we measured in terms of the number of operations (insertion, deletion, substitution) needed to make the sentence complete[5].

As shown in Table 4, revisions requiring more than two operations are categorized as "poor," those requiring one operation are "acceptable," and those requiring no operations are "perfect." We employed this measure because we found that grading detailed items such as grammaticality and insertion positions at fine levels was rather difficult. We also found that native Japanese speakers can correct errors easily. Notice the lead sentences are perfect and are supposed

[5] This was not an automatic process and may not be perfect. The evaluator simulated the correction in mind and judged whether it was done with one action.

to have an average score of 2 in sentential completeness. Since the revision does not improve the completeness further but elicits defects such as grammatical errors, it usually produces a score below 2. Some examples of the results with their scores are shown below. The underlined parts are the inserted body chunk phrases, and the parenthesized parts are the deleted lead chunks.

1) Concreteness 2, Completeness 2
民間団体の「コリア・ソサエティ」などが主催する「朝鮮半島平和フォーラム」に（催しに）出席する…
minkan-dantai-no 'private organization', korea-society-nado-ga 'Korea Society and others', shusai-suru 'sponsored', chousen-hantou-heiwa-forumu-ni 'Peace Forum in Korean Peninsula', (moyooshi-ni 'event'), shusseki-suru 'attend'

2) Concreteness 1, Completeness 2
部品に亀裂が入っているのが（）見つかった…
buhin-ni 'to the parts' ki-retsu-ga 'cracks', haitte-iru-no-ga 'being there' (), mitsuka-tta 'found'

3) Concreteness 2, Completeness 0
ヘリコプターから地上二十メートルの高さから（）落下し死亡しました。
Herikoputa-kara 'from a helicopter', chijou-niju-metoru-no-takasa-kara 'from 20 meters high' (), rakka-shi 'fell and', shibou-shima-shita 'killed'

Example 1 is the perfect substitution and had scores of 2 for both concreteness increase and completeness. Actually, the originally vaguely mentioned term 'event' was replaced by a more concrete phrase with proper names, 'Korean Peninsula Peace Forum sponsored by Korea Society and others.' Notice that this can be achieved by NP coreference based methods if they can identify that these two different phrases are coreferential. Our method does this through the dependency on the same trigger 出席する shusseki-suru 'attend.'

Example 2 is a perfect sentence, but its concreteness stayed at the same level. As a result, the scores were 1 for concreteness increase and 2 for completeness.

		Incorrect	Correct	Cor. Ratio
Parse	Succ.	70	353	0.83
	Fail.	31	149	0.83
Sent.	Body	50	464	0.90
	Supp.	51	38	0.43

Table 5. Results of semantic correctness

Score		0	1	2	Ave.
Parse	Succ.	0	55	298	1.84
	Fail.	1	19	129	1.86
Sent.	Body	1	61	402	1.86
	Supp.	0	13	25	1.66

Table 6. Results of concreteness increase

Score		0	1	2	Ave.
Parse	Succ.	78	60	215	1.39
	Fail.	66	55	28	0.74
Sent.	Body	120	110	234	1.25
	Supp.	24	5	9	0.61

Table 7. Results of sentential completeness

Actually, the original sentence that meant "They found a crack in the parts" was revised to "They found there was a crack in the parts," which did not add useful information. Example 3 has a grammatical problem although the revision supplied useful information.As a result, it had scores of 2 for concreteness increase and 0 for completeness. The added kara-case phrase (from phrase) 地上二十メートルの高さから chijou-niju-metoru-no-takasa-kara 'from 20 meters high' is useful, but since the original sentence already has the kara-case ヘリコプターから herikoputa-kara 'from helicopter,' the insertion invited a double kara-case, which is forbidden in Japanese. To correct the error, we need at least two operations, and thus, a completeness score of 0 was assigned.

5.2 Results of experiments

Table 5 presents the results of evaluation E2, the semantic correctness with the parsing status of evaluation E1 and the source sentence category from which the phrases for revision were obtained. Columns 2 and 3 list the number of revisions (insertions and substitutions) that were correct and incorrect and column 4 shows the correctness ratio. We obtained a total of 603 revisions and found that 30% (180/603) of them were derived with syntactic errors.

The semantic correctness ratio was unchanged regardless of the parsing success. On the contrary, it was affected by the source sentence type. The correctness ratio with the supplemental sentence was significantly[6] lower than that with the body sentence. Table 6 lists the results of the concreteness improvements with the parsing status and the source sentence type. Columns 2, 3 and 4 list the number of revisions that fell in the scores (0-2) listed in the first row. The average score in this table again was not affected by the parsing failure but was significantly affected by the source sentence category. The result with the supplement sentences was significantly worse than that with body sentences.

Table 7 lists the results of the sentential completeness in the same fashion as Table 6. The sentential completeness was significantly worsened by both the parsing failure and source sentence category.

These results indicate that the answers to the questions posed at the beginning of this section are as follows. From the semantic correctness evaluation, we infer that our trigger selection strategy worked well especially when the source sentence category was limited to the body.

From the concreteness-increase evaluation, the assumption that we made also worked reasonably well when the source sentence category was limited to the body.

The effect of parsing was much more limited than we had anticipated in that it did not degrade either the semantic correctness or the concreteness improvements. Parsing failure, however, degraded the sentential completeness of the revised sentences. This seems quite reasonable: parsing errors elicit problems such as wrong phrase attachment and wrong maximum phrase identification. The revisions with these errors invite incomplete sentences that need corrections.

It is worth noting that cases sometimes occurred where a parsing error did not cause any problem in the revision. We found that the phrases governed by a trigger pair in many cases were quite similar, and therefore, the parser makes the same error. In that case, the errors are often offset and cause no problems superficially.

We consider that the sentential completeness needs further improvements to make an automatic summarization system, although the semantic correctness and concreteness increase are at an almost satisfactory level. Our dependency-based revision is expected to be potentially useful to develop a summarization system.

[6] In this section, the "significance" was tested with the Mann-Whitney U test with Fisher's exact probability. We set the significance level at 5%.

6 Future work

Several problems remain to be solved, which will be addressed in future work. Obviously, we need to improve the parsing accuracy that degraded the sentential completeness in our experiments. Although we did not quantitatively evaluate the errors in phrase insertion position and redundancy, we could see these happening in the revised sentences because of the inaccurate parsing. Apart from this, we need to further refine the following problems.

Regarding the trigger selection, one particular problem we faced was the mixture of statements of different politicians in a news article. The statements were often included as direct quotations that end with the chunk 述べました nobe-mashi-ta 'said.' Our system takes the chunk as the trigger and does not care whose statements they are; thus, it ended up mixing them up. A similar problem happened when we had two different female victims of an incident in an article. Since our system has no means to distinguish them, the modifier phrases about these women were mixed up.

We think that we can improve our method by applying more general language generation techniques. An example is the kara-case collision that we explained in example 3 in section 5.1. The essence of the problem is that the added content is useful, but there is a grammatical problem. In other words, "what to say" is ok but "how to say" needs refinement. This particular problem can be solved by doing the case-collision check, and by synthesizing the colliding phrases into one. These can be better treated in the generation framework.

7 Conclusion

We proposed a lead sentence revision method based on the operations of phrases that have the same head in the lead and other sentences. This method is a type of sentence fusion and is more general than methods that use noun phrase coreferencing in that it can add phrases of any syntactic type. We described the algorithm and the rules extensively, conducted a lead revision experiment, and showed that the algorithm was able to find semantically appropriate revisions. We also showed that parsing errors mainly degrade the sentential completeness such as grammaticality and repetition.

Reference

Regina Barzilay and Kathleen R. McKeown. 2005. Sentence Fusion for Multidocument News Summarization. *Computational Linguistics*. 31(3): 298-327.

Katja Filippova and Michael Strube. 2008. Sentence Fusion via Dependency Graph Compression. *proc. of the EMNLP 2008*: 177-185

Hongyan Jing and Kathleen R. McKeown. 1999. The Decomposition of Human-Written Summary Sentences. *proc. of the 22nd International Conference on Research and Development in Information Retrieval SIGIR 99*: 129-136.

Hongyan Jing and Kathleen R. McKeown. 2000. Cut and Paste Based Text Summarization, *proc. of the 1st meeting of the North American Chapter of the Association for Computational Linguistics*: 178-185.

Taku Kudo and Yuji Matsumoto. 2002. Japanese Dependency Analysis using Cascaded Chunking. Proc. of the 6th Conference on Natural Language Learning 2002: 63-69.

Taku Kudo, Kaoru Yamamoto and Yuji Matsumoto. 2004. Applying Conditional Random Fields to Japanese Morphological Analysis, *proc. of the EMNLP 2004*: 230-237.

H. P. Luhn. 1958. The Automatic Creation of Literature Abstracts. *Advances in Automatic Text Summarization. The MIT Press*: 15-21.

Inderjeet Mani, Barbara Gates, and Eric Bloedorn. 1999. Improving Summaries by Revising Them. *Proc. of the 37th Annual Meeting of the Association for Computational Linguistics.*: 558-565.

Ruslan Mitkov 2002, Anaphora Resolution, Pearson Education.

Ani Nenkova. 2008. Entity-driven Rewrite for Multi-document Summarization, *proc. of the 3rd International Joint Conference on Natural Language Generation*: 118-125.

Jahna C. Otterbacher, Dragomir R. Radev, and Airong Luo 2002, Revisions that Improve Cohesion in Multi-document Summaries: A Preliminary Study. *Proc. of the ACL-02 Workshop on Automatic Summarization*: 27-36.

Jacques Robin and Kathleen McKeown. 1996. Empirically designing and evaluating a new revision-based model for summary generation. *Artificial Intelligence*. 85: 135-179.

A Parse-and-Trim Approach with Information Significance for Chinese Sentence Compression

Wei Xu **Ralph Grishman**
Computer Science Department
New York University
New York, NY, 10003, USA
{xuwei,grishman}@cs.nyu.edu

Abstract

In this paper, we propose an event-based approach for Chinese sentence compression without using any training corpus. We enhance the linguistically-motivated heuristics by exploiting event word significance and event information density. This is shown to improve the preservation of important information and the tolerance of POS and parsing errors, which are more common in Chinese than English. The heuristics are only required to determine possibly removable constituents instead of selecting specific constituents for removal, and thus are easier to develop and port to other languages and domains. The experimental results show that around 72% of our automatic compressions are grammatically and semantically correct, preserving around 69% of the most important information on average.

1 Introduction

The goal of sentence compression is to shorten sentences while preserving their grammaticality and important information. It has recently attracted much attention because of its wide range of applications, especially in summarization (Jing, 2000) and headline generation (which can be viewed as summarization with very short length requirement). Sentence compression can improve extractive summarization in coherence and amount of information expressed within a fixed length.

An ideal sentence compression will include complex paraphrasing operations, such as word deletion, substitution, insertion, and reordering. In this paper, we focus on the simpler instantiation of sentence simplification, namely word deletion, which has been proved a success in the literature (Knight and Marcu, 2002; Dorr et al, 2003; Clarke and Lapata, 2006).

In this paper, we present our technique for Chinese sentence compression without the need for a sentence/compression parallel corpus. We combine linguistically-motivated heuristics and word significance scoring together to trim the parse tree, and rank candidate compressions according to event information density. In contrast to probabilistic methods, the heuristics are more likely to produce grammatical and fluent compressed sentences. We reduce the difficulty and linguistic skills required for composing heuristics by only requiring these heuristics to identify possibly removable constituents instead of selecting specific constituents for removal. The word significance helps to preserve informative constituents and overcome some POS and parsing errors. In particular, we seek to assess the event information during the compression process, according to the previous successes in event-based summarization (Li et al, 2006) and a new event-oriented 5W summarization task (Parton et al, 2009).

The next section presents previous approaches to sentence compression. In section 3, we describe our system with three modules, viz. linguistically-motivated heuristics, word significance scoring and candidate compression selection. We also develop a heuristics-only approach for comparison. In section 4, we evaluate the compressions in terms of grammaticality, infor-

Proceedings of the 2009 Workshop on Language Generation and Summarisation, ACL-IJCNLP 2009, pages 48–55,
Suntec, Singapore, 6 August 2009. ©2009 ACL and AFNLP

mativeness and compression rate. Finally, Section 5 concludes this paper and discusses directions of future work.

2 Previous Work

Most previous studies relied on a parallel corpus to learn the correspondences between original and compressed sentences. Typically sentences are represented by features derived from parsing results, and used to learn the transformation rules or estimate the parameters in the score function of a possible compression. A variety of models have been developed, including but not limited to the noisy-channel model (Knight and Marcu, 2002; Galley and McKeown, 2007), the decision-tree model (Knight and Marcu, 2002), support vector machines (Nguyen et al, 2004) and large-margin learning (McDonald, 2006; Cohn and Lapata 2007).

Approaches which do not employ parallel corpora are less popular, even though the parallel sentence/compression corpora are not as easy to obtain as multilingual corpora for machine translation. Only a few studies have been done requiring no or minimal training corpora (Dorr et al, 2003; Hori and Furui, 2004; Turner and Charniak, 2005). The scarcity of parallel corpora also constrains the development in languages other than English. To the best of our knowledge, no study has been done on Chinese sentence compression.

An algorithm making limited use of training corpora was proposed originally by Hori and Furui (2004) for spoken text in Japanese, and later modified by Clarke and Lapata (2006) for English text. Their model searches for the compression with highest score according to the significance of each word, the existence of Subject-Verb-Object structures and the language model probability of the resulting word combination. The weight factors to balance the three measurements are experimentally optimized by a parallel corpus or estimated by experience.

Turner and Charniak (2005) present semi-supervised and unsupervised variants of the noisy channel model. They approximate the rules of compression from a non-parallel corpus (e.g. the Penn Treebank) based on probabilistic context free grammar derivation.

Our approach is most similar to the Hedge Trimmer for English headline generation (Dorr et al, 2003), in which linguistically-motivated heuristics are used to trim the parse tree. This method removes low content components in a preset order until the desired length requirement is reached. It reduces the risk of deleting subordinate clauses and prepositional phrases by delaying these operations until no other rules can be applied. This fixed order of applying rules limits the flexibility and capability for preserving informative constituents during deletions. It is likely to fail by producing a grammatical but semantically useless compressed sentence. Another major drawback is that it requires considerable linguistic skill to produce proper rules in a proper order.

3 Algorithms for Sentence Compression

Our system takes the output of a Chinese Treebank-style syntactic parser (Huang and Harper, 2009) as input and performs tree trimming operations to obtain compression. We propose and compare two approaches. One uses only linguistically-motivated heuristics to delete words and gets the compression result directly. The other one uses heuristics to determine which nodes in the parse tree are potentially removable. Then all removable nodes are deleted one by one according to their significance weights to generate a series of candidate compressions. Finally, the best compression is selected based on sentence length and informativeness criteria.

3.1 Linguistically-motivated Heuristics

This module aims to identify the nodes in the parse tree which may be removed without severe loss in grammaticality and information. Based on an analysis of the Penn Treebank corpus and human-produced compression, we decided that the following parse constituents are potential low content units.

Set 0 – basic:

- Parenthetical elements
- Adverbs except negative, some temporal and degree adverbs
- Adjectives except when the modified noun consists of only one character
- DNPs (which are formed by various phrasal categories plus "的" and appear as modifiers of NP in Chinese)
- DVPs (which are formed by various phrasal categories plus "地" in Chinese, and appear as modifiers of VP in Chinese)
- All nodes in noun coordination phrases except the first noun

Set 1 – fixed:

- All children of NP nodes except temporal nouns and proper nouns and the last noun word
- All simple clauses (IP) except the first one, if the sentence consists of more than one IP
- Prepositional phrases except those that may contain location or date information, according to a hand-made list of prepositions

Set 2 – flexible:

- All nodes in verb coordination phrases except the first one.
- Relative clauses
- Appositive clauses
- All prepositional phrases
- All children of NP nodes except the last noun word
- All simple clauses, if the sentence consists of more than one IP (at least one clause is required to be preserved in later trimming)

Set 0 lists all the fundamental constituents that may be removed and is used in both approaches. Set 1 and Set 2 are designed to handle more complex constituents for the two approaches respectively.

The heuristics-only approach exploits Set 0 and Set 1. It can be viewed as the Chinese version of Hedge Trimmer (Dorr et al, 2003), but differs in the following ways:

1) Chinese has different language constructions and grammar from English.
2) We eliminate the strict compression length constraint in order to yield more natural compressions with varying length.
3) We do not remove time expressions on purpose to benefit further applications, such as event extraction.

The heuristics-only approach deletes low content units mechanically while preserving syntactic correctness, as long as parsing is accurate. Our preliminary experiments showed that the heuristics in Set 0 and Set 1 can generate a comparatively satisfying compression, but is sensitive to part-of-speech and parsing errors, e.g. the proper noun "现代 (Hyundai)" as motor company is tagged as an adjective (shown in Figure 1) and thus removed since its literal meaning is "现代(modern)". Moreover, the rules in Set 1 reduce the sentence length in a gross manner, risking serious information or grammaticality loss. For example, the first clause may not be a complete grammatical sentence, and is not always the most important clause in the sentence though that is usually the case. We also want to point out that the heuristics tend to reduce the sentence length and preserve the grammar by removing most of the modifiers, even though modifiers may contain a lot of important information.

To address the above problems of heuristics, we exploit word significance to measure the importance of each constituent. Set 2 was created to work with Set 0 to identify removable low content units. The heuristics in this approach are used only to detect all possible candidates for deletion and thus are more general and easier to create than Set 1. For instance, we do not need to carefully determine which kinds of prepositional phrases are safe or dangerous to delete but instead mark all of them as potentially removable.

The actual word deletion is performed later by a compression generation and selection module, taking word significance and compression rate into consideration. The heuristics in Set 2 are able to cover more risky constituents than Set 1, e.g. clauses and parallel structures, since the risk will be controlled by the later processes.

```
( (IP
    (NP
        (*NP (NR 韩国))                          South Korean
        (#*ADJP (JJ 现代))                        Hyundai
        (NP
            (#*NN 汽车)                           motor
            (NN 公司)))                           company
    (VP (VC 是)                                   is
        (NP (#*DNP (NP (NR 沃尔沃))               Volvo
                   (DEG 的))                      's
            (#*ADJP (JJ 潜在))                    potential
            (NP (NN 买家))))                      buyer
    (PU .)))
```

Figure 1. Parse tree trimming by heuristics
(#: nodes trimmed out by Set0 & Set1;
*: nodes labeled as removable by Set0 & Set2.)

Figure 1 shows an example of applying heuristics to the parse tree of the sentence "韩国现代汽车公司是沃尔沃的潜在买家" (The South Korean Hyundai Motor Company is a potential buyer of Volvo.). The heuristics-only approach produces "韩国公司是买家" (The South Korean company is a buyer.), which is grammatical but semantically meaningless. We will see how word significance and information density scoring produce a better compression in section 3.3.

3.2 Event-based Word Significance

Based on our observations, a human-compressed sentence primarily describes an event or a set of relevant events and contains a large proportion of named entities, especially in the news article domain. Similar to event-based summarization (Li et al, 2006), we consider only the event terms, namely verbs and nouns, with a preference for proper nouns.

The word significance score $I_j(w_i)$ indicates how important a word w_i is to a document j. It is a tf-idf weighting scheme with additional weight for proper nouns:

$$I_j(w_i) = \begin{cases} tf_{ij} \times idf_i, & \text{if } w_i \text{ is verb or common noun} \\ tf_{ij} \times idf_i + \omega, & \text{if } w_i \text{ is proper noun} \\ 0, & \text{otherwise} \end{cases} \quad (1)$$

where

w_i : a word in the sentence of document j

tf_{ij} : term frequency of w_i in document j

idf_i : inverse document frequency of w_i

ω : additional weight for proper noun.

The nodes in the parse tree are then weighted by the word significance for leaves or the sum of the children's weights for internal nodes. The weighting depends on the word itself regardless of its part-of-speech tags in order to overcome some part-of-speech errors.

3.3 Compression Generation and Selection

In this module, we first apply a greedy algorithm to trim the weighted parse tree to obtain a series of candidate compressions. Recall that the heuristics Set 0 and 2 have provided the removability judgment for each node in the tree. The parse tree trimming algorithm is as follows:

1) remove one node with the lowest weight and get a candidate compressed sentence
2) update the weights of all ancestors of the removed node
3) repeat until no node is removable

The selection among candidate compressions is a tradeoff between sentence length and amount of information. Inspired by headlines in news articles, most of which contain a large proportion of named entities, we create an information density measurement $D(s_k)$ for sentence s_k to select the best compression:

$$D(s_k) = \frac{\sum_{w_i \in P} I(w_i)}{L(s_k)} \quad (2)$$

where

P : the set of words whose significance scores are larger than ω in (1)

$I(w_i)$: the significance score of word w_i

$L(s_k)$: the length of sentence in characters

Table 1 shows the effectiveness of information density to select a proper compression with a balance between length and meaningfulness. Table 1 lists all candidate compressions in sequence generated from the parse tree in Figure 1. The words in bold are considered in information density. The underlined compression is picked as final output as "韩国现代公司是沃尔沃的买家" (The South Korean Hyundai company is a buyer of Volvo.), which makes more sense than the one produced by heuristics-only approach as "韩国公司是买家" (The South Korean company is a buyer.). In our approach, "现代(Hyundai)" tagged as adjective and "沃尔沃的(Volvo's)" as a modifier to buyer are preserved successfully.

D(s)	Sentence
0.254	**韩国现代**汽车公司是**沃尔沃**的潜在买家. The South **Korean Hyundai** Motor Company is a potential buyer of **Volvo**.
0.288	韩国现代汽车公司是沃尔沃的买家. The South Korean Hyundai Motor Company is a buyer of Volvo.
<u>0.332</u>	<u>韩国现代公司是沃尔沃的买家.</u> <u>The South Korean Hyundai Company is a buyer of Volvo.</u>
0.282	韩国公司是沃尔沃的买家. The South Korean company is a buyer of Volvo.
0.209	公司是沃尔沃的买家. The company is a buyer of Volvo.
0.0	公司是买家. The company is a buyer.

Table 1. Compression generation and selection for the sentence in Figure 1

The compression with highest information density is chosen as system output. To achieve a better compression rate and avoids overly condensed sentences (i.e. very short sentences with only a proper noun), we further constrain the compression to a limited but varying length range [min_length, max_length] according to the length of the original sentence:

$$\begin{aligned} &min\_length = \min\{original\_length, \alpha\} \\ &max\_length = \begin{cases} \beta + \sqrt{orig\_length - \beta}, & \text{if } original\_length > \beta \\ original\_length, & \text{otherwise} \end{cases} \end{aligned} \quad (3)$$

where

orig_length : the length of original sentence in characters

α,β : fixed lengths in characters

In contrast to a fixed limitation of length, this varying length simulates human behavior in creating compression and avoid the overcompression caused by the density selection schema.

4 Experiments

4.1 Experiment Setup

Our experiments were designed to evaluate the quality of automatic compression. The evaluation corpus is 79 documents from Chinese newswires, and the first sentence of each news article is compressed.

The compression of the first sentences in the Chinese news articles is a comparatively challenging task. Unlike English, Chinese often connects two or more self-complete sentences together without any indicating word or punctuation; this is extremely frequent for the first sentence of news text. The average length of the first sentences in the 79 documents is 61.5 characters, compared to 46.8 characters for the sentences in the body of these news articles.

We compare the compressions generated by four different methods:

- Human [H]: A native Chinese speaker is asked to generate a headline-like compression (must be a complete sentence, not a fragment, and need not preserve original SVO structure) based on the first sentence of each news article. Only word deletion operations are allowed.
- Heuristics [R]: The heuristics-only approach mentioned in section 2.1.
- Heuristics + Word Significance [W]: The approach combines heuristics and word significance. The parameter ω in (1) is set to be 1, which is an upper bound of word's tf-idf value throughout the corpus.
- Heuristics + Word Significance + Length Constraints [L]: Compression is constrained to a limited but varying length, as mentioned in section 2.3. The length parameters α and β in (3) are set roughly to be 10 and 20 characters based on our experience.

4.2 Human Evaluation

Sentence compression is commonly evaluated by human judgment. Following the literature (Knight and Marcu, 2002; Dorr et al, 2003; Clarke and Lapata, 2006; Cohn and Lapata 2007), we asked three native Chinese speakers to rate the grammaticality of compressions using the 1 to 5 scale. We find that all three nonlinguist human judges tend to take semantic correctness into consideration when scoring grammaticality.

We also asked these three judges to give a list of keywords from the original sentence before seeing compressions, which they would preserve if asked to create a headline based on the sentence. Instead of a subjective score, the informativeness is evaluated by measuring the keyword coverage of the target compression on a percentage scale. The three judges give different numbers of keywords varying from 3.33 to 6.51 on average over the 79 sentences.

The compression rate is the ratio of the number of Chinese characters in a compressed sentence to that in its original sentence.

The experimental results in Table 2 show that our automatically generated compressions preserve grammaticality, with an average score of about 4 out of 5, because of the use of linguistically-motivated heuristics.

	Compression Rate	**Grammaticality (1 ~ 5)**	**Informativeness (0~100%)**
Human	38.5%	4.962	90.7%
Heuristics	54.1%	4.114	64.9%
Heu+Sig	52.8%	3.854	68.8%
Heu+Sig+L	34.3%	3.664	56.1%

Table 2. Mean rating from human evaluation on first sentence compression

Event-based word significance and information density increase the amount of important information by 6% with similar sentence length, but decreases the average grammaticality score by 6.5%. This is because the method using word significance sacrifices grammaticality to reduce the linguistic complexity of the heuristics. Nonetheless, this method does improve grammaticality for 16 of the 79 compressed sentences, typically for those with POS or parsing errors.

The compression rates of the two basic automatic approaches are around 53%, while it is 38.5% for manual compression. This is partially because our heuristics only trim the parse tree but do not transform the structure of it, while a human may change the grammatical structure, remove more linking words and even abbreviate some words. The length constraint boosts the compression rate of our combined approach by 35% with a loss of 18.5% in informativeness and 5% in grammaticality.

Grammaticality (1 ~ 5)	Number of Sentence	Compression Rate	Informativeness (0~100%)
Heuristics > 4.5	45	64.1%	75.9%
Heuristics >= 4	62	54.5%	70.6%
Heu+Sig > 4.5	35	59.8%	81.8%
Heu+Sig >= 4	57	56.7%	75.8%

Table 3. Compressions with good grammar

We further investigate the performance of our automatic system by considering only relatively grammatical compressions, as shown in Table 3. The compressions which receive an average score of more than 4.5 are comparatively readable. The combined approach generates 35 such compressions among a total of 79 sentences, preserving 81.8% important information on average, which is quite satisfying since human-generated compression only achieves 90.7%.

The infomativeness score of human-generated compression also demonstrates the difficulty of this task. We compare our automatically generated event words list with the keywords picked by human judges. 61.8% of human-selected keywords are included in the event words list, thus considered when calculating information significance. This fact demonstrates some success but also potential room for improving keyword selection.

4.3 Some Examples

We illustrate several representative samples of our system output in Table 4. In the first example, all three automatic compressions are acceptable, though different in preserving important information. [W] and [L] concisely contain the WHO, WHAT, WHOM information of the event, while [R] further preserves the WHY and WHEN information.

In the second example, the heuristics-only approach produced a decent compression by keeping only the first self-complete sub-sentence. The weight of word "白宫(White House)" is somewhat overwhelming and resulted in dense compressions in [W] and [L], which are too short to be good. Besides, [W] and [L] in this example show that not all the prepositional phrases, noun modifiers etc. can be removed in Chinese without affecting grammaticality, though in most cases the removals are safe. This is one of the main reasons for grammar errors in the compression results except POS and parsing errors.

The third example shows how the combined approach overcomes POS errors and how length constraints avoid overcompression. In [R], "纳达尔(Nadal)" is deleted because it is mistakenly tagged as an adverb modifying the action "claim the victory and progress through". Since Nadal is tagged as proper noun somewhere else in the document, its significance makes it survive the compression process. [L] produces a perfect compression with proper length, information and grammar, just as human-made compression. [W] selects a very condensed version of compression but loses some information.

1. [O] 由于对海域疆界划分各执一词, 为期三日的南北两韩高层军事会谈在今天不欢而散. Because both sides were immovable on the drawing of maritime borders, a three-day high-level military meeting between North and South Korea broke up in discord today. [H]两韩高层军事会谈今天不欢而散. A high-level military meeting between two Koreas broke up in discord today. [R]由于各执一词, 为期三日的两韩高层会谈在今天不欢而散. Because both sides were immovable, a three-day high-level meeting between two Koreas broke up in discord today. [L]两韩高层会谈不欢而散. A high-level meeting between two Koreas broke up in discord. [W]两韩高层会谈不欢而散. A high-level meeting between two Koreas broke up in discord.
2. [O]白宫今天呼吁尽快派遣核检人员, 以监督北韩关闭其核子反应炉; 白宫是在美国总统布希与南韩总统卢武铉电话交谈过后, 作出此一呼吁. The White House today called for nuclear inspectors to be sent as soon as possible to monitor North Korea's closure of its nuclear reactors. The White House made this call after US President Bush had telephone conversations with South Korean President Roh Moo-hyun. [H] 白宫今天呼吁派遣人员监督北韩关闭核反应炉. The White House today called for inspectors to be sent to monitor North Korea's closure of its nuclear reactors. [R]白宫今天呼吁派遣人员, 以监督北韩关闭反应炉. The White House today called for inspectors to be sent to monitor North Korea's closure of its reactors. [L]白宫今天呼吁派遣人员, 白宫是, 作出呼吁. The White House today called for inspectors to be sent. The White House is, made this call. [W]白宫是, 作出呼吁. The White House is, made this call.
3. [O]第四种子乔科维奇退赛, 让原以三比六, 六比一, 四比一领先的第二种子纳达尔获胜过关. Fourth seed Djokovic withdrew from the game, and allowed second seed Nadal , who was leading 3-6 , 6-1 , 4-1 , to claim the victory and progress through. [H]乔科维奇退赛让纳达尔获胜过关. Djokovic withdrew from the game, and allowed Nadal to claim the victory and progress through.

[R]乔科维奇退赛, 让以三比六, 六比一, 四比一领先的第二种子获胜过关. Djokovic withdrew from the game, and allowed second seed, who was leading 3-6 , 6-1 , 4-1 , to claim the victory and progress through. [L]乔科维奇退赛让种子纳达尔获胜过关. Djokovic withdrew from the game, and allowed seed Nadal to claim the victory and progress through. [W]乔科维奇退赛. Djokovic withdrew from the game.
4. [O]中新网 7 月 31 日电陈水扁 30 日质疑岛内司法人员企图介入台地区领导人选举. Chinanews.com , July 31 On the 30th Chen Shui-bian questioned that members of the judiciary on the island may have tried to get involved in elections for leaders in the Taiwan region. [H]陈水扁质疑司法人员介入台地区领导人选举. Chen Shui-bian questioned that members of the judiciary may get involved in elections for leaders in the Taiwan region. [R]中新网 7 月 31 日电陈水扁 30 日质疑岛内人员企图介入台地区领导人选举. Chinanews.com , July 31 On the 30th Chen Shui-bian questioned that members on the island may have tried to get involved in elections for leaders in the Taiwan region. [L]陈水扁 30 日质疑人员企图介入台地区领导人选举. On the 30th Chen Shui-bian questioned that members may have tried to get involved in elections for leaders in the Taiwan region. [W]陈水扁 30 日质疑人员企图介入台地区领导人选举. On the 30th Chen Shui-bian questioned that members may have tried to get involved in elections for leaders in the Taiwan region.
5. [O]帕蒂尔是印度史上第一位女性总统候选人, 如果她当选, 她将成为印度有史以来的首位女总统. Patil is India's first woman presidential candidate, if she is elected, she will become India's first woman president in history. [H] 帕蒂尔是印度史上第一位女性总统候选人. Patil is India's first woman presidential candidate. [R]帕蒂尔是印度史上第一位候选人. Patil is the first candidate in the history of India. [L]帕蒂尔是候选人, 她将成为印度有史以来的总统. Patil is the candidate, she will become president of Indian history. [W]帕蒂尔是候选人. Patil is the candidate.

Table 4. Compression examples including human and system results, with reference translation (O: Original sentence)

The fourth sample indicates an interesting linguistic phenomenon. The head of the noun phrase "岛内司法人员(members of the judiciary on the island)", "人员(members)" cannot stand alone making a fluent and valid sentence, though all the compressions are grammatically correct. Our human assessors also show a preference of [R] to [L, W] in grammaticality evaluation, taking semantic correctness into consideration as well. This is probably a reason that our combined approach performs worse than heuristic-only approach in grammaticality. The combined approach tends to remove risky constituents, but it is hard for word significance to control this risk properly in every case. This is another of the main reasons for bad compression.

In the fifth sample, all the automatic compressions are grammatically correct preserving well the heads of subject and object, but are semantically incorrect. This case should be hard to handle by any compression approach.

5 Conclusions and Future Work

In this paper, we propose a novel approach to combine linguistically-motivated heuristics and word significance scoring for Chinese sentence compression. We take advantage of heuristics to preserve grammaticality and not rely on a parallel corpus. We reduce the complexity involved in preparing complicated deterministic rules for constituent deletion, requiring people only to determine potentially removable constituents. Therefore, this approach can be easily extended to languages or domains for which parallel compression corpora are scarce. The word significance scoring is used to control the word deletion process, pursuing a balance between sentence length and information loss. The exploitation of event information improves the mechanical rule-based approach in preserving event-related words and overcomes some POS and parsing errors.

The experimental results prove that this combined approach is competitive with a finely-tuned heuristics-only approach to grammaticality, and includes more important information in the compressions of the same length.

In the future, we plan to apply the compression to Chinese summarization and headline generation tasks. A careful study on keyword selection and word weighting may further improve the performance of the current system. We also consider incorporating language models to produce fluent and natural compression and reduce semantically invalid cases.

Another important future direction lies in creating a parallel compression corpus in Chinese and exploiting statistical and machine learning techniques. We also expect that an abstractive approach involving paraphrasing operations besides word deletion will create more natural compression than an extractive approach.

Acknowledgments

This work was supported in part by the Defense Advanced Research Projects Agency (DARPA) under Contract HR0011-06-C-0023. Any opinions, findings, conclusions, or recommendations expressed in this material are the authors' and do not necessarily reflect those of the U.S. Government.

References

J. Clarke and M. Lapata, 2006. Models for Sentence Compression: A Comparison across Domains, Training Requirements and Evaluation Measures. In Proceedings of the COLING/ACL 2006, Sydney, Australia, pp. 377-384.

T. Cohn and M. Lapata. 2007. Large Margin Synchronous generation and its application to sentence compression. In the Proceedings of the EMNLP/ CoNLL 2007, Pragure, Czech Republic, pp. 73-82.

B. Dorr, D. Zajic and R. Schwartz. 2003. Hedge Trimmer: A Parse-and-Trim Approach to Headline Generation. In the Proceedings of the NAACL/HLT text summarization workshop, Edmonton, Canada, pp. 1-8.

M. Galley and K. McKeown, 2007. Lexicalized Markov Grammars for Sentence Compression. In the Proceedings of NAACL/HLT 2007, Rochester, NY, pp. 180-187.

C. Hori and S. Furui. 2004. Speech Summarization: An Approach through Word Extraction and a Method for Evaluation. IEICE Transactions on Information and Systems, E87-D(1): 15-25.

Z. Huang and M. Harper, 2009. Self-training PCFG Grammars with Latent Annotations Across Languages. In the proceedings of EMNLP 2009, Singapore.

H. Jing. 2000. Sentence Reduction for Automatic Text Summarization. In Proceedings of the 6th ANLP, Seattle, WA, pp. 310-315.

K. Knight and D. Marcu, 2002. Summarization beyond Sentence Extraction: a Probabilistic Approach to Sentence Compression. Artificial Intelligence, 139(1): 91-107.

W. Li, W. Xu, M. Wu, C. Yuan and Q. Lu. 2006. Extractive Summarization using Inter- and Intra-Event Relevance. In the Proceedings of COLING/ACL 2006, Sydney, Australia, pp 369-376.

R. McDonald. 2006. Discriminative Sentence Compression with Soft Syntactic Constraints. In the Proceedings of 11th EACL, Trento, Italy, pp. 297-304.

M. L. Nguyen, A. Shimazu, S. Horiguchi, T. B. Ho and M. Fukushi. 2004. Probabilistic Sentence Reduction using Support Vector Machines. In Proceedings of the 20th COLING, Geneva, Switzerland, pp. 743-749.

K. McKeown, R. Barzilay, S. Blair-Goldensohn, D. Evans, V. Hatzivassiloglou, J. Klavans, A. Nenkova, B. Schiffman and S. Sigelman. 2002. The Columbia Multi-Document Summarizer for DUC 2002. In the Proceedings of the ACL workshop on Document Understanding Conference (DUC) workshop, Philadelphia, PA, pp. 1-8.

K. Parton, K. McKeown, R. Coyne, M. Diab, R. Grishman, D. Hakkani-Tür, M. Harper, H. Ji, W. Ma, A. Meyers, S. Stolbach, A. Sun, G. Tur, W. Xu and S. Yaman. 2009. Who, What, When, Where, Why? Comparing Multiple Approaches to the Cross-Lingual 5W Task. In the Proceedings of ACL-IJCNLP, Singapore.

J. Turner and E. Charniak. 2005. Supervised and Unsupervised Learning for Sentence Compression. In the Proceedings of 43rd ACL, Ann Arbor, MI, pp. 290-297.

Short Papers

Visual Development Process for Automatic Generation of Digital Games Narrative Content

Maria Fernanda Caropreso[1] **Diana Inkpen**[1] **Shahzad Khan**[2] **Fazel Keshtkar**[1]

[1]University of Ottawa
{caropres,diana}@site.uottawa.ca
akesh081@uottawa.ca

[2]DISTIL Interactive
s.khan2@distilinteractive.com

Abstract

Users of Natural Language Generation systems are required to have sophisticated linguistic and sometimes even programming knowledge, which has hindered the adoption of this technology by individuals outside the computational linguistics research community. We have designed and implemented a visual environment for creating and modifying NLG templates which requires no programming ability and minimum linguistic knowledge. It allows specifying templates with any number of variables and dependencies between them. Internally, it uses SimpleNLG to provide the linguistic background knowledge. We tested the performance of our system in the context of an interactive simulation game. We describe the templates used for testing and show examples of sentences that our system generates from these templates.

1 Introduction

Natural Language Generation (NLG) is the process of constructing outputs from non-linguistic inputs (Bateman, 2002) (Dalianis, 1996) (Reiter and Dale, 2000).

NLG systems are useful in systems in which verbal or textual interaction with the users is required, as for example Gaming, Robotics, and Automatic Help Desks. Using NLG systems instead of manually authored sentences would enable the software to adapt the expressed messages to the context of the conversation, and express past and future actions that may form this interaction.

However, the use of the available NLG systems is far from simple. The most complete systems often require extensive linguistic knowledge. Some systems also require programming knowledge. This knowledge cannot be assumed for the content and subject matter experts who are members of a development team. However, these individuals do need to interact with the NLG system in order to make use of the message generation capability to support their product development efforts. It is then necessary to provide them with an environment that will allow them to have access in a simpler way to the features they need of a specific NLG system.

There are two widely adopted approaches to NLG, the 'deep-linguistic' and the 'template-based' (van Deemter et al., 2005). The deep-linguistic approach attempts to build the sentences up from a wholly logical representation. The template-based NLG systems provide scaffolding in the form of templates that contain a predefined structure and perhaps some of the final text.

SimpleNLG is an NLG system that allows the user to specify a sentence by giving its content words and its grammatical roles (such as subject or verb). SimpleNLG also permits the user to specify several features for the main verb, such as: tense (present, past or future); whether or not it is subjective, progressive, passive or perfect; whether or not it is in interrogative form; whether or not it is negated; and which, if any, modal to use (i.e. could, must).While some of these features affect only the verb, others affect the structure of the whole sentence, as for example when it has to be expressed in the passive voice.

SimpleNLG is implemented as a java library and it requires java programming knowledge to be used. Because of the programming nature of SimpleNLG, it allows the user to define flexible templates by using programming variables in the sentence specification. The variable parts of the templates could be filled with different values. When templates are defined using SimpleNLG they keep all the functionality of the NLG system (for example, being able to modify the verb fea-

Proceedings of the 2009 Workshop on Language Generation and Summarisation, ACL-IJCNLP 2009, pages 59–62,
Suntec, Singapore, 6 August 2009. ©2009 ACL and AFNLP

tures or the output format, and making use of the grammatical knowledge), while also allowing for the variable values to change.

We have designed an environment that provides simple access to the use of the SimpleNLG system in order to generate sentences with variable parts or templates. We developed this NLG Template Authoring Environment guided by the need of templates required for generating content for digital-based training games at DISTIL Interactive[1]. An early prototype of the tool, with a text-only interface, is presented in (Caropreso et al., 2009).

In training games the player is typically presented with challenging situations and is encouraged to practice different strategies at dealing with them, in a safe, virtual environment. Through tips and feedback, the player develops an understanding of the problem and what are the successful ways of confronting it (French et al., 1999).

In training games there is usually an explosion of possible scenarios and situations. The narrative should ideally reflect the past events and decisions taken. The considerable amount of textual information required in order to keep the feedback consistent with the updated narrative can be a burden on the game designers. It is then necessary to include templates that statically provide the basic information, combined with variable parts that adapt the narrative to the circumstances.

The goal of the NLG Template Authoring Environment was to provide the game content designers with an accessible tool they could use to create and manipulate the NLG templates, and thus generate sentences that would support the narrative progression of the game.

In the rest of this paper we describe our NLG Template Authoring Environment, its design, implementation and capabilities. We describe the templates that we used to test the system and we explain the user's knowledge required in order to create them. We finish the paper presenting our conclusions and future work.

2 Template Authoring Environment

The NLG Template Authoring Environment asks for a model sentence and allows the user to mark the sections that are variable. For each variable indicated, the user has to specify its type (i.e., personal pronoun, possessive pronoun, Employee_type) and which values of that type are allowed (i.e., all personal pronouns, or only "she" and "he"). Additionally, the user can also indicate dependencies between variable elements and information for the verb (i.e., tense, form, modals). The system then shows the user all the possible sentences that could be generated from the given template by calculating all the possible combinations of variable values that respect the specified dependencies and follow the verb selections. The user can then refine the template by changing the given example or the specified variables, dependencies or verb options, in order to adjust the generated sentences to the needs of the game.

The NLG Template Authoring Environment has been implemented in Java. The SimpleNLG library was used to automatically generate correct sentences and provide the user with the possibility of exploring different attributes to the verb. It has a user-friendly intuitive graphical interface, part of which is shown in Figure 1.

Figure 1: Graphical Interface

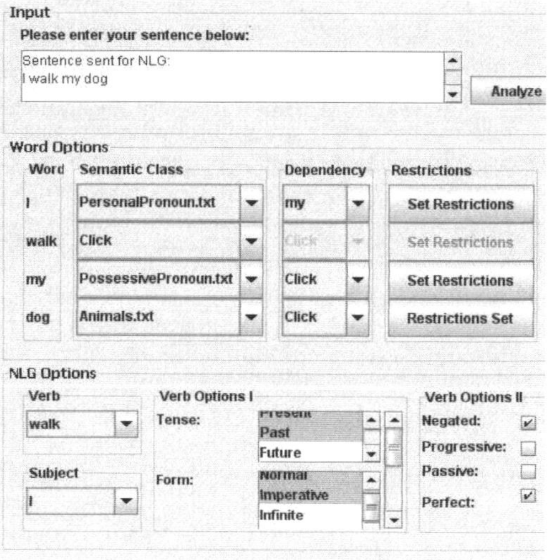

After entering an example sentence and clicking on Analyze, the user indicates that a section is variable by giving a type or semantic class to the word in that section. The values of a semantic class are stored in a text file, which allows the user to create new semantic classes as needed. These files contain all the possible values and their respective syntactic information (person, number and gender) which will be used for agreement with the verb and for dependency between variables purposes. Restrictions to the values that a variable can take are also indicated

[1] http://www.distilinteractive.com/

through the graphical interface. Dependencies can be indicated only between already declared variables. The main verb and all its options are indicated in the section at the bottom of the graphical interface.

In the template shown in Figure 1, the example sentence is "I walk my dog", "I" is a variable of type personal pronoun, "walk" is the main verb, "my" is a variable of type possessive pronoun, "dog" is a variable of type animal and there is a dependency between "I" and "my" (which will allow to make their values agree in person, number and gender when generating all possible combinations).

In Figure 1 we also see that the user has selected the values "present and past" for the verb tense and "normal" and "imperative" for the verb form. Therefore, four sentences will be generated for each combination of the variables' values (one sentence for each combination of the tense and form selections). All these sentences will have the verb negated and will use the perfect tenses (as indicated by the extra verb options).

3 Testing the NLG Template Authoring Environment

In order to verify the correct functioning of the NLG Template Authoring Environment, we selected a set of sentence templates from the game "Business in Balance: Implementing an Environmental Management System" from DISTIL Interactive. The templates were selected manually, while keeping in mind the need to cover different aspects, as for example the number and type of the variables and dependencies. The testing of these examples covers for many more templates of the same type. The five selected sentence templates that form our testing set are displayed in Table 1 and are identified in the rest of this section by their reference number or order in the table.

Table 1. Testing examples

Ref. number	Template
1	`The ACTORS (ME/US) could help DEPARTMENTS.`
2	`The ACTORS IS/ARE now available to help.`
3	`I/WE struggled because of MY/OUR lack of knowledge.`
4	`I/WE AM/ARE pleased to report that I/WE completed the task TASKS.`
5	`I/WE WAS/WERE not the greatest choice for keeping things moving along quickly.`

In these template examples, we show in capitals the variable parts of the templates. `ACTORS`, `DEPARTMENTS` and `TASKS` refer to one of several possible nouns previously defined for each of the classes with those names. The terms in capitals separated by a "/" already display all the accepted values for that variable (for example `I/WE` represent a variable of type personal pronoun which could take only the selected values "I" or "we" and the rest are filtered out).

The first template example has two variables of predefined closed class nouns, `ACTORS` and `DEPARTMENTS`. The latter is independent, while the former has a dependency with a variable of type personal pronoun (in objective case form) that could only take the values "me" or "us". This template is used in the game when the actor/character available to help is the same actor/character that is providing the information. This template can be successfully generated with our system by declaring the variables, restricting the values of the pronoun variable, and establishing the dependency. When filtering non-valid sentences, the system will eliminate those cases where the value's number of the variable `ACTOR` and the personal pronoun do not agree (i.e., it will only allow sentences that use "me" if the actor is singular, and sentences that use "us", if the actor is plural). When creating this template, the user will have to be aware that the main verb is "to help" and indicate "could" as a modal to be used. This is important as otherwise SimpleNLG will modify the main verb in order to agree with the number of the subject. It is also necessary in case some of the options to change the main verb are specified.

Two examples of the generated sentences using the first template are shown below.

- `The HR Training Manager (me) could help the Design Department.`
- `The Implementation Team (us) could help the Deputy Management Representative.`

The second template is one that found a problem with our system and provided us with a reason and an opportunity to improve it. This example template also uses a variable of the closed class noun `ACTOR` together with the verb "to be" in the present tense, agreeing in number with the actor. It might seem trivial to indicate this dependency between the actor variable and the verb. But in our system the verbs are not treated as a regular variable (even when their values can be variable), but they are left for SimpleNLG to find the correct verb form. We needed then to inform SimpleNLG the number to which the verb should agree (by default it would assume singular). In this case we needed to inform SimpleNLG that the number to agree with would be the number of the variable ACTOR. We also have to consider the case when the subject number does not depend on a variable and is plural, as for example in a template where the subject is "The members of DEPARTMENT". To accommodate for these cases, we improved our system by asking the user to indicate in a pull down menu whether the template's verb should agree with a variable value or it should be always used in plural or in singular. (This option is displayed in the bottom right corner of the interface and not shown in the partial screen shot on Figure 1.)

The third template presents a dependency between a variable of type personal pronoun in the subjective case form, and a variable of type possessive pronoun in the complement. Both variables accept only a pair of their possible values, and the dependency between them establishes that they have to agree in person, number and gender. That is not a problem for our system. With respect to the verb, the user has to indicate the past tense as the only option.

In the fourth and fifth template, there is a personal pronoun variable taking the place of the subject, which should agree in person and number with the verb. This is, as mentioned before, left to SimpleNLG to solve. As the subject in these cases consists of only a personal pronoun and SimpleNLG can detect this fact, no extra information is required. In the fourth template, there is also a dependency between the personal pronoun variable in the subject role and the personal pronoun variable in the complement. Once again the person and number of these two variables have to agree, and the sentences not satisfying this restriction are filtered out by our system. Finally, for the fifth template the user is forced to specify that the verb "to be" has to be used in its past tense.

4 Conclusions and Future Work

We have identified the need for an NLG Template Authoring Environment that allows game content designers without linguistic and programming background to experiment with and finally create language templates.

We have designed and implemented a system that allows the user to specify an example sentence together with variables, its dependencies, and verb options that complete the template. This system shows the user all the possible sentences that could be generated with the specified template. It can be used to refine the template until it satisfies the user's needs.

The system makes use of the SimpleNLG java library which provides us with correct sentences and the possibility of including many verb variations, such as tense, form and modals.

We have evaluated our NLG Template Authoring Environment in a set of sentence templates from a digital-based interactive simulation game that covered different characteristics.

We have implemented a user-friendly intuitive graphical interface for the system. The convenience of use of this interface will be evaluated in the context of the development of a new game.

Acknowledgements

This work is supported by the Ontario Centres of Excellence (OCE) and Precarn Incorporated.

References

J. A. Bateman. 2002. Natural Language Generation: an introduction and open-ended review of the state of the art.

M. F. Caropreso, D. Inkpen, S. Khan and F. Keshtkar. 2009. Novice Friendly Natural Language Generation Template Authoring Environment. Proceeding of the Canadian Artificial Intelligence Conference 2009, Kelowna, BC, pp.195-198.

H. Dalianis. 1996. Concise Natural Language Generation from Formal Specifications, Ph.D. Thesis, (Teknologie Doktorsavhandling), Department of Computer and Systems Sciences, Royal Institute of Technology/ Stockholm University. Report Series No. 96-008, ISSN 1101-8526, SRN SU-KTH/DSV/R 96/8 SE.

K. van Deemter, E. Krahmer and M. Theune. 2005. Real versus Template-Based Natural Language Generation: A False Opposition? In Computational Linguistics, 31(1): 15-24.

D. French, C. Hale, C. Johnson and G. Farr. 1999. Internet Based Learning: An introduction and framework for higher education and business. London, UK: Kogan Page.

E. Reiter and R. Dale. 2000. Building Natural Language Generation Systems (Studies in Natural Language Processing), Cambridge University Press.

E. Reiter. 2007. SimpleNlg package: http://www.csd.abdn.ac.uk/ereiter/simplnlg

Reducing redundancy in multi-document summarization using lexical semantic similarity

Iris Hendrickx, Walter Daelemans
University of Antwerp
Antwerpen, Belgium
iris.hendrickx@ua.ac.be
walter.daelemans@ua.ac.be

Erwin Marsi, Emiel Krahmer
Tilburg University
Tilburg, The Netherlands
e.j.krahmer@uvt.nl
e.c.marsi@uvt.nl

Abstract

We present an automatic multi-document summarization system for Dutch based on the MEAD system. We focus on redundancy detection, an essential ingredient of multi-document summarization. We introduce a semantic overlap detection tool, which goes beyond simple string matching. Our results so far do not confirm our expectation that this tool would outperform the other tested methods.

1 Introduction

One of the main issues in automatic multi-document summarization is avoiding redundancy. As the source documents are all related to the same topic, at least some of their content is likely to overlap. In fact, this is in part what makes multi-document summarization feasible. For example, news articles that report on a particular event, or that are based on the same source, often contain similar information expressed in different ways. A multi-document summarizer should include this overlapping information not more than once. The backbone of most current approaches to automatic summarization is a vector space model in which a sentence is regarded as a bag of words and a weighted cosine similarity measure is used to quantify the amount of shared information between a pair of sentences. Cosine similarity (in this context) essentially amounts to calculating word overlap, albeit with weighting of the terms and normalization for differences in sentence length. It is clear that this approach to detecting redundancy is far from satisfactory, because it only covers redundancy in its most trivial form, i.e., identical words. In contrast, the redundancy that we ultimately want to avoid in summarization is that at the semantic level. As an extreme case in point, two sentences with no words in common can still carry virtually the same meaning.

The remainder of this paper is structured in the following way. In Section 2 we introduce a tool for detecting semantic overlap. In section 3 we present a Dutch multi-document summarization system, based on the MEAD summarization toolkit (Radev et al., 2004). Next, in section 4 we describe the experimental setup and the data set that we used. Section 5 reports on the results, and we conclude in section 6.

2 Detecting semantic overlap

In this section, we detail the semantic overlap detection tool and the resources we build on.

Parallel/comparable text corpus The basis for our semantic overlap detection tool is a monolingual parallel/comparable tree-bank of 1 million words of Dutch text (Marsi and Krahmer, 2007). Half of the text material has so far been manually aligned at the sentence level. Subsequently, the sentences have been parsed and the resulting parse trees have been aligned at the level of syntactic nodes. Moreover, aligned nodes have been labeled according to a set of semantic similarity labels that express the type of similarity relation between the nodes. The following five labels are used: *generalize, specify, intersect, restate*, and *equal*. The corpus serves as the basis for developing tools for automatic alignment and relation labeling.

Word aligner The word alignment tool takes as input a pair of source and target sentences and produces a matching between the words, that is, a (possibly partial) one-to-one mapping of source to target words. This aligner is a part of the full fledged tree aligner currently under development.

The alignment task comprises several subtasks. First, the input sentences are tokenized and parsed with the Alpino syntactic parser for Dutch (Bouma et al., 2001). Apart from the syntactic analysis, which we disregard in the current work, the parser

Proceedings of the 2009 Workshop on Language Generation and Summarisation, ACL-IJCNLP 2009, pages 63–66,
Suntec, Singapore, 6 August 2009.

performs lemmatization, part-of-speech tagging and compound analysis, all of which are used here.

In addition, the aligner uses lexical-semantic knowledge from Cornetto, a lexical database for Dutch (40K entries) similar to the well-known English WordNet (Vossen et al., 2008). The relations we use are *synonym*, *hyperonym*, and *xpos-near-synonym* (align near synonyms with different POS labels). In addition we check whether a pair of content words has a least common subsumer (LCS) in the hyperonym hierarchy. As path length has been shown to be a poor predictor in this respect, we calculate the Lin similarity, which combines the Information Content of the words involved (Lin, 1998). A current limitation is that we lack word sense disambiguation, hence we take the maximal score over all the senses of the words.

The components described above can be considered as experts which predict word alignments with a certain probability. Since alignments can support, complement or contradict each other, we are faced with the problem of how to combine the evidence. Our approach is to view the alignment as a weighted bipartite multigraph. That is, a graph where source and target nodes are in disjoint sets, multiple edges are allowed between the same pair of nodes, and edges have an associated weight. Our goal is on the one hand to maximize the sum of the edge weights, and on the other hand to reduce this graph to a model in which every node can have at most one associated edge. This is a combinatorial optimization problem known as *the assignment problem* for which efficient algorithms exist. We use a variant of the *The Hungarian Algorithm*[1] (Kuhn, 1955), for the computation of the matches.

Sentence similarity score Given a word alignment between a pair of sentences, a similarity score is required to measure the amount of semantic overlap or redundancy. Evidently the similarity score should be proportional to the relative number of aligned words. However, some alignments are more important than others. For example, the alignment between two determiners (e.g. *the*) is less significant than that between two common nouns. This is modeled in our similarity score by weighting alignments according to the idf (inverse document frequency) (Spärck Jones, 1972) of the words involved.

$$sim(s_1, s_2) = \frac{\sum_{w_i \in A} idf(w_i)}{\sum_{w_j \in S} idf(w_j)} \quad (1)$$

Here s_1 and s_2 are sentences, S is the longest of the two sentences, w_j are the words in S, A is the subsequence of aligned words in S, and w_i are the words in A.

3 Multi-document summarization

The Dutch Multi-Document Summarizer presented here is based on the MEAD summarization toolkit (Radev et al., 2004), which offers a wide range of summarization algorithms and has a flexible structure. The system creates a summary by extracting a subset of sentences from the original documents. The summarizer reads in a cluster of documents, i.e. a set of documents relevant for the same topic, and for each sentence it extracts a set of features. These features are combined to determine an importance score for each sentence. Next the sentences are sorted according to their importance score. The system starts a summary by adding the sentence with the highest weight. Then it examines the second most important sentence and measures the similarity with the sentence that is already added. If the overlap is limited, the sentence is added to the summary, otherwise it is disregarded. This process is repeated until the intended summary size is reached. The module that performs this last step of determining which sentences end up in the final summary is called the *reranker*.

We use two baseline systems: the random baseline system randomly selects a set of sentences and the lead-based system which selects a subset of initial sentences as summary. We investigated the following features. A simple and effective features is the *position*: each sentence gets a score of $1/position$ where 'position' is the place in the document. The *length* feature is a filter that removes sentences shorter than the given threshold. The *simwf* feature presents the overlap of a sentence with the title of the document computed with cosine similarity. One of MEAD's main features is *centroid*-based summarization. Centroids of clusters are used to determine which words are important for the cluster and sentences containing these words are considered to be central sentences. The words are weighted with tf*idf.

[1] Also known as the *Munkres algorithm*

The aim of query-based summarization is to create summaries that are relevant with respect to a particular query. This can easily be done with features that express the overlap between the query and a source sentence. We examined three different query-based features that measure simple word overlap between the query and the sentence, cosine similarity with tf*idf weighting of words and cosine similarity without tf*idf weighting.

The MEAD toolkit implements multiple reranker modules, we investigated the following three: the *cosine*-reranker, the *mmr*-reranker and *novelty*-reranker. We compare these rerankers against the semantic overlap detection (sod) tool detailed in section 2. The cosine-reranker represents two sentences as tf*idf weighted word vectors and computes a cosine similarity score between them. Sentences with a cosine similarity above the threshold are disregarded. The mmr-reranker module is based on the maximal margin relevance criterion (Carbonell and Goldstein, 1998). MMR models the trade-off between a focused summary and a summary with a wide scope. The novelty-reranker is an extension of the cosine-reranker and boosts sentences occurring after an important sentence by multiplying with 1.2. The reranker tries to mimic human behavior as people tend to pick clusters of sentences when summarizing.

4 Experimental setup

To perform proper evaluation of the summarization system we constructed a new data set for evaluating Dutch multi-document summarization. It consists of 30 query-based document clusters. The document clusters were created manually following the guidelines of DUC 2006 (Dang, 2006). Each cluster contains a query description and 5 to 25 newspaper articles relevant for that particular question. For each cluster five annotators wrote an abstract of approximately 250 words. These summaries serve as a gold standard for comparison with automatically generated extracts.

We split our data set in a test set of 20 clusters and a development set of 10 clusters. We use the development set for parameter tuning and feature selection for the summarizer. We try out each of the characteristics discussed in section 3. The best combination found on the development set is the feature combination *position*, *centroid*, *length* with cut-off 13, and *queryCosine*. We tested the different rerankers and vary the similarity thresholds to determine their optimal threshold value. As the novelty-reranker scored lower than the other rerankers on the development set, we did not include it in our experiments on the test set.

For the experiments on the development set, we compare each of the automatically produced extracts with five manually written summaries and report macro-average Rouge-2 and Rouge-SU4 scores (Lin and Hovy, 2003). For the experiments on the test set, we also perform a manual evaluation. We follow the DUC 2006 guidelines for manual evaluation of responsiveness and the linguistic quality of the produced summaries. The responsiveness scores express the information content of the summary with respect to the query. The linguistic quality is evaluated on five different objectives: *grammaticality, non-redundancy, coherence, referential clarity* and *focus*. The annotators can choose a value on a five point scale where 1 means 'very poor' and 5 means 'very good'. We use two independent annotators to evaluate the summaries and we report the average scores.

5 Results

The evaluation of the results on the test set are shown in table 1. The Rouge scores of the different rerankers are all above both baselines, and they are very close to each other. The scores for the content measure and responsiveness show that the values for the automatic summaries are between 2 (poor) and 3 (barely acceptable). The optimized summarizers score higher than the two baselines on this point.

We are most interested in the aspect of 'non-redundancy'. The random baseline system achieves a good result here, and the optimized summarizers all score lower. The chance of overlap between randomly selected sentences seems to be lower than when an automatic summarizer tries to select only the most important sentences. When we compare the three optimized systems with different rerankers on this aspect we see that the scores are very close. Our semantic overlap detection (sod) reranker does not do any better than the other two. The optimized summarizers do perform better than the baseline systems with respect to focus and structure.

setting	Rouge-2	Rouge-SU4	gram	redun	ref	focus	struct	respons
rand baseline	0.101	0.153	4.08	3.9	2.58	2.6	2	2.25
lead baseline	0.139	0.179	3.05	3.6	3.25	2.88	2.38	2.4
optim-cosine	0.152	0.193	3.9	3.18	2.65	3.15	2.43	2.75
optim-mmr	0.149	0.191	3.98	3.13	2.55	3.13	2.38	2.7
optim-sod	0.150	0.193	4.05	3.13	2.85	3.23	2.5	2.7

Table 1: Macro-average Rouge scores and manual evaluation on the test set on these aspects: *gram*maticality, non-*redun*dancy, *ref*erential clarity, *focus*, *struct*ure and *respons*iveness.

6 Discussion and conclusion

We presented an automatic multi-document summarization system for Dutch based on the MEAD system, supporting the claim that MEAD is largely language-independent. We experimented with different features and parameter settings of the summarizer, and optimized it for summarization of Dutch newspaper text. We presented a semantic overlap detection tool, developed on the basis of a monolingual corpus of parallel/comparable Dutch text, which goes beyond simple string matching. We expected this tool to improve the sentence reranking step, thereby reducing redundancy in the summaries. However, we were unable to show a significant effect. We have several possible explanations for this. First, many of the sentence pairs that share the same semantic content, also share a number of identical words. To detect these cases, therefore, computing cosine similarity may be just as effective. Second, the accuracy of the alignment tool may not be good enough, partly because of errors in the linguistic analysis or lack of coverage, and partly because certain types of knowledge (word sense, syntactic structure) are not yet exploited. Third, reranking of sentences is unlikely to improve the summary in cases where the preceding step of sentence ranking within documents performs poorly. We are currently still investigating this matter and hope to obtain significant results with an improved version of our tool for detecting semantic overlap.

We plan to work on a more refined version that not only uses word alignment but also considers alignments at the parse tree level. This idea is in line with the work of Barzilay and McKeown (2005) who use this type of technique to fuse similar sentences for multi-document summarization.

Acknowledgements This work was conducted within the DAESO `http://daeso.uvt.nl` project funded by the Stevin program (De Nederlandse Taalunie). The construction of the evaluation corpus described in this paper was financed by KP BOF 2008, University of Antwerp. We would like to thank NIST for kindly sharing their DUC 2006 guidelines.

References

Regina Barzilay and Kathleen R. McKeown. 2005. Sentence fusion for multidocument news summarization. *Computational Linguistics*, 31(3):297–328.

Gosse Bouma, Gertjan van Noord, and Robert Malouf. 2001. Alpino: Wide-coverage computational analysis of Dutch. In *Computational Linguistics in the Netherlands 2000.*, pages 45–59. Rodopi, Amsterdam, New York.

Jaime Carbonell and Jade Goldstein. 1998. The use of mmr, diversity-based reranking for reordering documents and producing summaries. In *Proceedings of SIGIR 1998*, pages 335–336, New York, NY, USA. ACM.

H.T. Dang. 2006. Overview of DUC 2006. In *Proceedings of the Document Understanding Workshop*, pages 1–10, Brooklyn, USA.

Harold W. Kuhn. 1955. The Hungarian Method for the assignment problem. *Naval Research Logistics Quarterly*, 2:83–97.

C.-Y. Lin and E.H. Hovy. 2003. Automatic evaluation of summaries using n-gram co-occurrence statistics. In *Proceedings of HLT-NAACL*, pages 71 – 78, Edmonton, Canada.

D. Lin. 1998. An information-theoretic definition of similarity. In *Proceedings of the ICML*, pages 296–304.

Erwin Marsi and Emiel Krahmer. 2007. Annotating a parallel monolingual treebank with semantic similarity relations. In *Proceedings of the 6th International Workshop on Treebanks and Linguistic Theories*, pages 85–96, Bergen, Norway.

Dragomir Radev et al. 2004. Mead - a platform for multidocument multilingual text summarization. In *Proceedings of LREC 2004*, Lisabon, Portugal.

Karen Spärck Jones. 1972. A statistical interpretation of term specificity and its application in retrieval. *Journal of Documentation*, 28(1):11–21.

P. Vossen, I. Maks, R. Segers, and H. van der Vliet. 2008. Integrating lexical units, synsets and ontology in the Cornetto Database. In *Proceedings of LREC 2008*, Marrakech, Morocco.

Non-textual Event Summarization by Applying Machine Learning to Template-based Language Generation

Mohit Kumar and **Dipanjan Das** and **Sachin Agarwal** and **Alexander I. Rudnicky**
Language Technologies Institute
Carnegie Mellon University, Pittsburgh, USA
mohitkum,dipanjan,sachina,air@cs.cmu.edu

Abstract

We describe a learning-based system that creates draft reports based on observation of people preparing such reports in a target domain (conference replanning). The reports (or briefings) are based on a mix of text and event data. The latter consist of task creation and completion actions, collected from a wide variety of sources within the target environment. The report drafting system is part of a larger learning-based cognitive assistant system that improves the quality of its assistance based on an opportunity to learn from observation. The system can learn to accurately predict the briefing assembly behavior and shows significant performance improvements relative to a non-learning system, demonstrating that it's possible to create meaningful verbal descriptions of activity from event streams.

1 Introduction

We describe a system for recommending items for a briefing created after a session with a crisis management system in a conference replanning domain. The briefing system is learning-based, in that it initially observes how one set of users creates such briefings then generates draft reports for another set of users. This system, the Briefing Assistant(BA), is part of a set of learning-based cognitive assistants each of which observes users and learns to assist users in performing their tasks faster and more accurately.

The difference between this work from most previous efforts, primarily based on text-extraction approaches is the emphasis on learning to summarize event patterns. This work also differs in its emphasis on learning from user behavior in the context of a task.

Report generation from non-textual sources has been previously explored in the Natural Language Generation (NLG) community in a variety of domains, based on, for example, a database of events. However, a purely generative approach is not suitable in our circumstances, as we want to summarize a variety of tasks that the user is performing and present a summary tailored to a target audience, a desirable characteristic of good briefings (Radev and McKeown, 1998). Thus we approach the problem by applying learning techniques combined with a template-based generation system to instantiate the briefing-worthy report items. The task of instantiating the briefing-worthy items is similar to the task of Content Selection (Duboue, 2004) in the Generation pipeline however our approach minimizes linguistic involvement. Our choice of a template-based generative system was motivated by recent discussions in the NLG community (van Deemter et al., 2005) about the practicality and effectiveness of this approach.

The plan of the paper is as follows. We describe relevant work from existing literature in the next section. Then, we provide brief system description followed by experiments and results. We conclude with a summary of the work.

2 Related Work

Event based summarization has been studied in the summarization community. (Daniel et al., 2003) described identification of sub-events in multiple documents. (Filatova and Hatzivassiloglou, 2004) mentioned the use of event-based features in extractive summarization and (Wu, 2006; Li et al., 2006) describe similar work based on events occurring in text. However, unlike the case at hand, all the work on event-based summarization used text as source material.

Non-textual summarization has also been explored in the Natural Language Generation (NLG) community within the broad task of generating

Proceedings of the 2009 Workshop on Language Generation and Summarisation, ACL-IJCNLP 2009, pages 67–71,
Suntec, Singapore, 6 August 2009.

reports based on database of events in specific domains such as medical (Portet et al., 2009), weather (Belz, 2007), sports (Oh and Shrobe, 2008) etc. However, in our case we want to summarize a variety of tasks that the user is performing and present a summary to an intended audience (as defined by a report request).

Recent advances in NLG research use statistical approaches at various stages of processing in the generation pipeline like content selection (Duboue and McKeown, 2003; Barzilay and Lee, 2004), probabilistic generation rules (Belz, 2007). Our proposed approach differs from these in that we apply machine learning after generation of all the templates, as a post-processing step, to rank them for inclusion in the final briefing. We could have used a general purpose template-based generation framework like TG/2 (Busemann, 2005), but since the number of templates and their corresponding aggregators is limited, we chose an approach based on string manipulation.

We found in our work that an approach based on modeling individual users and then combining the outputs of such models using a voting scheme gives the best results, although our approach is distinguishable from collaborative filtering techniques used for driving recommendation systems (Hofmann, 2004). We believe this is due to the fact that the individual sessions from which ranking models are learned, although they range over the same collection of component tasks, can lead to very different (human-generated) reports. That is, the particular history of a session will affect what is considered to be briefing-worthy.

3 System Overview

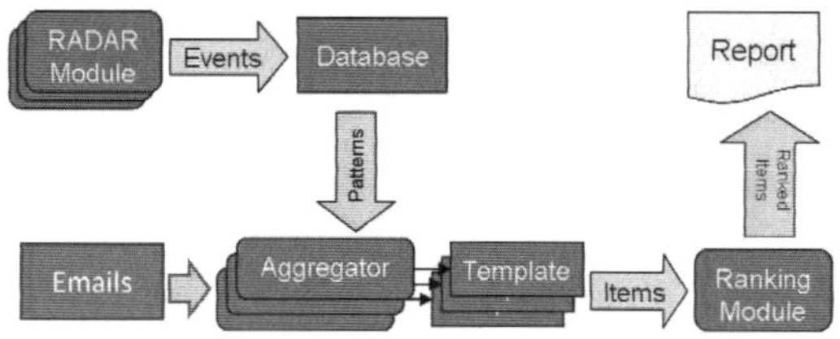

Figure 1: Briefing Assistant Data Flow.

The Briefing Assistant Model: We treat the task of briefing generation in the current domain[1] as non-textual event-based summarization. The events are the task creation and task completion actions logged by various cognitive assistants in the system (so-called specialists). As part of the design phase for the template-based generation component, we identified a set of templates, based on the actual briefings written by users in a separate experiment. Ideally, we would like to adopt a corpus-based approach to automatically extract the templates in the domain, like (Kumar et al., 2008), but since the sample briefings available to us were very few, the application of such corpus-based techniques was not necessary. Based on this set of templates we identified the patterns that needed to be extracted from the event logs in order to populate the templates. A ranking model was also designed for ordering instantiations of this set of templates and to recommend the top 4 most relevant ones for a given session.

[1]More details about the domain and the interaction of BA with the larger system are mentioned in a longer version of the paper (Kumar et al., 2009)

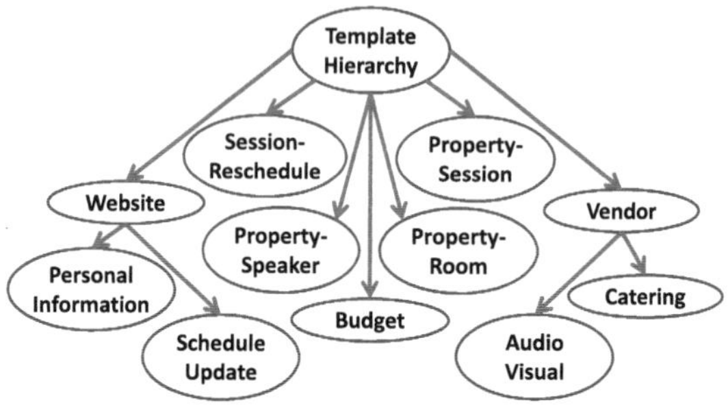

Figure 2: The category tree showing the information types that we expect in a briefing.

The overall data flow for BA during a session (runtime) is shown in Figure 1. The various specialist modules generate task related events that are logged in a database. The aggregators operate over this database and emails to extract relevant patterns. These patterns in turn are used to populate templates which constitute candidate briefing items. The candidate briefing items are then ordered by the ranking module and presented to the user.

Template Design and Aggregators: The set of templates used in the current instantiation of the BA was derived from a corpus of human-generated briefings collected in a previous experiment using the same crisis management system. The set of templates was designed to cover the range of items that users in that experiment chose to include in their reports corresponding to nine categories shown in Figure 2. We found that information can be conveyed at different levels of granularity (for example, qualitatively or quantitatively). The appropriate choice of granularity for a particular session is a factor that the system can learn[2].

Ranking Model, Classifiers and Features: The ranking module orders candidate templates so that the four most relevant ones appear in the briefing draft. The ranking system consists of a consensus-based classifier, based on individual classifier models for each user in the training set. The prediction from each classifier are combined (averaged) to produce a final rank of each template.

We used the Minorthird package (Cohen, 2004) for modeling. Specifically we allowed the system to experiment with eleven different learning schemes and select the best one based on cross-validation within the training corpus. The schemes were Naive Bayes, Voted Perceptron, Support Vector Machines, Ranking Perceptron, K Nearest Neighbor, Decision Tree, AdaBoost, Passive Aggressive learner, Maximum Entropy learner, Balanced Winnow and Boosted Ranking learner.

The features[3] used in the system are static or dynamic. Static features reflect the properties of the templates irrespective of the user's activity whereas the dynamic features are based on the actual events that took place. We used the Information Gain (IG) metric for feature selection, experimenting with seven different cut-off values $All, 20, 15, 10, 7, 5, 4$ for the total number of selected features.

4 Experiments and Results

Experimental Setup: Two experimental conditions were used to differentiate performance based on knowledge engineering, designated MinusL and performance based on learning, designated PlusL.[4]

Email Trigger: In the simulated conference replanning crisis, the briefing was triggered by an email containing explicit information requests, not known beforehand. To customize the briefing according to the request, a natural language processing module identified the categories of information requested. The details of the module are beyond the scope of the current paper as it is external to our system; it took into account the template categories we earlier identified. Figure 4 shows a sample briefing email stimulus. The mapping from the sample email in the figure to the categories is as follows: "expected attendance" - Property-Session; "how many sessions have been rescheduled", "how many still need to be rescheduled", "any problems you see as you try to reschedule" - Session-Reschedule; "status of food service (I am worried about the keynote lunch)" - Catering Vendors.

Training: Eleven expert users[5] were asked to provide training by using the system then generating the end of session briefing using the BA GUI. For this training phase, no item ranking was performed by the system, i.e. all the templates were populated by the aggregators and recommendations were random. The expert user was asked to select the best possible four items and was further asked to judge the usefulness of the remaining items. The resulting training data consists of the activity log, extracted features and the user-labeled items. The trigger message for the training users did not contain any specific information request.

Test: Subjects were recruited to use the crisis management system in MinusL and PlusL condition, although they were not aware of the condition of the system and they were not involved with the project. There were 54 test runs in the MinusL condition and 47 in the PlusL condition. Out of these runs, 29 subjects in MinusL and 43 subjects in PlusL wrote a briefing using the BA. We report the evaluation scores for this latter set.

Evaluation: The base performance metric is Recall, defined in terms of the briefing templates recommended by the system compared to the templates ultimately selected by the user. We justify this by noting that Recall can be directly linked to the expected time savings for the users. We calculate two variants of Recall: *Category-based*— calculated by matching the categories of the BA recommended templates and user selected ones ignoring the granularity and *Template-based*— calculated by matching the exact templates. The first metric indicates whether the right category of information was selected and the latter indicates whether the information was presented at the appropriate level of detail.

We also performed subjective human evaluation

[2] The details of template design process including sample templates, categories of templates and details of aggregators are presented in (Kumar et al., 2009)

[3] Detailed description of the features are mentioned in (Kumar et al., 2009)

[4] The details of the experimental setup as part of the larger cognitive assistant system are presented in (Kumar et al., 2009).

[5] Members of the project from other groups who were aware of the scenario and various system functionalities but not the ML methods

using a panel of three judges. The judges assigned scores (0-4) to each of the bullets based on the coverage of the crisis, clarity and conciseness, accuracy and the correct level of granularity. They were advised about certain briefing-specific characteristics (e.g. negative bullet items are useful and hence should be rated favorably). They were also asked to provide a global assessment of report quality, and evaluate the coverage of the requests in the briefing stimulus email message. This procedure was very similar to the one used as the basis for template selection.

Experiment: The automatic evaluation metric used for the trained system configuration is the *Template-based* recall measure. To obtain the final system configuration, we automatically evaluate the system under the various combinations of parameter settings with eleven different learning schemes and seven different feature selection threshold (as mentioned in previous sections). Thus a total of 77 different configurations are tested. For each configuration, we do a eleven-fold cross-validation between the 11 training users i.e. we leave one user as the test user and consider the remaining ten users as training users. We average the performance across the 11 test cases and obtain the final score for the configuration. We choose the configuration with the highest score as the final trained system configuration. The learned system configuration in the current test includes Balanced Winnow (Littlestone, 1988) and top 7 features.

Results: We noticed that four users in PlusL condition took more than 8 minutes to complete the briefing when the median time taken by the users in PlusL condition was 55 seconds, so we did not include these users in our analysis in order to maintain the homogeneity of the dataset. These four data points were identified as extreme outliers using a procedure suggested by (NIST, 2008)[6]. There were no extreme outliers in MinusL condition.

Figure $3a$ shows the Recall values for the MinusL and PlusL conditions. The learning delta i.e. the difference between the recall values of PlusL and MinusL is 33% for *Template-based* recall and 21% for *Category-based* recall. These differences are significant at the $p < 0.001$ level. The statistical significance for the *Template-based* metric, which was the metric used for selecting system parameters during the training phase, shows that learning is effective in this case. Since the email stimulus processing module extracts the briefing categories from the email the *Category-based* and *Template-based* recall is expected to be high for the baseline MinusL case. In our test, the email stimuli had 3 category requests and so the *Category-based* recall of 0.77 and *Template-based* recall of 0.67 in MinusL is not unexpected.

Figure $3b$ shows the Judges' panel scores for the briefings in MinusL and PlusL condition. The learning delta in this case is 3.6% which is also statistically significant, at $p < 0.05$. The statistical significance of the learning delta validates that the briefings generated during PlusL conditions are better than MinusL condition. The absolute difference in the qualitative briefing scores between the two conditions is small because MinusL users can select from all candidates, while the recommendations they receive are random. Consequently they need to spend more time in finding the right items. The average time taken for a briefing in MinusL condition is about 83 seconds and 62 seconds in PlusL (see Figure $3c$). While the time difference is high (34%) it is not statistically significant due to high variance.

Four of the top 10 most frequently selected features across users for this system are dynamic features. This indicates that the learning model is capturing the user's world state and the recommendations are related to the underlying events. We believe this validates the process we used to generate briefing reports from non-textual events.

5 Summary

The Briefing Assistant is not designed to learn the generic attributes of good reports; rather it's meant to rapidly learn the attributes of good reports within a particular domain and to accommodate specific information needs on a report-by-report basis. We found that learned customization produces reports that are judged to be of better quality. We also found that a consensus-based modeling approach, which incorporates information from multiple users, yields the best performance. We believe that our approach can be used to create flexible summarization systems for a variety of applications.

[6] Extreme outliers are defined as data points that are outside the range $[Q1-3*IQ, Q3+3*IQ]$ in a box plot. $Q1$ is lower quartile, $Q3$ is upper quartile and IQ is the difference $(Q3 - Q1)$ is the interquartile range.

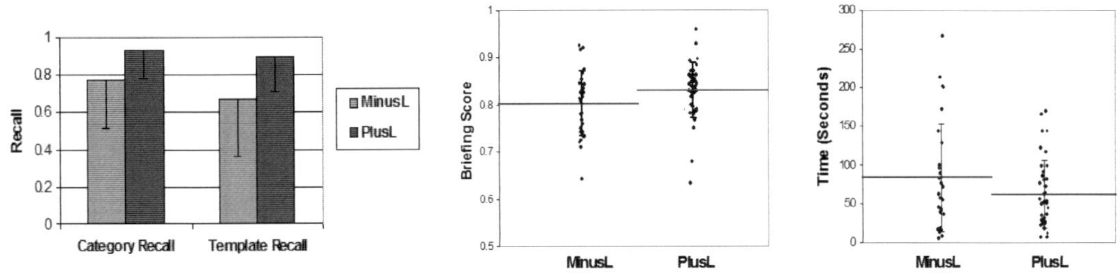

(a) (b) (c)

Figure 3: (a) Recall values for MinusL and PlusL conditions (b) Briefing scores from the judges' panel for MinusL and PlusL conditions (c) Briefing time taken for MinusL and PlusL conditions.

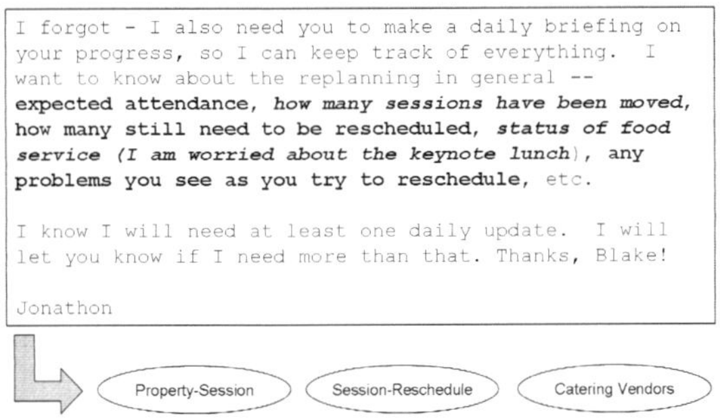

Figure 4: Template categories corresponding to the Briefing request email.

References

Regina Barzilay and Lillian Lee. 2004. Catching the drift: probabilistic content models, with applications to generation and summarization. In *Proceedings of NAACL*.

Anja Belz. 2007. Probabilistic generation of weather forecast texts. In *Proceedings of HLT-NAACL*.

Stephan Busemann. 2005. Ten years after: An update on TG/2 (and friends). In *Proceedings of European Natural Language Generation Workshop*.

William W. Cohen. 2004. Minorthird: Methods for identifying names and ontological relations in text using heuristics for inducing regularities from data. http://minorthird.sourceforge.net, 10th Jun 2009.

Naomi Daniel, Dragomir Radev, and Timothy Allison. 2003. Sub-event based multi-document summarization. In *Proceedings of HLT-NAACL*.

Pablo A. Duboue and Kathleen R. McKeown. 2003. Statistical acquisition of content selection rules for natural language generation. In *Proceedings of EMNLP*.

Pablo A. Duboue. 2004. Indirect supervised learning of content selection logic. In *Proceedings of INLG*.

Elena Filatova and Vasileios Hatzivassiloglou. 2004. Event-based extractive summarization. In *Text Summarization Branches Out: Proceedings of the ACL-04 Workshop*.

Thomas Hofmann. 2004. Latent semantic models for collaborative filtering. *ACM Transactions on Information Systems*, 22(1):89–115.

Mohit Kumar, Dipanjan Das, and Alexander I. Rudnicky. 2008. Automatic extraction of briefing templates. In *Proceedings of IJCNLP*.

Mohit Kumar, Dipanjan Das, Sachin Agarwal, and Alexander I. Rudnicky. 2009. Non-textual event summarization by applying machine learning to template-based language generation. Technical Report CMU-LTI-09-012, Language Technologies Institute, Carnegie Mellon University.

Wenjie Li, Mingli Wu, Qin Lu, Wei Xu, and Chunfa Yuan. 2006. Extractive summarization using inter- and intra- event relevance. In *Proceedings of ACL*.

Nick Littlestone. 1988. Learning quickly when irrelevant attributes abound: A new linear-threshold algorithm. *Machine Learning*, 2(4):285–318.

NIST. 2008. NIST/SEMATECH e-handbook of statistical methods. http://www.itl.nist.gov/div898/handbook/, 10th Jun 2009.

Alice Oh and Howard Shrobe. 2008. Generating baseball summaries from multiple perspectives by reordering content. In *Proceedings of INLG*.

François Portet, Ehud Reiter, Albert Gatt, Jim Hunter, Somayajulu Sripada, Yvonne Freer, and Cindy Sykes. 2009. Automatic generation of textual summaries from neonatal intensive care data. *Artificial Intelligence*, 173(7-8):789–816.

Dragomir R. Radev and Kathleen R. McKeown. 1998. Generating natural language summaries from multiple on-line sources. *Computational Linguistics*, 24(3):470–500.

Kees van Deemter, Emiel Krahmer, and Mariet Theune. 2005. Real versus template-based natural language generation: A false opposition? *Computational Linguistics*, 31(1):15–24.

Mingli Wu. 2006. Investigations on event-based summarization. In *Proceedings of ACL*.

Creating an Annotated Corpus for Generating Walking Directions

Stephanie Schuldes† **Michael Roth**‡ **Anette Frank**‡ **Michael Strube**†

†EML Research gGmbH
Heidelberg, Germany
http://www.eml-research.de/nlp

‡Department of Computational Linguistics
University of Heidelberg, Germany
http://www.cl.uni-heidelberg.de

Abstract

This work describes first steps towards building a system that synchronously generates multimodal (textual and visual) route directions for pedestrians. We pursue a corpus-based approach for building a generation model that produces natural instructions in multiple languages. We conducted an empirical study to collect verbal route directions, and annotated the acquired texts on different levels. Here we describe the experimental setting and an analysis of the collected data.

1 Introduction

Route directions guide a person unfamiliar with the environment to their designated goal. We plan to generate route instructions that are similar to those given by humans by referring to landmarks and by structuring the route in a way that it is easy to memorize (Denis, 1997).

We develop a system for synchronously generating natural language route directions and 3D scenes of a route. The core of the architecture is a unified representation providing information for both verbal and graphical output. The direct correspondence between linguistic references and shown objects facilitates the identification of the visual scene in the real world and the choice of the correct action while following the route. To create a reusable system that is adaptable to different navigational domains and languages, we use machine learning techniques to build a statistical generation model from annotated corpora. We report on an empirical study to collect human-produced walking directions to be used for statistical generation from underlying semantic structures. While our scenario is ultimately multilingual, here we give an analysis of the German dataset.

2 Related Work

The task of analyzing and generating cognitively adequate route instructions has been addressed by a number of authors (Taylor & Tversky, 1996; Tappe, 2000; Habel, 2003; Richter, 2008; Viethen & Dale, 2008; Kelleher & Costello, 2009). Marciniak & Strube (2005) showed that a system for generating route directions can be successfully trained on a small set of 75 route direction texts (8418 tokens). In their approach directions are represented in a graph, which encodes information on various conceptual levels. While their approach is restricted to reproducing directions for the learned graphs, we will generate directions for a wide range of possible routes. Dale et al. (2005) developed a system that takes GIS data as input and uses a pipeline architecture to generate verbal route directions. In contrast to their approach, our approach will be based on an integrated architecture allowing for more interaction between the different stages of generation. The idea of combining verbal directions with scenes from a virtual 3D environment has recently lead to a new framework for evaluating NLG systems: The Challenge on Generating Instructions in Virtual Environments (GIVE) (Byron et al., 2009) is planned to become a regular event for the NLG community.

3 Corpus Acquisition

For collecting naturally produced route instructions, we conducted a study with 29 native speakers of German (66% female and 33% male). The participants in our study were students from various fields aged between 20 and 34 years. We designed two different settings: one *on-site setting*, in which participants walked around in a real world situation (specifically our university campus), and one *desk-based setting*, in which they interacted with a web application. The former was further divided into indoor and outdoor routes,

Proceedings of the 2009 Workshop on Language Generation and Summarisation, ACL-IJCNLP 2009, pages 72–76,
Suntec, Singapore, 6 August 2009.

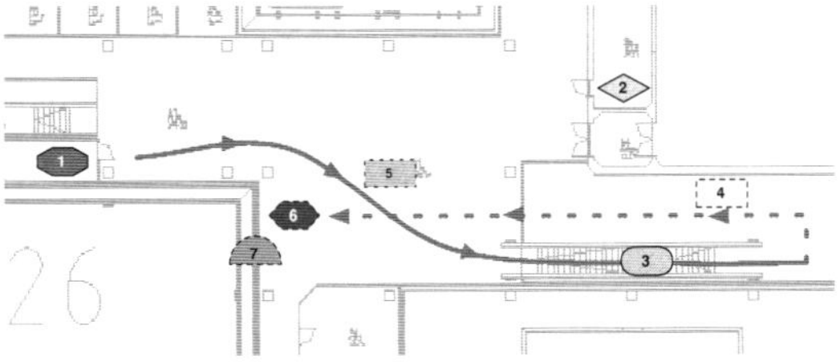

Figure 1: Example route from the indoor setting (first task), leading from a room with photocopiers (1) across an open space and downstairs (3) to a students' union room (6), passing an information board (4) and a coffee machine (5). A lecture room (2) and a glass wall (7) are visible from the route.

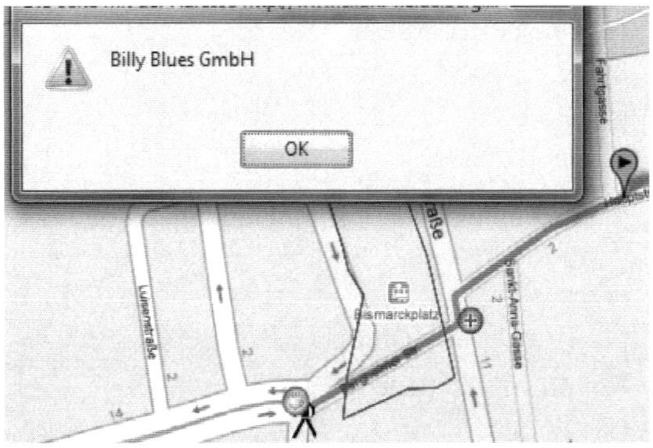

Figure 2: Web application used in the second task. Landmarks were introduced successively via pop-ups as the animated walker encountered them.

while the latter was restricted to an outdoor scenario. This design enables us to study possible differences and commonalities between linguistic realizations obtained for different environments as well as different presentation modes.

For both scenarios, the task was to give written directions to a person unfamiliar with the area as to how to get to the destination the participants just reached, taking the same route. First, participants were led along a route to a given destination point (on-site). Each participant was asked to give directions for two routes inside buildings of the university campus (e.g. from an office to a seminar room, cf. Figure 1), and one outside route (e.g. from the building entrance to a bus stop).

Second, participants were shown a web application that guided them along a route by means of a 2D animation (desk-based). Subjects were allowed to use all information displayed by the web application: named places, buildings, street and bridge names, etc. (cf. Figure 2).

Setting	GM	CI	CO	Total
physical routes	9	6	3	18
directions	59	58	28	145
tokens	5353	4119	2674	12146
tokens/dir. (∅)	91	71	96	

Table 1: Number of routes, directions, and tokens for the different settings. GM = Google Maps, CI = Campus Indoor, CO = Campus Outdoor.

4 Corpus Annotation

The acquired texts were processed in several steps. To ensure that all route directions consist of syntactically and semantically correct sentences, we manually corrected spelling mistakes, omissions resulting in grammatical errors, and removed elliptical and unclear directions.

The preprocessed texts were annotated on the following three levels:

pos_lemma – part-of-speech and lemma

syn_dep – dependency relations

sem_frame – frames and semantic roles

For the *pos_lemma* and *syn_dep* levels, we used *TreeTagger* (Schmid, 1997) and XLE (Maxwell & Kaplan, 1993). The corpus was parsed with the German ParGram LFG grammar (Forst, 2007). The outputs were corrected manually by two annotators. On the *sem_frame* level annotation was carried out using the annotation tool SALTO (Burchardt et al., 2006) and following the definiton of the FrameNet frames SELF_MOTION, PERCEPTION, BEING_LOCATED and LOCATIVE_RELATION (Baker et al., 1998). In terms of accuracy for unlabeled/labeled relations, the annotation agreement was 78.88%/65.17% on the *syn_dep* level and 79.27%/68.39% for frames and semantic roles.

5 Data Analysis

5.1 Corpus Statistics

We examined word frequencies with respect to the experimental settings in order to determine similarities and dissimilarities in lexical choice. Table 2 shows the three most frequent verbs and nouns found in each corpus part.

The data reveals that the most frequent verbs are typical among all settings. However, we found a number of lower-frequency verbs that are rather

Top verbs (Campus)	GM	CI	CO
gehen 'to walk'	11%	18%	14%
sein 'to be'	3.9%	8.2%	6.6%
stehen 'to stand'	**0.0%**	6.3%	5.3%
Top verbs (GM)	**GM**	**CI**	**CO**
folgen 'to follow'	12%	2.9%	2.6%
gehen 'to walk'	11%	18%	14%
abbiegen 'to turn into'	9.0%	3.8%	8.9%
Top nouns (Campus)	**GM**	**CI**	**CO**
Tür 'door'	**0.0%**	12%	0.9%
Treppe 'stairs'	**0.0%**	8.3%	**0.0%**
Gang 'hallway'	**0.0%**	6.6%	**0.0%**
Top nouns (GM)	**GM**	**CI**	**CO**
...straße '... Street'	28%	**0.0%**	2.2%
Richtung 'direction'	3.5%	2.8%	2.6%
...platz '... Square'	3.4%	**0.0%**	6.1%

Table 2: Relative frequency of the three most common verbs and nouns in both studies

scenario-specific. In many cases, the occurrence or absence of a verb can be attributed to a verb's selectional restrictions. For example, some of the verbs describing movements along streets (e.g. *folgen* 'to follow', *abbiegen* 'to turn into') do not occur within the indoor corpus whereas verbs describing "3D movements" (e.g. *durchqueren* 'to walk through', *hinuntergehen* 'to walk down') are not mentioned with the Google Maps setting.

The most frequent nouns significantly differ between the indoor and outdoor settings. This correlation does not come as a surprise, as most of the mentioned objects cannot be found in all scenarios. On the other hand, nouns that are common to both indoor and outdoor scenarios can be divided into two categories: Nouns denoting (1) objects that appear in both scenarios (e.g. *Gebäude* 'building') and (2) abstract concepts typical for route directions in general, e.g. *Richtung* 'direction', *Nummer* 'number', *Ziel* 'goal', and *Startpunkt* 'starting point'.

5.2 Landmark Alignment

Landmark alignment serves the purpose of detecting objects that are most frequently mentioned across directions, and how the same object is referred to differently. We created a graph-based representation of the landmarks mentioned in each route instruction (*single route representation, SRR*) for use in two types of alignment. Figure 3 shows an example from the indoor study. First, we created a combined graph for each physical route by merging the respective SRRs, taking into account several criteria:

String matching of landmark names;

Semantic similarity using *GermaNet* (Lemnitzer & Kunze, 2002), a lexical-semantic network for German similar to WordNet;

Frequency of references across all directions;

Spatio-temporal proximity of references to the same object;

Number of landmarks mentioned in a single direction (i.e. length of the SRR).

The combined graphs show that there are strong correspondences between the directions for the same route. We also found that, in the campus settings, there was a small number of frequently used general objects and a large number of less frequently used specific objects. This facilitates merging and shows the importance of the objects for people's orientation, and at the same time supports our claim that other modalities are needed to disambiguate references during navigation. For generating informative referential expressions, the combined graph needs to be refined so that object properties are represented (Krahmer et al., 2003).

Second, we aligned the SRRs with the physical route graph. Comparing the landmarks mentioned in the campus settings revealed that, in 97.8% of the cases, people adhere to the sequence in which objects are encountered. Reversed order was only found in special cases like distant objects.

5.3 Discourse Phenomena

We analyzed the use of anaphora, the temporal order of instructions, and occurrences of prototypical event chains in the collected texts in order to identify coherence-inducing elements.

Spatio-temporal adverbials: Most anaphors mention intermediate goals on the route in order to refer to the starting point of a new action (e.g. *da/hier* 'here', *dort* 'there'). This finding goes hand in hand with the observation that the collected route directions are typically structured in a linear temporal order (cf. Table 3) as for example indicated by the use of **adverbs indicating temporal succession** (e.g. *jetzt* 'now', *dann* 'then' and *danach* 'afterwards') and conjunctions (e.g. *bis* 'until', *wenn* 'when'). Interestingly, a reversed order can be found in a few cases, where

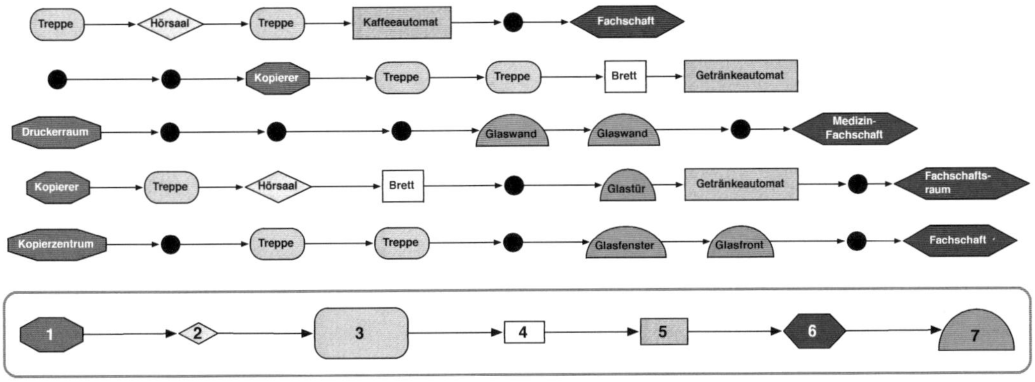

Figure 3: Each line shows one SRR for the route in Figure 1. Correspondences are indicated by identical node shapes, black dots substitute non-matched tokens. The bottom graph shows the physical route seen as sequence of landmarks. Node size reflects the importance of the referred object as conveyed by SRRs.

Adverbs $>_t$	**GM**	**CI**	**CO**
dann 'then'	55	43	30
jetzt 'now'	4	7	5
danach 'afterwards'	12	5	3
Adverbs $<_t$	**GM**	**CI**	**CO**
vorher 'beforehand'	0	1	0
davor 'before'	1	0	2

Table 3: Frequencies of temporal adverbs indicating linear ($>_t$) and reversed linear order ($<_t$)

the following action or situation is not supposed to take place (e.g. *Gehen Sie vorher rechts* 'beforehand turn right').

Backward-looking event anaphors and references to result states: We also found explicit references to past events (e.g. *Nach dem Durchqueren* 'after traversing') and result states of events, e.g. the adverbial phrase *unten angekommen* (here: 'downstairs') was frequently used following an instruction to 'walk downstairs'.

6 Conclusions and Future Work

The lexical corpus analysis confirms our hypothesis that there are strong commonalities in lexical choice for directions that persist across scenarios and presentation modes, with a small number of focused differences, and obvious domain-dependent lexical differences regarding the nature of objects in the respective scenarios. While our current corpus data is rather broad, environment-specific data can be extended quickly by setting up web studies using 2D and 3D environments.

The alignment of the physical routes and verbal instructions shows a clear tendency that linear route structure is observed in verbal realization, with only few exceptions. Since temporal order is observed by default, temporal annotation can be restricted to capture exceptional orderings, which are recoverable from linguistic cues. The study of discourse coherence effects yielded a number of elements that will be given special attention in the surface generation model. We observed a variety of coherence-inducing elements that are generic in nature and thus seem well-suited for a corpus-based generation model. As other languages are known to exhibit differences in verbal realization of directions (von Stutterheim et al., 2002), we have to extend our data collection in order to generate systematic linguistic variations from a single underlying semantic structure for all languages.

The linguistic annotation levels of frames and roles, syntactic dependencies, and basic word categories have been tested successfully with a similar corpus (Roth & Frank, 2009). The next steps will consist in the alignment of physical routes and landmarks with semantic representations in an integrated generation architecture.

Acknowledgements: This work is supported by the DFG-financed innovation fund FRONTIER as part of the Excellence Initiative at Heidelberg University (ZUK 49/1) and partially funded by the Klaus Tschira Foundation, Heidelberg, Germany. We thank the participants in our study, our annotators Tim Krones and Anna Schmidt, and student assistants Jonathan Geiger and Carina Silberer.

References

Baker, Collin F., Charles J. Fillmore & John B. Lowe (1998). The Berkeley FrameNet Project. In *Proceedings of the 17th International Conference on Computational Linguistics and 36th Annual Meeting of the Association for Computational Linguistics,* Montréal, Québec, Canada, 10–14 August 1998, pp. 86–90.

Burchardt, Aljoscha, Katrin Erk, Anette Frank, Andrea Kowalski & Sebastian Pado (2006). SALTO: A versatile multi-level annotation tool. In *Proceedings of the 5th International Conference on Language Resources and Evaluation,* Genoa, Italy, 22–28 May 2006, pp. 517–520.

Byron, Donna, Alexander Koller, Kristina Striegnitz, Justine Cassell, Robert Dale, Johanna Moore & Jon Oberlander (2009). Report on the First NLG Challenge on Generating Instructions in Virtual Environments (GIVE). In *Proceedings of the 12th European Workshop on Natural Language Generation (ENLG 2009),* Athens, Greece, 30-31 March 2009, pp. 165–173.

Dale, Robert, Sabine Geldof & Jean-Philippe Prost (2005). Using natural language generation in automatic route description. *Journal of Research and Practice in Information Technology*, 37(1):89–106.

Denis, Michel (1997). The description of routes: A cognitive approach to the production of spatial discourse. *Current Psychology of Cognition*, 16:409–458.

Forst, Martin (2007). Filling statistics with linguistics – Property design for the disambiguation of German LFG parses. In *Proceedings of the ACL 2007 Workshop on Deep Linguistic Processing,* Prague, Czech Republic, 28 June 2007, pp. 17–24.

Habel, Christopher (2003). Incremental generation of multimodal route instructions. In Reva Freedman & Charles Callaway (Eds.), *Working Papers of the 2003 AAAI Spring Symposium on Natural Language Generation in Spoken and Written Dialogue*, pp. 44–51. Menlo Park, California: AAAI Press.

Kelleher, John D. & Fintan J. Costello (2009). Applying computational models of spatial prepositions to visually situated dialog. *Computational Linguistics*, 35(2):271–306.

Krahmer, Emiel, Sebastiaan van Erk & André Verleg (2003). Graph-based generation of referring expressions. *Computational Linguistics*, 29(1):53–72.

Lemnitzer, Lothar & Claudia Kunze (2002). GermaNet – representation, visualization, application. In *Proceedings of the 3rd International Conference on Language Resources and Evaluation,* Las Palmas, Canary Islands, Spain, 29–31 May 2002, pp. 1485–1491.

Marciniak, Tomacz & Michael Strube (2005). Beyond the pipeline: Discrete optimization in NLP. In *Proceedings of the 9th Conference on Computational Natural Language Learning,* Ann Arbor, Mich., USA, 29–30 June 2005, pp. 136–145.

Maxwell, John T. & Ronald M. Kaplan (1993). The interface between phrasal and functional constraints. *Computational Linguistics*, 19(4):571–590.

Richter, Kai-Florian (2008). *Context-Specific Route Directions – Generation of Cognitively Motivated Wayfinding Instructions*. Amsterdam: IOS Press.

Roth, Michael & Anette Frank (2009). A NLG-based application for walking directions. In *Companion Volume to the Proceedings of the 47th Annual Meeting of the Association for Computational Linguistics and the 4th International Joint Conference on Natural Language Processing of the Asian Federation of Natural Language Processing,* Singapore, 2-7 August 2009. To appear.

Schmid, Helmut (1997). Probabilistic Part-of-Speech tagging using decision trees. In Daniel Jones & Harold Somers (Eds.), *New Methods in Language Processing*, pp. 154–164. London, U.K.: UCL Press.

Tappe, Heike (2000). Perspektivenwahl in Beschreibungen dynamischer und statischer Wegeskizzen. [Choice of perspective in descriptions of dynamic and static sketchmaps]. In Christopher Habel & Christiane v. Stutterheim (Eds.), *Räumliche Konzepte und sprachliche Strukturen*, pp. 69–97. Tübingen: Niemeyer.

Taylor, Holly & Barbara Tversky (1996). Perspective in spatial descriptions. *Journal of Memory and Language*, 35:371–391.

Viethen, Jette & Robert Dale (2008). The use of spatial relations in referring expression generation. In *Proceedings of the Fifth International Natural Language Generation Conference,* Salt Fork OH, USA, 12–14 June 2008, pp. 59–67.

von Stutterheim, Christiane, Ralf Nüse & Jorge M. Serra (2002). Crosslinguistic differences in the conceptualisation of events. In Hilde Hasselgård, Stig Johansson, Bergljot Behrens & Cathrine Fabricius-Hansen (Eds.), *Information Structure in a Cross-lingustic Perspective*, pp. 179–198. Amsterdam: Rodopi.

The 2009 Generation of Referring Expressions in Context Challenges

GREC 2009

Organisers:
Anja Belz, Eric Kow, Jette Viethen, Albert Gatt

The GREC Main Subject Reference Generation Challenge 2009: Overview and Evaluation Results

Anja Belz **Eric Kow**
NLT Group
University of Brighton
Brighton BN2 4GJ, UK
{asb,eykk10}@bton.ac.uk

Jette Viethen
Centre for LT
Macquarie University
Sydney NSW 2109
jviethen@ics.mq.edu.au

Albert Gatt
Computing Science
University of Aberdeen
Aberdeen AB24 3UE, UK
a.gatt@abdn.ac.uk

Abstract

The GREC-MSR Task at Generation Challenges 2009 required participating systems to select coreference chains to the main subject of short encyclopaedic texts collected from Wikipedia. Three teams submitted one system each, and we additionally created four baseline systems. Systems were tested automatically using existing intrinsic metrics. We also evaluated systems extrinsically by applying coreference resolution tools to the outputs and measuring the success of the tools. In addition, systems were tested in an intrinsic evaluation involving human judges. This report describes the GREC-MSR Task and the evaluation methods applied, gives brief descriptions of the participating systems, and presents the evaluation results.

1 Introduction

The GREC-MSR Task is about how to generate appropriate references to an entity in the context of a piece of discourse longer than a sentence. Rather than requiring participants to generate referring expressions from scratch, the GREC-MSR data provides sets of possible referring expressions for selection. This was the second time we ran a shared task using the GREC-MSR data (following a first run in 2008). The task definition was again kept fairly simple, but in the 2009 round the main aim for participating systems was to select an appropriate word string to serve as a referring expression, whereas in 2008 it was to select an appropriate *type* of referring expression (name, common noun, pronoun, or empty reference).

The immediate motivating application context for the GREC-MSR Task is the improvement of referential clarity and coherence in extractive summaries by regenerating referring expressions in them. There has recently been a small flurry of work in this area (Steinberger et al., 2007; Nenkova, 2008). In the longer term, the GREC-MSR Task is intended to be a step in the direction of the more general task of generating referential expressions in discourse context.

The GREC-MSR data is an extension of the GREC 1.0 Corpus which had about 1,000 texts in the subdomains of cities, countries, rivers and people (Belz and Varges, 2007a). For the purpose of the GREC-MSR shared task, an additional 1,000 texts in the new subdomain of mountain texts were obtained and a new XML annotation scheme (Section 2.2) was developed.

Team	System Name
University of Delaware	UDel
ICSI, Berkeley	ICSI-CRF
Jadavpur University	JUNLG

Table 1: GREC-MSR'09 participating teams.

Nine teams from seven countries registered for GREC-MSR'09, of which three teams (Table 1) submitted one system each.[1] Participants had to submit their system reports before downloading test data inputs, and had to submit test data outputs within 48 hours of downloading the test data inputs. In addition to the participants' systems, we also used the corpus texts themselves as 'system' outputs, and created 4 baseline systems; we evaluated the resulting 8 systems using a range of intrinsic and extrinsic evaluation methods (for details see Sections 5 and 6). This report presents the results of all evaluations (Section 6), along with descriptions of GREC-MSR data and task (Section 2), test sets (Section 3), evaluation methods (Section 4), and participating systems (Section 5).

2 Data and Task

The GREC Corpus (version 2.0) consists of about 2,000 texts in total, all collected from introduc-

[1] One team submitted by the original deadline (Jan. 2009), one by the revised deadline (1 June 2009), one slightly later.

Proceedings of the 2009 Workshop on Language Generation and Summarisation, ACL-IJCNLP 2009, pages 79–87, Suntec, Singapore, 6 August 2009. ©2009 ACL and AFNLP

tory sections in Wikipedia articles, in five different subdomains (cities, countries, rivers, people and mountains). In each text, three broad categories of Main Subject Reference (MSR)[2] have been annotated, resulting in a total of about 13,000 annotated REs. The GREC-MSR shared task version of the corpus was randomly divided into 90% training data (of which 10% were randomly selected as development data) and 10% test data. Participants used the training data in developing their systems, and (as a minimum requirement) reported results on the development data.

2.1 Types of referential expression annotated

Three broad categories of main subject referring expressions (MSREs) are annotated in the GREC corpus[3] — subject NPs, object NPs, and genitive NPs and pronouns which function as subject-determiners within their matrix NP. These categories of referring expressions (RE) are relatively straightforward to identify and to achieve high inter-annotator agreement on (complete agreement among four annotators in 86% of MSRs), and account for most cases of overt main subject reference in the GREC texts. The annotators were asked to identify subject, object and genitive subject-determiners and decide whether or not they refer to the main subject of the text. More detail is provided in Belz and Varges (2007b).

In addition to the above, relative pronouns in supplementary relative clauses (as opposed to integrated relative clauses, Huddleston and Pullum, 2002, p. 1058) were annotated, e.g.:

(1) *Stoichkov is a football manager and former striker <u>who</u> was a member of the Bulgaria national team that finished fourth at the 1994 FIFA World Cup.*

We also annotated 'non-realised' subject MSREs in those cases of VP coordination where an MSRE is the subject of the coordinated VPs, e.g.:

(2) *He stated the first version of the Law of conservation of mass, __ introduced the Metric system, and __ helped to reform chemical nomenclature.*

The motivation for annotating the approximate place where the subject NP would be if it were realised (the gap-like underscores above) is that from a generation perspective there is a choice to be made about whether to realise the subject NP in the second and third coordinates or not.

[2]The main subject of a Wikipedia article is simply taken to be given by its title, e.g. in the cities domain the main subject (and title) of one text is *London*.

[3]In terminology and view of grammar the annotations rely heavily on Huddleston and Pullum (2002).

2.2 XML format

Figure 1 is one of the texts distributed in the GREC-MSR training/development data set. The REF element indicates a reference, in the sense of 'an instance of referring' (which could, in principle, be realised by gesture or graphically, as well as by a string of words, or a combination of these). REFs have three attributes: `ID`, a unique reference identifier; `SEMCAT`, the semantic category of the referent, ranging over `city`, `country`, `river`, `person`, `mountain`; and `SYNCAT`, the syntactic category required of referential expressions for the referent in this discourse context (`np-obj`, `np-subj`, `subj-det`). A `REF` is composed of one `REFEX` element (the 'selected' referential expression for the given reference; in the training/development data texts it is simply the referential expression found in the corpus) and one `ALT-REFEX` element which in turn is a list of `REFEX`s which are possible alternative referential expressions (see following section).

`REFEX` elements have four attributes. The `HEAD` attribute has the possible values `nominal`, `pronoun`, and `rel-pron`; the `CASE` attribute has the possible values `nominative`, `accusative` and `genitive` for pronouns, and `plain` and `genitive` for nominals. The binary-valued `EMPHATIC` attribute indicates whether the RE is emphatic; in the GREC-MSR corpus, the only type of RE that has `EMPHATIC=yes` is one which incorporates a reflexive pronoun used emphatically (e.g. *India itself*). The `REG08-TYPE` attribute indicates basic RE type. The choice of types is motivated by the hypothesis that one of the most basic decisions to be taken in RE selection for named entities is whether to use an RE that includes a name, such as *Modern India* (the corresponding `REG08-TYPE` value is `name`); whether to go for a common-noun RE, i.e. with a category noun like *country* as the head (`common`); whether to use a pronoun (`pronoun`); or whether it can be left unrealised (`empty`).

2.3 The GREC-MSR Task

The task for participating systems was to develop a method for selecting one of the `REFEX`s in the `ALT-REFEX` list, for each `REF` in each `TEXT` in the test sets. The test data inputs were identical to the training/development data, except that `REF` elements contained only an `ALT-REFEX` list, not the preceding 'selected' `REFEX`. `ALT-REFEX` lists are generated for each text by an automatic method

```
<?xml version="1.0" encoding="utf-8"?>
<!DOCTYPE TEXT SYSTEM "reg08-grec.dtd">
<TEXT ID="36">
<TITLE>Jean Baudrillard</TITLE>
<PARAGRAPH>
 <REF ID="36.1" SEMCAT="person" SYNCAT="np-subj">
  <REFEX REG08-TYPE="name" EMPHATIC="no" HEAD="nominal" CASE="plain">Jean Baudrillard</REFEX>
  <ALT-REFEX>
   <REFEX REG08-TYPE="name" EMPHATIC="no" HEAD="nominal" CASE="plain">Jean Baudrillard</REFEX>
   <REFEX REG08-TYPE="name" EMPHATIC="yes" HEAD="nominal" CASE="plain">Jean Baudrillard himself</REFEX>
   <REFEX REG08-TYPE="empty">_</REFEX>
   <REFEX REG08-TYPE="pronoun" EMPHATIC="no" HEAD="pronoun" CASE="nominative">he</REFEX>
   <REFEX REG08-TYPE="pronoun" EMPHATIC="yes" HEAD="pronoun" CASE="nominative">he himself</REFEX>
   <REFEX REG08-TYPE="pronoun" EMPHATIC="no" HEAD="rel-pron" CASE="nominative">who</REFEX>
   <REFEX REG08-TYPE="pronoun" EMPHATIC="yes" HEAD="rel-pron" CASE="nominative">who himself</REFEX>
  </ALT-REFEX>
 </REF>
 (born June 20, 1929) is a cultural theorist, philosopher, political commentator,
 sociologist, and photographer.
 <REF ID="36.2" SEMCAT="person" SYNCAT="subj-det">
  <REFEX REG08-TYPE="pronoun" EMPHATIC="no" HEAD="pronoun" CASE="genitive">His</REFEX>
  <ALT-REFEX>
   <REFEX REG08-TYPE="name" EMPHATIC="no" HEAD="nominal" CASE="genitive">Jean Baudrillard's</REFEX>
   <REFEX REG08-TYPE="pronoun" EMPHATIC="no" HEAD="pronoun" CASE="genitive">his</REFEX>
   <REFEX REG08-TYPE="pronoun" EMPHATIC="no" HEAD="rel-pron" CASE="genitive">whose</REFEX>
  </ALT-REFEX>
 </REF>
 work is frequently associated with postmodernism and post-structuralism.
</PARAGRAPH>
</TEXT>
```

Figure 1: Example text from the GREC-MSR Training Data.

which collects all the (manually annotated) MSREs in a text including the title, and adds several defaults: pronouns and reflexive pronouns in all subdomains; and category nouns (e.g. *the river*), in all subdomains except people. The main objective in the 2009 GREC-MSR Task was to get the word strings contained in REFEXs right (whereas in REG'08 it was the REG08-TYPE attributes).

3 Test Data

1. Test Set C-1: a randomly selected 10% subset (183 texts) of the GREC corpus (with the same proportions of texts in the 5 subdomains as in the training/testing data).

2. Test Set C-2: the same subset of texts as in C-1; however, for C-2 we did not use the MSREs in the corpus, but replaced them with human-selected alternatives. These were obtained in an online experiment as described in Belz & Varges (2007a) where subjects selected MSREs in a setting that duplicated the conditions in which the participating systems in the GREC-MSR Task make selections.[4] We obtained three versions of each text, where in each version all MSREs were selected by the same person. The motivation for this version of Test Set C was that having several human-produced chains of MSREs to compare the outputs of participating ('peer') systems against is more reliable than having one only; and that Wikipedia texts are edited by multiple authors which sometimes adversely affects MSR chains; we wanted to have additional reference texts where all references are selected by a single author.

3. Test Set L: 74 Wikipedia introductory texts from the subdomain of lakes (there were no lake texts in the training/development set).

4. Test Set P: 31 short encyclopaedic texts in the same 5 subdomains as in the GREC corpus, in approximately the same proportions as in the training/testing data, but of different origin. We transcribed these texts from printed encyclopaedias published in the 1980s which are not available in electronic form. The texts in this set are much shorter and more homogeneous than the Wikipedia texts, and the sequences of MSRs follow very similar patterns. It seems likely that it is these properties that have resulted in better scores overall for Test Set P than for the other test sets in both the 2008 and 2009 runs of the GREC-MSR task (for the latter, see Section 6).

Each test set was designed to test peer systems for generalisation to different kinds of unseen data. Test Set C tests for generalisation to unseen material from the same corpus and the same subdomains as the training set; Test Set L tests for generalisation to unseen material from the same corpus but different subdomain; and Test Set P for generalisation to a different corpus but the same subdomains.

[4]The experiment can be tried out here: http://www.nltg.brighton.ac.uk/home/Anja.Belz/TESTDRIVE/

4 Evaluation methods

4.1 Automatic intrinsic evaluations[5]

Accuracy of REFEX word strings: when computed against test sets (C-1, L and P), Word String Accuracy is simply the proportion of REFEX word strings selected by a participating system that are identical to the one in the corpus. When computed against test set C-2, which has three versions of each text, Word String Accuracy is computed as follows: first the number of correct REFEX word strings is computed at the text level for each of the three versions of a text and the maximum of these is determined; then the maximum text-level numbers are summed and divided by the total number of REFs in all the texts, which gives the global Word String Accuracy score. The rationale behind computing the Word String Accuracy scores in this way for multiple-RE test sets (maximising scores on RE chains rather than individual REs) is that an RE is not good or bad in its own right, but depends on other MSREs in the same text.

Accuracy of REG08-Type: similarly to Word String Accuracy above, when computed against test sets C-1, L and P, REG08-Type Accuracy is the proportion of REFEXs selected by a participating system that have a REG08-TYPE value identical to the one in the corpus. When computed against test set C-2, first the number of correct REG08-Types is computed at the text level for each of the three versions of a corpus text and the maximum of these is determined; then the maximum text-level numbers are summed and divided by the total number of REFs in all the texts, which gives the global REG08-Type Accuracy score.

String-edit distance metrics: String-edit distance (SE) is straightforward Levenshtein distance with a substitution cost of 2 and insertion/deletion cost of 1. We also used a length-normalised version of string-edit distance (denoted 'norm. SE' in results tables below). For test sets C-1, L and P, the global score is simply the mean of all RE-level scores. For Test Set C-2, the global score is the mean of the mean of the three text-level scores.

Other metrics: BLEU is a precision metric from machine translation that assesses peer translations in terms of the proportion of word n-grams ($n \leq 4$ is standard) they share with several reference translations. We used BLEU-3 rather than the more standard BLEU-4 because most REs in the corpus are less than 4 tokens long. We also used the NIST version of BLEU which weights in favour of less frequent n-grams. In both cases, we assessed just the MSREs selected by peer systems (leaving out the surrounding text), and computed scores globally (rather than averaging over RE-level scores), as this is standard for these metrics. BLEU, and NIST are designed to work with one or multiple reference texts, so we did not need to use a different method for Test Set C-2.

4.2 Automatic extrinsic evaluation

As in GREC-MSR'08, we used an automatic extrinsic evaluation method based on coreference resolution performance.[6] The basic idea is that it seems likely that badly chosen reference chains affect the ability to resolve REs in automatic coreference resolution tools which will tend to perform worse with poorly selected MSR reference chains.

To counteract the possibility of results being a function of a specific coreference resolution algorithm or tool, we used two different resolvers—those included in LingPipe[7] and OpenNLP (Morton, 2005)—and averaged results.

There does not appear to be a single standard evaluation metric in the coreference resolution community, so we opted to use three: MUC-6 (Vilain et al., 1995), CEAF (Luo, 2005), and B-CUBED (Bagga and Baldwin, 1998), which seem to be the most widely accepted metrics. All three metrics compute Recall, Precision and F-Scores on aligned gold-standard and resolver-tool coreference chains. They differ in how the alignment is obtained and what components of coreference chains are counted for calculating scores. Results for the automatic extrinsic evaluations are reported below in terms of the F-Scores from these three metrics, as well as in terms of their mean.

4.3 Human intrinsic evaluation

The intrinsic human evaluation involved 24 randomly selected items from Test Set C and outputs for these produced by peer and basline systems as

[5]For GREC-MSR'09 we updated the tool that computes all automatic intrinsic scores and in the course of this eliminated a character encoding issue; as a result the results for baseline systems and corpus texts reported here are on the whole very slightly higher than those reported for GREC-MSR'08.

[6]However, for GREC'09 we overhauled the tool; the current version no longer uses JavaRAP, and uses the most recent versions of the other resolvers; the GREC-MSR'08 and GREC-MSR'09 results for this method are not entirely comparable for this reason.

[7]http://alias-i.com/lingpipe/

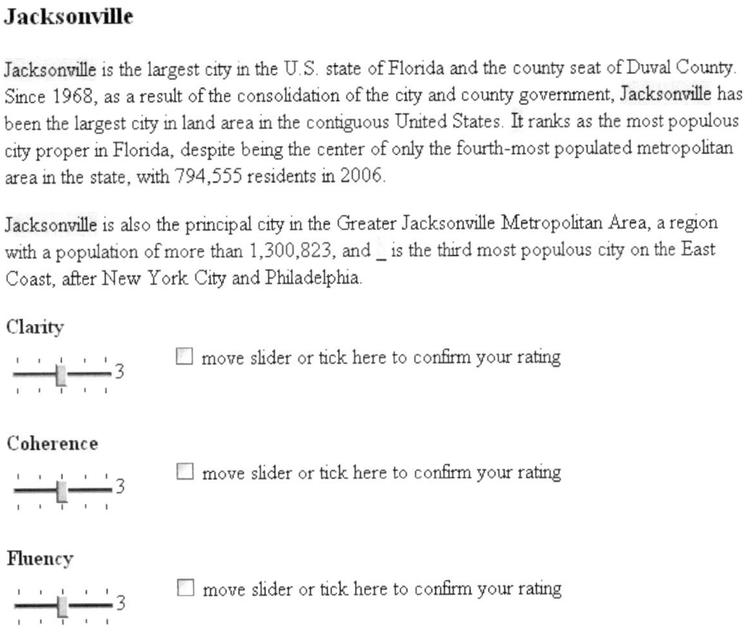

Figure 2: Example of text presented in human intrinsic evaluation of GREC-MSR systems.

well as those found in the original corpus texts (8 systems in total). We used a Repeated Latin Squares design which ensures that each subject sees the same number of outputs from each system and for each test set item. There were three 8x8 squares, and a total of 576 individual judgments in this evaluation (72 per system: 3 criteria x 3 articles x 8 evaluators).

We recruited 8 native speakers of English from among post-graduate students currently doing a linguistics-related degree at University College London (UCL) and University of Sussex.

Following detailed instructions, subjects did two practice examples, followed by the 24 texts to be evaluated, in random order. Subjects carried out the evaluation over the internet, at a time and place of their choosing. They were allowed to interrupt and resume the experiment (though discorouged from doing so). According to self-reported timings, subjects took between 25 and 45 minutes to complete the evaluation (not counting breaks).

Figure 2 shows what subjects saw during the evaluation of an individual text. All references to the MS are highlighted in yellow, and the task is to evaluate the quality of the REs in terms of three criteria which were explained in the introduction as follows (the wording of the explanations of Criteria 1 and 3 were taken from the DUC evaluations):

1. **Referential Clarity**: It should be easy to identify who or what the referring expressions in the text are referring to. If a person or other entity is mentioned, it should be clear what their role in the story is. So, a reference would be unclear if an entity is referenced, but their identity or relation to the story remains unclear.
2. **Fluency**: A referring expression should 'read well', i.e. it should be written in good, clear English, and the use of titles and names etc. should seem natural. Note that the Fluency criterion is independent of the Referential Clarity criterion: a reference can be perfectly clear, yet not be fluent.
3. **Structure and Coherence**: The text should be well structured and well organised. The text should not just be a heap of related information, but should build from sentence to sentence to a coherent body of information about a topic. This criterion too is independent of the others.

Subjects selected evaluation scores by moving sliders (see Figure 2) along scales ranging from 1 to 5. Slider pointers started out in the middle of the scale (3). These were continuous scales and we recorded scores with one decimal place (e.g. 3.2). The meaning of the numbers was explained in terms of integer scores (1=very poor, 2=poor, 3=neither poor nor good, 4=good, 5=very good).

5 Systems

Base-rand, Base-freq, Base-1st, Base-name: Baseline system *Base-rand* selects one of the REFEXS at random. *Base-freq* selects the REFEX that is the overall most frequent given the SYNCAT and SEMCAT of the reference. *Base-1st* always selects the REFEX which appears first in the ALT-REFEX list; and *Base-name* selects the shortest REFEX with attributes REG08-TYPE=name, HEAD=nominal and EMPHATIC=no.[8]

[8] Attributes are considered in this order. If for one attribute, the right value is not found, the process ignores that attribute and moves on the next one.

UDel: The UDel system consists of a preprocessing component performing sentence segmentation and identification of non-referring occurrences of main subject (MS) names, an RE type selection component (two C5.0 decision trees, one optimised for people and mountains, the other for the other subdomains), and a word string selection component. The RE type selection decision trees use the following features: is the MS the subject of the current, preceding and preceding but one sentence; was the last MSR in subject position; are there interfering references to other entities between the current and the previous MSR; distance to preceding non-referring occurrences of an MS name; sentence and reference IDs; other features indicating whether the reference occurred before and after certain words and punctuation marks. Given a selected RE type, the word-string selection component selects the longest non-emphatic name for the first named reference in an article, and the shortest for subsequent named references; for other types, the first matching word-string is used, backing off to pronoun or name.

ICSI-CRF: The ICSI-CRF system construes the GREC-MSR task as a sequence labelling task and determines the most likely current label given preceding labels using a Conditional Random Field model trained using the follow features for the current, preceding and preceding but one MSR: preceding and following word unigram and bigram; suffix of preceding and following word; preceding and following punctuation; reference ID; is this is the beginning of a paragraph. If more than one label remains, the last in the list of possible REs in the GREC-MSR data is selected.

JUNLG: The JUNLG system is based on co-occurrence statistics between REF feature sets and REFEX feature sets as found in the GREC-MSR data. REF feature sets were augmented by a paragraph counter and a within-paragraph REF counter. For each given set of REF features, the system selects the most frequent REFEX feature set (as determined from co-occurrence counts in the training data). If the current set of possible REFEXs does not include a REFEX with the selected feature set, then the second most likely feature set is selected. Several hand-coded default rules override the frequency-based selections, e.g. if the preceding word is a conjunction, and the current SYNCAT is np-subj, then the REG08-Type is empty.

6 Results

This section presents the results of all evaluation methods described in Section 4. We start with Word String Accuracy, the intrinsic automatic metric which participating teams were told was going to be the chief evaluation method, followed by REG08-Type Accuracy and other intrinsic automatic metrics (Section 6.2), the intrinsic human evaluation (Section 6.3) and the extrinsic automatic evaluation (Section 6.4).

System	Word String Acc.	REG08-Type Acc.	Norm. Edit Dist.
ICSI-CRF	0.67	0.75	0.28
UDel	0.6357	0.7027	0.3383
JUNLG	0.532	0.62	0.421

Table 2: Self-reported evaluation scores for development set.

6.1 Word String Accuracy

Participants computed Word String Accuracy for the development set (97 texts) themselves, using an evaluation tool provided by us. These scores are shown in column 2 of Table 2, and are also included in the participants' reports in this volume. Corresponding results for test set C-1 are shown in column 2 of Table 3. Surprisingly, Word String Accuracy results on the test data are better (than on the development data) for the UDel and JUNLG systems. Also included in this table are results for the four baseline systems, and it is clear that selecting the most frequent word string given SEMCAT and SYNCAT (as done by the Base-freq system) provides a strong baseline.

The other two parts of Table 3 contain results for test sets L and P. As expected, results for Test Set L are lower than for Test Set C-1, because in addition to consisting of unseen texts (like C-1), Test Set L is also from an unseen subdomain (unlike C-1). The Word String Accuracy results for Test Set P are higher than for any other set, probably for the reasons discussed at the end of Section 3.

For each test set in Table 3 we carried out a univariate ANOVA with System as the fixed factor, 'Number of REFEXs in a text' as a random factor, and Word String Accuracy as the dependent variable. We found significant main effects of System on Word String Accuracy at $p < .001$ in the case of all three test sets (C-1: $F_{(7,1272)} = 90.058$; L: $F_{(7,440)} = 44.139$; P: $F_{(7,168)} = 21.991$).[9] The columns containing capital letters in Table 3

[9]We included the corpus texts themselves in the analysis, hence 7 degrees of freedom (8 systems).

Test Set C-1						Test Set L				Test Set P				
UDel	67.68	A				UDel	52.89	A		UDel	77.16	A		
ICSI-CRF	62.98	A				JUNLG	50.80	A		ICSI-CRF	72.22	A		
JUNLG	61.94	A				ICSI-CRF	49.20	A		JUNLG	71.60	A		
Base-freq	47.05		B			Base-name	21.06		B	Base-freq	53.09		B	
Base-name	28.74			C		Base-freq	20.74		B	Base-name	27.78			C
Base-1st	28.26			C		Base-1st	20.74		B	Base-1st	27.16			C
Base-rand	18.95				D	Base-rand	15.11		B	Base-rand	18.52			C

Table 3: Word String Accuracy scores against Test Sets C-1, L and P; homogeneous subsets (Tukey HSD, alpha = .05) for each test set (systems that do not share a letter are significantly different).

System	Word String Accuracy for multiple-RE Test Set C-2											
	All							Cities	Countries	Rivers	People	Mountains
Corpus	*71.58*	A						*65.25*	*69.11*	*76.47*	*80.40*	*66.87*
UDel	70.22	A	B					68.09	71.20	76.47	76.63	64.84
JUNLG	64.57		B	C				54.61	51.83	73.53	71.86	65.85
ICSI-CRF	63.69			C				58.87	56.54	64.71	72.11	60.98
Base-freq	57.01				D			51.06	57.07	58.82	63.82	53.05
Base-name	40.21					E		51.06	46.07	29.41	29.90	43.90
Base-1st	39.65					E		47.52	41.88	38.24	25.63	47.97
Base-rand	26.99						F	28.37	29.32	23.53	21.61	30.28

Table 4: Word String Accuracy scores against Test Set C-2 for complete set and for subdomains; homogeneous subsets (Tukey HSD, alpha = .05) for complete set only (systems that do not share a letter are significantly different).

show the homogeneous subsets of systems as determined by post-hoc Tukey HSD comparisons of means. Systems whose Word String Accuracy scores are not significantly different (at the .05 level) share a letter.

The results for Word String Accuracy computed against Test Set C-2 are shown in Table 4. These should be considered the chief results of the GREC-MSR'09 Task evaluations, as stated in the participants' guidelines. Here too we performed a univariate ANOVA with System as the fixed factor, Number of REFEXS as the random factor and Word String Accuracy as the dependent variable. There was a significant main effect of System ($F_{(7,1272)} = 74.892$, $p < .001$). We compared the mean scores with Tukey's HSD. As can be seen from the resulting homogeneous subsets, there is no significant difference between the corpus texts (C-1) and the UDel system, but also there is no significant difference between the latter and the JUNLG system. In this analysis, all peer systems outperform all baselines; the Base-freq baseline outperforms all other baselines; and Base-name and Base-1st outperform the random baseline.

Overall, there is a marked improvement in Word String Accuracy compared to GREC-MSR'08 where peer systems' scores ranged from 50.72 to 65.61.

6.2 Other automatic intrinsic metrics

In addition to the chief evaluation measure reported on in the preceding section, we computed REG08-Type Accuracy and the string similarity metrics described in Section 4.1. The resulting scores for Test Set C-2 are shown in Table 5 (recall that in Test Set C-2 corpus texts are evaluated against 3 texts with human-selected alternative REs). The corpus texts again receive the best scores across the board. Ranks for peer systems are very similar to those reported in the last section.

We performed a univariate ANOVA with System as the fixed factor, Number of REFEXS as the random factor, and REG08-Type Accuracy as the dependent variable. The main effect of System was $F_{(7,1272)} = 75.040$, $p < .001$; the homogeneous subsets resulting from the Tukey HSD post-hoc analysis are shown in columns 3–5 of Table 5. The differences between the scores of the peer systems and the corpus texts were not found to be significant.

6.3 Human-assessed intrinsic measures

Table 6 shows the results of the human intrinsic evaluation. In each of the three parts of the table (showing the results for Fluency, Clarity and Coherence, respectively) systems are ordered in terms of their mean scores (shown in the second column of each part of the table). We first established that the main effect of Evaluator was weak (F between 2.1 and 2.6) on Fluency, Clarity and Coherence, and only of borderline significance (just below .05); and that the interaction between System and Evaluator was very weak and

System	Other similarity measures for Triple-RE Test Set C-2								
	REG08-Type				BLEU-3	NIST	SE	norm. SE
Corpus	*79.30*	*A*			*0.77*	*5.60*	*1.04*	*0.34*
UDel	77.71	A			0.74	5.32	1.11	0.37
JUNLG	75.40	A			0.53	4.69	1.34	0.40
ICSI-CRF	75.16	A			0.54	4.68	1.32	0.41
Base-freq	62.50		B		0.54	4.30	1.93	0.50
Base-name	51.04			C	0.46	4.76	1.80	0.63
Base-1st	50.32			C	0.39	4.42	1.93	0.63
Base-rand	48.09			C	0.26	3.02	2.30	0.72

Table 5: REG08-Type Accuracy, BLEU, NIST and string-edit scores, computed on test set C-2 (systems in order of REG08-Type Accuracy); homogeneous subsets (Tukey HSD, alpha = .05) for REG08-Type Accuracy only (systems that do not share a letter are significantly different).

Fluency						Clarity				Coherence			
Corpus	4.43	A				Base-name	4.62	A		*Corpus*	4.40	A	
UDel	4.27	A				*Corpus*	4.56	A		JUNLG	4.33	A	
JUNLG	4.26	A				JUNLG	4.50	A		UDel	4.27	A	B
ICSI-CRF	4.15	A	B			ICSI-CRF	4.45	A		ICSI-CRF	4.02	A	B
Base-freq	3.33		B	C		UDel	4.35	A		Base-freq	3.96	A	B
Base-name	2.84			C	D	Base-1st	4.27	A		Base-name	3.85	A	B
Base-1st	2.76			C	D	Base-freq	4.10	A		Base-1st	3.7	A	B
Base-rand	2.15				D	Base-rand	3.18		B	Base-rand	3.46		B

Table 6: Clarity, Fluency and Coherence scores (with homogeneous subsets) for all systems.

not significant in the case of Clarity and Coherence, and borderline significant in the case of Fluency. We then ran a (non-factorial) multivariate ANOVA, with Fluency, Coherence and Clarity as the dependent variables, and (just) System as the fixed factor. The main effect of System was as follows: Fluency: $F_{(7,128)} = 20.444, p < 0.001$; Clarity: $F_{(7,128)} = 5.248, p < 0.001$; Coherence: $F_{(7,128)} = 2.680, p < 0.012$. The homogeneous subsets resulting from a post-hoc Tukey analysis are shown in the letter columns in Table 6.

The effect of System was strongest on Fluency; here, the system ranks are also the same as for Word String Accuracy and REG08-Type Accuracy for Test Set C-2. This, together with the fair amount of significant differences found, indicates that the evaluators were able to make sense of the Fluency criterion and that there were interesting differences between systems under this criterion. However, differences between the three peer systems were not significant.

For Clarity, there were no significant differences among the peer systems and non-random baseline systems; all of these were significantly better than the random baseline. Base-name had the highest mean Clarity score, possibly because always chosing the name of an entity when referring to it ensures high referential clarity.

The Coherence results are perhaps the most difficult to interpret. Both the main effect of System on Coherence and its significance were weaker than for Fluency and Clarity. Only two significant pairwise differences were found: Corpus and JUNLG were better than the random baseline. The system ranks are roughly the same as for Fluency, but the mean scores cover a smaller range (from 3.46 to 4.4) than in the case of either of the other two criteria. Overall, the Coherence results probably indicate that the evaluators found it somewhat difficult to make sense of the Coherence criterion.

Computing Pearson's r for the three criteria on individual (text-level) scores showed that there were only moderate correlations between them (all around $r = 0.5$) which were all significant at $\alpha = 0.05$. This gives some indication that the evaluators were able to assess the three criteria independently from each other.

6.4 Automatic extrinsic measures

We fed the outputs of all eight systems through the two coreference resolvers, and computed mean MUC, CEAF and B-CUBED F-Scores as described in Section 4.2. The second column in Table 7 shows the mean of these three F-Scores, to give a single overall result for this evaluation method. A univariate ANOVA with mean F-Score as the dependent variable and System as the fixed factor revealed a significant main effect of System on mean F-Score ($F_{(7,1456)} = 73.061, p < .001$). A post-hoc comparison of the means (Tukey HSD, alpha = .05) found the significant differences indicated by the homogeneous subsets in columns 3–4 (Table 7). The numbers shown in the last three columns are the separate MUC, CEAF and B-CUBED F-Scores for each system, averaged over the two resolver tools. ANOVAs revealed the following effects of System on the separate scoring methods: on CEAF $F_{(7,1456)} = 43.471, p < .001$; on MUC: $F_{(7,1456)} =, p < .001$; on B-CUBED: $F_{(7,1456)} = 38.574, p < .001$. All three scoring methods separately and their mean yielded the same significant differences (as shown in columns 3–4 of Table 7).

The three F-Score measures (MUC, CEAF and B-CUBED) are all significantly correlated ($p < .001$, 2-tailed). However it is not a strong correlation, with Pearson's correlation coefficient around 0.5.

System	(MUC+CEAF+B3)/3			MUC	CEAF	B3
Base-name	65.19	A		62.35	63.14	70.06
Base-1st	63.77	A		59.95	62.08	69.28
Base-freq	63.14	A		59.08	62.04	68.3
UDel	46.19		B	34.85	46.86	56.86
ICSI-CRF	44.47		B	31.61	45.58	56.21
JUNLG	44.19		B	31.27	45.21	56.10
Base-rand	42.99		B	30.24	43.04	55.7
Corpus	*42.52*		*B*	*29.53*	*43.57*	*54.47*

Table 7: MUC, CEAF and B-CUBED F-Scores for all systems; homogeneous subsets (Tukey HSD), alpha = .05, for mean of F-Scores.

6.5 Correlations

When assessed on the system-level scores and using Pearson's r, all evaluation methods above were strongly and significantly correlated with each other (at the 0.01 level, 2-tailed), with the following exceptions. Clarity was not significantly correlated with *any* of the other methods except NIST ($r = .902, p < .01$); apart from this, NIST was only correlated with Word String Accuracy on test set C-2, with non-normalised string-edit distance, Fluency and Coherence, moreover all at the weaker 0.05 level. Finally, the extrinsic method was not correlated with any of the intrinsic methods (and in fact showed signs of being negatively correlated with all of them except Clarity).

7 Concluding Remarks

The GREC-MSR Task is still a relatively new task not only for an NLG shared-task challenge, but also as a research task in general (post-processing extractive summaries in order to improve their quality seems to be just taking off as a research subfield). There was substantial interest in the GREC-MSR Task this year (as indicated by the nine teams that originally registered). However, only three teams were ultimately able to participate.

We continued the traditions of previous NLG shared tasks in that we used a wide range of evaluation metrics to obtain a well-rounded view of the quality of the participating systems. This included intrinsic human evaluations for the first time. However, we decided against an extrinsic human evaluation this year, given time constraints as well as the fact that this evaluation type yielded barely any significant results last year.

Overall, there was an improvement in system performance compared to last year, to the point where the performance of the top system was barely distinguishable from the human topline. We are not currently planning to run the GREC-MSR task again next year.

Acknowledgments

Many thanks to the UCL and Sussex students who participated in the intrinsic evaluation experiment.

References

A. Bagga and B. Baldwin. 1998. Algorithms for scoring coreference chains. In *Proceedings of the Linguistic Coreference Workshop at LREC'98*, pages 563–566.

A. Belz and S. Varges. 2007a. Generation of repeated references to discourse entities. In *Proceedings of ENLG'07*, pages 9–16.

A. Belz and S. Varges. 2007b. The GREC corpus: Main subject reference in context. Technical Report NLTG-07-01, University of Brighton.

R. Huddleston and G. Pullum. 2002. *The Cambridge Grammar of the English Language*. Cambridge University Press.

X. Luo. 2005. On coreference resolution performance metrics. *Proc. of HLT-EMNLP*, pages 25–32.

T. Morton. 2005. *Using Semantic Relations to Improve Information Retrieval*. Ph.D. thesis, University of Pensylvania.

A. Nenkova. 2008. Entity-driven rewrite for multi-document summarization. In *Proceedings of IJCNLP'08*.

L. Qiu, M. Kan, and T.-S. Chua. 2004. A public reference implementation of the rap anaphora resolution algorithm. In *Proceedings of LREC'04*, pages 291–294.

J. Steinberger, M. Poesio, M. Kabadjov, and K. Jezek. 2007. Two uses of anaphora resolution in summarization. *Information Processing and Management: Special issue on Summarization*, 43(6):1663–1680.

M. Vilain, J. Burger, J. Aberdeen, D. Connolly, and L. Hirschman. 1995. A model-theoretic coreference scoring scheme. *Proceedings of MUC-6*, pages 45–52.

The GREC Named Entity Generation Challenge 2009: Overview and Evaluation Results

Anja Belz **Eric Kow**
NLT Group
University of Brighton
Brighton BN2 4GJ, UK
{asb,eykk10}@bton.ac.uk

Jette Viethen
Centre for LT
Macquarie University
Sydney NSW 2109
jviethen@ics.mq.edu.au

Abstract

The GREC-NEG Task at Generation Challenges 2009 required participating systems to select coreference chains for all people entities mentioned in short encyclopaedic texts about people collected from Wikipedia. Three teams submitted six systems in total, and we additionally created four baseline systems. Systems were tested automatically using a range of existing intrinsic metrics. We also evaluated systems extrinsically by applying coreference resolution tools to the outputs and measuring the success of the tools. In addition, systems were tested in an intrinsic evaluation involving human judges. This report describes the GREC-NEG Task and the evaluation methods applied, gives brief descriptions of the participating systems, and presents the evaluation results.

1 Introduction

The GREC-NEG task is about how to generate appropriate references to people entities in the context of a piece of discourse longer than a sentence. Rather than requiring participants to generate referring expressions (REs) from scratch, the GREC-NEG data provides sets of possible REs for selection. This was the first time we ran a shared task using this data. GREC-NEG is a step further from the related GREC-MSR Task in that it requires systems to generate plural as well as singular references, for all people entities mentioned in a text (GREC-MSR in contrast only had singular references to a single entity). Moreover in GREC-NEG, possible REs for each entity are provided as one set for each entity (rather than one set for each context), so the task of selecting an appropriate RE for a given context is harder than in GREC-MSR. The main aim for participating systems in GREC-NEG'09 was to select an appropriate *type* of RE (name, common noun, pronoun, or empty reference).

The immediate *motivating application context* for the GREC Tasks is the improvement of referential clarity and coherence in extractive summaries and multiply edited texts (such as Wikipedia articles) by regenerating REs contained in them.

The *motivating theoretical interest* for the GREC Tasks is to discover what kind of information is useful in the input when making decisions about different properties of referring expressions when such expressions are being generated in context (this is in contrast to most traditional referring expression generation work in NLG which views the REG task as context-independent).

The GREC-NEG data is derived from the newly created GREC-People corpus which consists of 1,000 annotated introduction sections from Wikipedia articles in the category People.

Nine teams from seven countries registered for the GREC-NEG'09 Task, of which three teams ultimately submitted six systems in total (see Table 1). We also used the corpus texts themselves as 'system' outputs, and created four baseline systems. We evaluated the resulting 11 systems using a range of intrinsic and extrinsic evaluation methods. This report presents the results of all evaluations (Section 6), along with descriptions of the GREC-NEG data (Sections 2) and task (Section 3), the test sets and evaluation methods (Section 4), and the participating systems (Section 5).

Team	System name(s)
Univ. Delaware	UDel-NEG-1, UDel-NEG-2, UDel-NEG-3
ICSI, Berkeley	ICSI-CRF
Univ. Wolverhampton	WLV-STAND, WLV-BIAS

Table 1: GREC-NEG'09 teams and systems.

2 GREC-NEG Data

The GREC-NEG data is derived from the newly created GREC-People corpus which consists

Proceedings of the 2009 Workshop on Language Generation and Summarisation, ACL-IJCNLP 2009, pages 88–98,
Suntec, Singapore, 6 August 2009.

of 1,000 annotated introduction sections from Wikipedia articles in the category People. An introduction section was defined as the textual content of a Wikipedia article from the title up to (and excluding) the first section heading, the table of contents or the end of the text, whichever comes sooner. Each text belongs to one of three subcategories: inventors, chefs and early music composers. For the purposes of the GREC-NEG'09 competition, the GREC-People corpus was divided into training, development and test data. The number of texts in the 3 data sets and 3 subdomains are as follows:

	All	Inventors	Chefs	Composers
Total	1,000	307	306	387
Training	809	249	248	312
Development	91	28	28	35
Test	100	31	30	39

In these texts we have annotated mentions of people by marking up the word strings that function as referential expressions (REs) and annotating them with coreference information as well as syntactic and semantic features. The subject of each text is a person, so there is at least one coreference chain in each text. The numbers of coreference chains (entities) in the 900 texts in the training/development sets are as shown in Table 2. The texts vary greatly in length, from 13 words to 935, with an average of 128.98 words.

2.1 Annotation of REs in GREC-People

This section describes the different types of referring expression (RE) that we annotated in the GREC-People corpus. These manual annotations were then automatically checked and converted to the XML format described in Section 2.2 (which encodes slightly less information, as explained below). In terminology and the treatment of syntax used in the annotation scheme and discussion of it in this report we rely heavily on *The Cambridge Grammar of the English Language* by Huddleston and Pullum which we will refer to as *CGEL* for short below (Huddleston and Pullum, 2002).

In the example sentences below, (unbroken) underlines are used for referential expressions (REs) that are an example of the specific type of RE they are intended to illustrate, whereas dashed underlines are used for other annotated REs. Coreference between REs is indicated by subscripts $i, j, ...$ immediately to the right of an underline (their scope is one example sentence, i.e. an i in one example sentence does not represent the same entity as an i in another example sentence). Square brackets indicate supplements. The syntactic component relativised by a relative pronoun is indicated by vertical bars. Supplements and their anchors (in the case of appositive supplements), and relative clauses and the component they relativise (in the case of relative-clause supplements) are coindexed by superscript $x, y, ...$. Dependents integrated in an RE are indicated by curly brackets. Supplements and dependents are highlighted in bold where they specifically are being discussed.

In the XML format of the annotations, the beginning and end of a reference is indicated by `<REF><REFEX>... </REFEX></REF>` tags, and other properties discussed in the following sections (e.g. syntactic category) are encoded as attributes on these tags (for details see Section 2.2). For GREC-NEG'09 we decided not to transfer the annotations of integrated dependents and relative clauses to the XML format. Such dependents are included within `<REFEX>...</REFEX>` annotations where appropriate, but without being marked up as separate constituents.

2.1.1 Syntactic Category and Function

This section describes the types of REs we annoted in the GREC-People Corpus.

I Subject NPs: referring subject NPs, including pronouns and special cases of VP coordination:

1. *He*$_i$ *was born in Ramsay township, near Almonte, Ontario, Canada, the eldest son of |Scottish immigrants, {John Naismith and Margaret Young}|*$^x_{j,k}$ *[who*$_{j,k}$ *had arrived in the area in 1851 and __*$_{j,k}$ *worked in the mining industry]*^{x}.

2. *The Banū Mūsā brothers*$_{i,j,k}$ *were three 9th century Persian scholars, of Baghdad, active in the House of Wisdom.*

Ia Subjects of gerund-participials:

1. *His*$_i$ *research on hearing and speech eventually culminated in Bell*$_i$ *being awarded the first U.S. patent for the invention of the telephone in 1876.*

2. *Fessenden*$_i$ *used the alternator-transmitter to send out a short program from Brant Rock, which included his*$_i$ *playing the song O Holy Night on the violin and __*$_i$ *reading a passage from the Bible.*

II Object NPs: referring NPs including pronouns that function as direct or indirect objects of VPs and prepositional phrases; e.g.:

1. *Many of the alpinists arrested with Vitaly Abalakov*$_i$ *were executed.*

2. *He*$_i$ *entrusted them*$_{j,k,l}$ *to Ishaq bin Ibrahim al-Mus'abi*^x_m, *[a former governor of Baghdad]*^x_m.

Entities	1	2	3	4	5	6	7	8	9	10	11	12	13	14	15	16	17	18	19	20	21	22	23
Texts	437	192	80	63	38	31	16	18	4	7	9	1	1	0	0	0	0	0	0	1	1	0	1

Table 2: Numbers of person entities (hence coreference chains) in texts in the training/development data, e.g. there are 38 texts which mention exactly 5 person entities.

IIa Reflexive pronouns:

1. *Smith$_i$ called himself$_i$ the "Komikal Konjurer".*

III Subject-determiner genitives: genitive NPs (including genitive forms of pronouns) that function as subject-determiners, i.e. syntactic components that "combine the function of determiner, marking the NP as definite, with that of complement (more specifically subject)." (*CGEL*, p. 56):

1. *They$_{i,j,k}$ shared the 1956 Nobel Prize in Physics for their$_{i,j,k}$ invention.*
2. *On the eve of his$_i$ death in 1605, the Mughal empire spanned almost 500 million acres (doubling during Akbar's$_i$ reign).*

Note that this category excludes lexicalised cases, e.g. *the so-called "Newton's method"*.

IIIa REs in composite nominals: this is the only type of RE we have annotated that is not an NP, but a nominal. This type functions as integrated attributive complement, e.g.:

1. *The Eichengrün$_i$ version was ignored by historians ...*
2. *The new act was a great success, largely despite the various things Blackton$_i$ and Smith$_j$ were doing between the Edison$_k$ films.*

Note that this category too excludes lexicalised cases, e.g. *the Nobel Prizes; the Gatling gun*.

2.1.2 Annotation of supplements

We have annotated two kinds of supplements in the GREC-People corpus, **supplementary relative clauses** (*CGEL*, p. 1058), and **appositive supplements**. The former is not transferred to the XML annotation, for more information see (Belz, 2009).

The following examples illustrate annotation of appositive supplements (which are in bold):

1. *John W. Campbell, Jr.$_i^x$ [**the editor of Astounding magazine$_i$**]^x.*
2. was *the eldest of the six children of Thomas Aspdin$_i^x$, [**a bricklayer living in the Hunslet district of Leeds$_i$**]^x*

In the XML version, anchor and supplement are simply annotated as two (or occasionally three) independent, usually adjacent REs (REFEXs); the syntactic function of the second (and third) RE is marked as appositive supplement (SYNFUNC="app-supp").

2.1.3 Further aspects of the annotation

As can be seen from some of the examples above, we annotated all **embedded references**. The maximum depth of embedding that occurs in the GREC-People corpus is 3.

We annotated all **plural REs** that refer to groups of people where the number of group members is known. For an explanation of our treatment of REs that are coordinations of NPs, see the GREC-NEG'09 documentation (Belz, 2009).

We have annotated all mentions of individual person entities even if they are not actually named anywhere in the text, and including cases of both definite and indefinite references, e.g.:

1. *The resolution's sponsor$_i$ described it as ...*
2. ... *with the help of Robert Cailliau$_j$ and a {young} student staff {at CERN}$_k$.*

2.2 XML Annotation

Figure 1 shows one of the XML-annotated texts from the GREC-NEG data. Each such text consists of two initial lines of XML declarations followed by a GREC-ITEM. A GREC-ITEM consists of a TEXT element followed by an ALT-REFEX element. A TEXT has one attribute (an ID unique within the corpus), and is composed of one TITLE followed by any number of PARAGRAPHS. A TITLE is just a string of characters. A PARAGRAPH is any combination of character strings and REF elements.

The REF element indicates a reference, in the sense of 'an instance of referring' (which could, in principle, be realised by gesture or graphically, as well as by a string of words, or a combination of these). A REF is composed of one REFEX element (the 'selected' referential expression for the given reference; in the corpus texts it is the referential expression found in the corpus).

The attributes of the REF element are ENTITY (entity identifier), MENTION (mention identifier), SEMCAT (semantic category), SYNCAT (syntactic category), and SYNFUNC (syntactic function). For full details and ranges of values see (Belz, 2009). ENTITY and MENTION together constitute a unique identifier for a reference within a text; together

```
<?xml version="1.0" encoding="utf-8"?>
<!DOCTYPE GREC-ITEM SYSTEM "genchal09-grec.dtd">
<GREC-ITEM>
<TEXT ID="15">
<TITLE>Alexander Fleming</TITLE>

<PARAGRAPH> <REF ENTITY="0" MENTION="1" SEMCAT="person" SYNCAT="np" SYNFUNC="subj">
  <REFEX ENTITY="0" REG08-TYPE="name" CASE="plain">Sir Alexander Fleming</REFEX>
</REF> (6 August 1881 - 11 March 1955) was a Scottish biologist and pharmacologist.
<REF ENTITY="0" MENTION="2" SEMCAT="person" SYNCAT="np" SYNFUNC="subj">
  <REFEX ENTITY="0" REG08-TYPE="name" CASE="plain">Fleming</REFEX>
</REF> published many articles on bacteriology, immunology, and chemotherapy.
<REF ENTITY="0" MENTION="3" SEMCAT="person" SYNCAT="np" SYNFUNC="subj-det">
  <REFEX ENTITY="0" REG08-TYPE="pronoun" CASE="genitive">his</REFEX>
</REF> best-known achievements are the discovery of the enzyme lysozyme in 1922 and the discovery
of the antibiotic substance penicillin from the fungus Penicillium notatum in 1928, for which
<REF ENTITY="0" MENTION="4" SEMCAT="person" SYNCAT="np" SYNFUNC="subj">
  <REFEX ENTITY="0" REG08-TYPE="pronoun" CASE="nominative">he</REFEX>
</REF> shared the Nobel Prize in Physiology or Medicine in 1945 with
<REF ENTITY="1" MENTION="1" SEMCAT="person" SYNCAT="np" SYNFUNC="obj">
  <REFEX ENTITY="1" REG08-TYPE="name" CASE="plain">Florey</REFEX>
</REF> and
<REF ENTITY="2" MENTION="1" SEMCAT="person" SYNCAT="np" SYNFUNC="obj">
  <REFEX ENTITY="2" REG08-TYPE="name" CASE="plain">Chain</REFEX>
</REF>.</PARAGRAPH>
</TEXT>

<ALT-REFEX>
  <REFEX ENTITY="0" REG08-TYPE="empty" CASE="no_case">_</REFEX>
  <REFEX ENTITY="0" REG08-TYPE="name" CASE="genitive">Fleming's</REFEX>
  <REFEX ENTITY="0" REG08-TYPE="name" CASE="genitive">Sir Alexander Fleming's</REFEX>
  <REFEX ENTITY="0" REG08-TYPE="name" CASE="plain">Fleming</REFEX>
  <REFEX ENTITY="0" REG08-TYPE="name" CASE="plain">Sir Alexander Fleming</REFEX>
  <REFEX ENTITY="0" REG08-TYPE="pronoun" CASE="accusative">him</REFEX>
  <REFEX ENTITY="0" REG08-TYPE="pronoun" CASE="genitive">his</REFEX>
  <REFEX ENTITY="0" REG08-TYPE="pronoun" CASE="nominative">he</REFEX>
  <REFEX ENTITY="0" REG08-TYPE="pronoun" CASE="nominative">who</REFEX>
  <REFEX ENTITY="1" REG08-TYPE="empty" CASE="no_case">_</REFEX>
  <REFEX ENTITY="1" REG08-TYPE="name" CASE="genitive">Florey's</REFEX>
  <REFEX ENTITY="1" REG08-TYPE="name" CASE="plain">Florey</REFEX>
  <REFEX ENTITY="1" REG08-TYPE="pronoun" CASE="accusative">him</REFEX>
  <REFEX ENTITY="1" REG08-TYPE="pronoun" CASE="genitive">his</REFEX>
  <REFEX ENTITY="1" REG08-TYPE="pronoun" CASE="nominative">he</REFEX>
  <REFEX ENTITY="1" REG08-TYPE="pronoun" CASE="nominative">who</REFEX>
  <REFEX ENTITY="2" REG08-TYPE="empty" CASE="no_case">_</REFEX>
  <REFEX ENTITY="2" REG08-TYPE="name" CASE="genitive">Chain's</REFEX>
  <REFEX ENTITY="2" REG08-TYPE="name" CASE="plain">Chain</REFEX>
  <REFEX ENTITY="2" REG08-TYPE="pronoun" CASE="accusative">him</REFEX>
  <REFEX ENTITY="2" REG08-TYPE="pronoun" CASE="genitive">his</REFEX>
  <REFEX ENTITY="2" REG08-TYPE="pronoun" CASE="nominative">he</REFEX>
  <REFEX ENTITY="2" REG08-TYPE="pronoun" CASE="nominative">who</REFEX>
</ALT-REFEX>
</GREC-ITEM>
```

Figure 1: Example XML-annotated text from the GREC-NEG'09 data.

with the TEXT ID, they constitute a unique identifier for a reference within the entire corpus.

A REFEX element indicates a referential expression (a word string that can be used to refer to an entity). The attributes of the REFEX element are REG08-TYPE (name, common, pronoun, empty), and CASE (nominative, accusative, etc.).

We allow arbitrary-depth embedding of references. This means that a REFEX element may have REF element(s) embedded in it. See also next but one paragraph for embedding in REFEX elements that are contained in ALT-REFEX lists.

The second (and last) component of a GREC-ITEM is an ALT-REFEX element which is a list of REFEX elements. For the GREC-NEG'09 Task, these were obtained by collecting the set of all REFEXs that are in the text, and adding several defaults including pronouns and other cases (e.g. genitive) of REs already in the list.

REF elements that are embedded in REFEX elements contained in an ALT-REFEX list have an unspecified MENTION id (the '?' value). Furthermore, such REF elements have had their enclosed REFEX removed. For example:

```
<ALT-REFEX>
  ...
  <REFEX ENTITY="2" REG08-TYPE="common" CASE="plain">
    a friend of <REF ENTITY="1" MENTION="?" SEMCAT=
    "person" SYNCAT="np" SYNFUNC="obj"></REF></REFEX>
  ...
</ALT-REFEX>
```

3 The GREC-NEG Task

The test data inputs were identical to the training/development data (Figure 1), except that REF elements in the test data do not contain a REFEX element, i.e. they are 'empty'. The task for participating systems is to select one REFEX from the ALT-REFEX list for each REF in each TEXT in the test sets. If the selected REFEX contains an embedded REF then participating systems also need to select a REFEX for this embedded REF and to set the value of its MENTION attribute. The same applies to all further embedded REFEXs, at any depth of embedding.

4 Evaluation Procedures

The GREC-NEG data set was divided into training, development and test data. We performed evaluations on the test data, using a range of different evaluation methods, including intrinsic and extrinsic, automatically assessed and human-evaluated, as described in the following sections.

Participants computed evaluation scores on the development set, using the `geval-2.0.pl` code provided by us which computes Word String Accuracy, REG'08-Type Recall and Precision, string-edit distance and BLEU.

4.1 Test sets

We created two versions of the test data for the GREC-NEG Task:

1. GREC-NEG Test Set 1a: randomly selected 10% subset (100 texts) of the GREC-People corpus (with the same proportion of texts in the 3 subdomains as in the training/development data).
2. GREC-NEG Test Set 1b: the same subset of texts as in (1a); for this set we did not use the REs in the corpus, but replaced each of them with human-selected alternatives obtained in an online experiment as described in (Belz and Varges, 2007); this test set therefore contains three versions of each text where all the REFEXs in a given version were selected by one 'author'.

Test Set 1a has a single version of each text, and the scoring metrics below that are based on counting matches (Word String Accuracy counts matching word strings, REG08-Type Recall/Precision count matching REG08-Type attribute values) simply count the number of matches a system achieves against that single text.

Test Set 1b, however, has three versions of each text, so the match-based metrics first calculate the number of matches for each of the three versions and then use (just) the highest number of matches.

4.2 Automatic intrinsic evaluations

The chief humanlikeness measures we computed were REG08-Type Recall and Precision. REG08-Type Precision is defined as the proportion of REFEXs selected by a participating system which match the reference REFEXs (where match counts are obtained as explained in the preceding section). REG08-Type Recall is defined as the proportion of reference REFEXs for which a participating system has produced a match.

The reason why we use REG08-Type Recall and Precision for GREC-NEG rather than REG08-Type Accuracy as in GREC-MSR is that in GREC-NEG (unlike in GREC-MSR) there may be a different number of REFEXs in system outputs and the reference texts in the test set (because there are embedded references in GREC-People, and systems may select REFEXs with or without embedded references for any given REF).

We also computed String Accuracy, defined as the proportion of word strings selected by a participating system that match those in the reference texts. This was computed on complete, 'flattened' word strings contained in the outermost REFEX i.e. embedded REFEX word strings were not considered separately.

We also computed BLEU-3, NIST, string-edit distance and length-normalised string-edit distance, all on word strings defined as for String Accuracy. BLEU and NIST are designed for multiple output versions, and for the string-edit metrics we computed the mean of means over the three text-level scores (computed against the three versions of a text). For details, see GREC-MSR report in this volume.

4.3 Human-assessed intrinsic evaluations

Given that the motivating application context for the GREC-NEG Task is improving referential clarity and coherence in multiply edited texts, we designed the human-assessed intrinsic evaluation as a preference-judgment test where subjects expressed their preference, in terms of two criteria, for either the original Wikipedia text or the version of it with system-generated referring expressions in it. The intrinsic human evaluation involved outputs for 30 randomly selected items from the test set from 5 of the 6 participating systems,[1] the four baselines and the original corpus texts (10 systems in total). We used a Repeated Latin Squares design which ensures that each subject sees the same number of outputs from each system and for each test set item. There were three 10x10 squares, and a total of 600 individual judgments in this evaluation (60 per system: 2 criteria x 3 articles x 10

[1]We left out UDel-NEG-1 given our limited resources and the fact that this is a kind of baseline system.

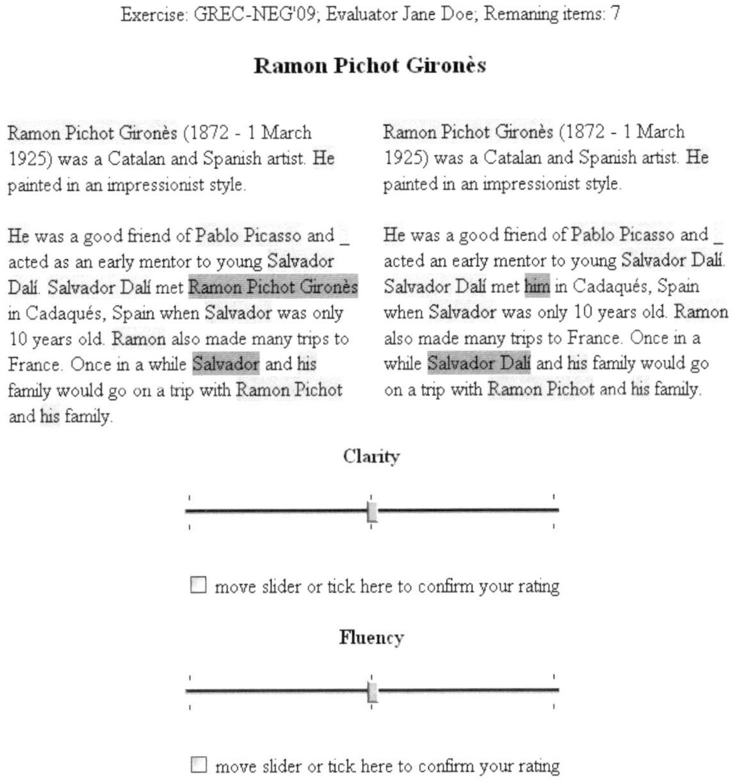

Figure 2: Example of text pair presented in human intrinsic evaluation of GREC-NEG systems.

evaluators). We recruited 10 native speakers of English from among students currently completing a linguistics-related degree at Kings College London and University College London.

Following detailed instructions, subjects did two practice examples, followed by the 30 texts to be evaluated, in random order. Subjects carried out the evaluation over the internet, at a time and place of their choosing. They were allowed to interrupt and resume the experiment (though discouraged from doing so).

Figure 2 shows what subjects saw during the evaluation of an individual text pair. The place (left/right) of the original Wikipedia article was randomly determined for each individual evaluation of a text pair. People references are highlighted in yellow/orange, those that are identical in both texts are yellow, those that are different are orange. The evaluator's task is to express their preference in terms of each quality criterion by moving the slider pointers. Moving the slider to the left means expressing a preference for the text on the left, moving it to the right means preferring the text on the right; the further to the left/right the slider is moved, the stronger the preference. The two criteria were explained in the introduction as follows (the wording of the first is from DUC):

1. **Referential Clarity**: It should be easy to identify who the referring expressions are referring to. If a person is mentioned, it should be clear what their role in the story is. So, a reference would be unclear if a person is referenced, but their identity or relation to the story remains unclear.
2. **Fluency**: A referring expression should 'read well', i.e. it should be written in good, clear English, and the use of titles and names should seem natural. Note that the Fluency criterion is independent of the Referential Clarity criterion: a reference can be perfectly clear, yet not be fluent.

It was not evident to the evaluators that sliders were associated with numerical values. Slider pointers started out in the middle of the scale (no preference). The values associated with the points on the slider ranged from -10.0 to +10.0.

4.4 Extrinsic automatic evaluation

An evaluation we piloted in REG'08 was an automatic approach to extrinsic evaluation (for a more detailed description, see the GREC-MSR results report elsewhere in this volume). The basic premise is that poorly chosen reference chains seem likely to affect the reader's ability to resolve REs. In our automatic extrinsic method, the role of the reader is played by an automatic coreference resolution tool and the expectation is that the tool performs worse (is less able to identify coreference chains) with more poorly chosen referential expressions.

To counteract the possibility of results being a function of a specific coreference resolution algorithm or tool, we used two different resolvers—those included in LingPipe[2] and OpenNLP (Morton, 2005)—and averaged results. For the same reason we used three different performance measures: MUC-6 (Vilain et al., 1995), CEAF (Luo, 2005), and B-CUBED (Bagga and Baldwin, 1998).

5 Systems

Base-rand, Base-freq, Base-1st, Base-name: We created four baseline systems each with a different way of selecting a REFEX from those REFEXS in the ALT-REFEX list that have matching entity IDs. *Base-rand* selects a REFEX at random. *Base-1st* selects the first REFEX. *Base-freq* selects the first REFEX with a REG08-TYPE that is the overall most frequent (as determined from the training/development data) given the SYNCAT, SYNFUNC and SEMCAT of the reference. *Base-name* selects the shortest REFEX with attribute REG08-TYPE=name.

UDel: The UDel-NEG-1 system is identical to the UDel system that was submitted to the GREC-MSR Task (for a description of that system see GREC-MSR'09 results report in this volume), except that it was adapted to the different data format of GREC-NEG. UDel-NEG-2 is identical to UDel-NEG-1 except that it was retrained on GREC-NEG data and the feature set was extended by entity and mention IDs. UDel-NEG-3 additionally utilised improved identification of other entities.

ICSI-CRF: The ICSI-CRF system construes the GREC-MSR task as a sequence labelling task and determines the most likely current class label given preceding labels using a Conditional Random Field model trained using the follow features for the current reference, the most recent preceding reference, and the most recent reference to the same entity: preceding and following word unigram and bigram; suffix of preceding and following word; preceding and following punctuation; reference ID; and whether this is the beginning of a paragraph. If more than one class label remains, the last in the list of possible REs in the GREC-MSR data is selected.

WLV: The WLV systems start with sentence splitting and POS tagging. WLV-STAND then employs a J48 decision tree classifier to obtain a probability for each REF/REFEX pair that it is a good pair in the current context. The context is represented by the following set of features. Features of the REFEX word string: is it the longest of the possible REFEXS; number of words; all REFEX features supplied in GREC-NEG data. Features of the REF: is it part of the first chain in the text; is it the first mention of the entity; is it at the beginning of the sentence; all REF features supplied in GREC-NEG data. Other features: do the preceding words match ", but", "and then" and similar phrases; distance in sentences to last mention; REG08-Type selected for the two preceding REFS; POS tags of 4 words before and 3 words after; correlation between SYNFUNC and CASE values; size of the chain.

WLV-BIAS is the same except that it is retrained on reweighted training instances. The reweighting scheme assigns a cost of 3 to false negatives and 1 to false positives.

6 Results

This section presents the results of all the evaluation methods described in Section 4. We start with REG08-Type Precision and Recall, the intrinsic automatic metrics which participating teams were told was going to be the chief evaluation method, followed by Word String Accuracy and other intrinsic automatic metrics (Section 6.2), the intrinsic human evaluation (Section 6.3) and the extrinsic automatic evaluation (Section 6.4).

System	REG08-Type		WS Acc.	Norm. SE
	Recall	Precision		
ICSI-CRF	83.05	83.05	0.786	0.197
WLV-BIAS	77.61	80.26	0.735	0.239
UDelNEG-3	75.27	75.27	0.333	0.636
UDelNEG-2	74.95	74.95	0.323	0.646
UDelNEG-1	68.87	68.87	0.315	0.658
WLV-STAND	66.20	68.46	0.626	0.351

Table 5: Self-reported evaluation scores for development set.

6.1 REG08-Type Precision and Recall

Participants computed scores for the development set (91 texts) themselves, using the geval evaluation tool provided by us. These scores are shown in Table 5, and are also included in the participants' reports elsewhere in this volume.[3]

REG08-Type Recall and Precision results for Test Set 1a are shown in column 2 of Table 3. As would be expected, results on the test data are

[2] http://alias-i.com/lingpipe/

[3] ICSI-CRF scores obtained directly from ISCI team.

System	REG08-Type Precision and Recall Scores against Corpus (Test Set 1a)																		
	All													Chefs		Composers		Inventors	
	Precision							Recall						R	P	R	P	R	P
ICSI-CRF	79.12	A						76.92	A					70.01	73.54	78.11	80.18	80.05	81.86
WLV-BIAS	73.77		B					72.70	A					69.82	71.52	73.53	74.38	73.65	74.56
WLV-STAND	64.49			C				63.55		B				58.28	59.70	65.38	66.14	64.78	65.59
Base-freq	61.52			C				59.6		B				49.41	51.86	63.95	65.74	60.59	62.12
UDel-NEG-2	53.21				D			51.14			C			44.38	47.17	50.50	52.22	57.88	59.80
UDel-NEG-3	52.49				D			50.45			C			43.49	46.23	49.79	51.48	57.39	59.29
UDel-NEG-1	50.47				D			48.51			C			42.90	45.60	47.78	49.41	54.43	56.23
Base-rand	43.32					E		42.00				D		38.76	40.43	41.77	43.00	45.07	46.21
Base-name	40.60					E		39.09				D		44 97	47.80	39.06	40.32	34.24	35.28
Base-1st	10.99						F	10.81					E	12.43	12.73	9.30	9.43	12.07	12.22

Table 3: REG08-Type Precision and Recall scores against corpus version of Test Set for complete set and for subdomains; homogeneous subsets (Tukey HSD, alpha = .05) for complete set only.

System	REG08-Type Precision and Recall Scores against human topline (Test Set 1b)																			
	All														Chefs		Composers		Inventors	
	Precision							Recall							R	P	R	P	R	P
Corpus	82.67	A						84.01	A						84.24	82.25	84.47	83.26	83.04	82.02
ICSI-CRF	79.33	A	B					78.38		B					76.36	77.54	78.81	79.74	79.30	80.10
WLV-BIAS	77.78		B					77.78		B					77.58	77.58	77.86	77.86	77.81	77.81
WLV-STAND	67.51			C				67.51			C				65.76	65.76	68.60	68.60	67.08	67.08
Base-freq	65.38			C				64.37			C				58.48	59.94	68.07	68.97	62.84	63.64
UDel-NEG-2	57.39				D			56.06				D			55.15	57.23	54.86	55.92	58.85	60.05
UDel-NEG-3	57.25				D			55.92				D			55.76	57.86	54.57	55.62	58.35	59.54
Base-name	55.22				D			54.01				D			54.24	56.29	57.04	58.05	48.63	49.49
UDel-NEG-1	53.57				D			52.32				D	E		51.21	53.14	50.80	51.78	55.86	57.00
Base-rand	48.46					E		47.75					E		47.88	48.77	46.44	47.13	49.88	50.51
Base-1st	12.54						F	12.54						F	13.94	13.94	10.45	10.45	14.96	14.96

Table 4: REG08-Type Recall and Precision scores against human topline version of Test Set for complete set and for subdomains; homogeneous subsets (Tukey HSD, alpha = .05) for complete set only.

somewhat worse (than on the development data). Also included in this table are results for the 4 baseline systems, and it is clear that selecting the most frequent RE type given SEMCAT, SYNFUNC and SYNCAT (as done by the Base-freq system) provides a strong baseline for RE type selection.

The last 6 columns in Table 3 contain Recall (R) and Precision (P) results for the three subdomains. For most of the systems results are slightly better for Inventors than for Composers, and better for Composers than for Chefs. A contributing factor to this may be the fact that texts in Chefs tend to be much more colloquial. Base-1st has by far the worst results; this is because it selects the empty reference in almost all cases (because ALT-REFEX lists are sorted and if a list contains an empty reference it will end up at the beginning).

We carried out univariate ANOVAs with System as the fixed factor, and 'Number of REFEXS in a text' as a random factor, and REG08-Type Recall as the dependent variable in one ANOVA, and REG08-Type Precision in the other. The result for Recall was $F_{(10,704)} = 81.547, p < 0.001$.[4] The result for Precision was $F_{(10,722)} = 79.359, p < 0.001$. The columns containing capital letters in Table 3 show the homogeneous subsets of systems as determined by a post-hoc Tukey HSD analysis. Systems whose scores are not significantly different (at the .05 level) share a letter.

Table 4 shows analogous results computed against Test Set 1b (which has three versions of each text). These should be considered as the chief results of the GREC-NEG'09 Task evaluations, as stated in the participants' guidelines. Table 4 includes results for the corpus texts, computed (as are results for the system outputs in Table 4) against the three versions of each text in Test Set 1b. We performed univariate ANOVAs with System as the fixed factor, Number of REFEXS as a random factor, and Recall as the dependent variable in one, and Precision in the other. The result for Recall was $F_{(10,724)} = 72.528$, $p < .001$), and for Precision $F_{(10,722)} = 75.476$, $p < .001$. For both cases, we compared the mean scores with Tukey's HSD. As can be seen from the resulting homogeneous subsets (letter columns in Table 4), system ranks are the same for Precision and for Recall. In terms of Precision, the difference between the corpus texts and the ICSI-CRF system was not significant.

6.2 Other automatic intrinsic metrics

In addition to the chief evaluation measure reported on in the preceding section, we computed

[4]We included the corpus texts themselves in the analysis, hence 10 degrees of freedom (11 systems).

System	String similarity against Corpus (Test Set 1a)														
	Word String Accuracy											BLEU-3	NIST	SE	norm. SE
	All								Chefs	Composers	Inventors				
ICSI-CRF	74.84	A							68.24	76.63	77.10	0.75	5.78	0.70	0.23
WLV-BIAS	68.57		B						66.35	69.08	69.47	0.76	5.62	0.82	0.29
WLV-STAND	59.55			C					54.72	61.24	60.56	0.73	5.34	1.01	0.39
Base-name	28.48				D				35.53	27.51	24.43	0.5	4.09	1.80	0.67
UDel-NEG-1	16.58					E			20.13	15.09	16.28	0.43	2.47	2.1	0.82
UDel-NEG-2	16.44					E			19.81	14.79	16.54	0.45	2.37	2.08	0.83
UDel-NEG-3	16.37					E			19.18	15.09	16.28	0.45	2.41	2.08	0.83
Base-rand	8.22						F		8.49	7.10	9.92	0.17	0.9	2.43	0.89
Base-1st	7.28						F		7.23	6.36	8.91	0.16	0.98	2.54	0.90
Base-freq	2.52							G	4.40	2.37	1.27	0.31	1.91	2.34	0.90

Table 6: Word String Accuracy, BLEU, NIST, and string-edit scores, computed on Test Set 1a (systems in order of Word String Accuracy); homogeneous subsets (Tukey HSD, alpha = .05) for String Accuracy only.

System	String similarity against human topline (Test Set 1b)															
	Word String Accuracy												BLEU-3	NIST	SE	norm. SE
	All									Chefs	Composers	Inventors				
Corpus	81.90	A								83.33	82.25	80.15	0.95	7.15	0.71	0.25
ICSI-CRF	74.55		B							71.70	75.15	75.83	0.86	6.35	0.92	0.31
WLV-BIAS	69.07			C						69.50	68.49	69.72	0.88	6.17	1.03	0.36
WLV-STAND	59.70				D					58.18	60.36	59.80	0.84	5.81	1.21	0.45
Base-name	37.27					E				42.14	36.83	34.10	0.65	5.57	1.73	0.63
UDel-NEG-1	19.25						F			22.96	17.60	19.08	0.51	2.62	2.17	0.82
UDel-NEG-2	18.96						F			22.96	17.31	18.58	0.53	2.42	2.15	0.83
UDel-NEG-3	18.89						F			22.64	17.75	17.81	0.53	2.49	2.15	0.82
Base-rand	10.45							G		10.06	9.91	11.70	0.25	1.11	2.49	0.89
Base-1st	8.65							G		8.49	7.54	10.69	0.24	1.29	2.64	0.92
Base-freq	3.24								H	4.40	3.55	1.78	0.39	2.1	2.40	0.90

Table 7: Word String Accuracy, BLEU, NIST, and string-edit scores, computed on Test Set 1b (systems in order of Word String Accuracy); homogeneous subsets (Tukey HSD, alpha = .05) for String Accuracy.

Word String Accuracy and the other string similarity metrics described in Section 4.2. The resulting scores for Test Set 1a (the corpus texts) are shown in Table 6. Ranks for peer systems relative to each other are very similar to the results reported in the last section. However, the ranks of the baseline systems have changed substantially, both in relation to each other and to the peer systems. In particular, Base-freq has moved all the way down to the bottom of the table. The reason is that this method is geared towards selecting the correct type of RE, but pays no attention to whether it selects a syntactically appropriate RE for the given context, instead simply selecting the first RE from the ALT-REFEX list that has the selected type; in the GREC-NEG'09 Task (unlike the GRE-MSR task) this just happens to be an RE in the genitive case most of the time which is overall rarer than nominative/plain. It is likely that the Word String scores for the UDel-NEG systems are low for a similar reason.

We performed a univariate ANOVA with System as the fixed factor and Number of REFEXS as a random factor and Word String Accuracy as the dependent variable. The result for System was $F_{(10,726)} = 103.339$; the homogeneous subsets resulting from the Tukey HSD post-hoc analysis are shown in columns 3–9 of Table 6.

Table 7 shows analogous results for human topline Test Set 1b (which has three versions of each text). We carried out the same kind of ANOVA as for Test Set 1a; the result for System on Word String Accuracy was $F_{(10,726)} = 106.755, p < 0.001$. System rankings and homogeneous subsets are the same as for Test Set 1a; scores across the board are somewhat higher, because of the way scores are computed for Test Set 1b: it is the highest score a system achieves (at text-level) against any of the three versions of a test set text that is taken into account.

Results for BLEU-3, NIST and the two string-edit distance metrics are shown in the rightmost 4 columns of Tables 6 and 7. Systems whose Word String Accuracy scores differ significantly are assigned the same ranks by NIST and the two string-edit distance metrics as by Word String Accuracy (except for Base-1st and Base-freq which swap ranks in some. BLEU-3 does the same and also flips ICSI-CRF and WLV-BIAS.

6.3 Human-assessed intrinsic measures

In the human intrinsic evaluation, evaluators rated system outputs in terms of whether they preferred them over the original Wikipedia texts. As a re-

Clarity										
System	Mean							+	0	−
Corpus	0	A						0	30	0
ICSI-CRF	-1.447	A	B					3	17	10
WLV-BIAS	-2.437	A	B	C				3	14	13
Base-name	-2.583		B	C				7	7	16
WLV-STAND	-4.477			C	D			1	9	20
UDelNEG-3	-6.427				D	E		1	4	26
UDelNEG-2	-6.667				D	E		1	3	26
Base-rand	-8.183					E	F	0	1	29
Base-freq	-8.26					E	F	0	0	30
Base-1st	-9.357						F	0	0	30

Fluency									
System	Mean						+	0	−
Corpus	0	A					0	30	0
ICSI-CRF	-0.353	A					9	14	7
WLV-BIAS	-2.257	A	B				2	14	14
WLV-STAND	-5.823		B	C			1	3	26
Base-name	-4.257			C	D		2	5	23
UDelNEG-3	-6.263			C	D	E	1	3	26
UDelNEG-2	-7.13				D	E	0	3	27
Base-rand	-7.513				D	E	0	0	30
Base-freq	-7.57				D	E	0	0	30
Base-1st	-8.477					E	0	0	30

Table 8: Results for Clarity and Fluency preference judgement experiment. Mean = mean of individual scores (where scores ranged from -10.0 to + 10.0); + = number of times system was preferred; − = number of times corpus text (Wikipedia) was preferred; 0 = number of times neither was preferred.

sult of the experiment we had for each system and each evaluation criterion a set of scores ranging from -10.0 to +10.0, where 0 meant no preference, negative scores meant a preference for the Wikipedia text, and positive scores a preference for the system-produced text.

The second column of the left half of Table 8 summarises the Clarity scores for each system in terms of their mean; if the mean is negative the evaluators overall preferred the Wikipedia texts, if it is positive evaluators overall preferred the system. The more negative the score, the more strongly evaluators preferred the Wikipedia texts. Columns 9-11 show corresponding counts of how many times each system was preferred (+), dispreferred (−), and neither (0), when compared to Wikipedia.

The other half of Table 8 shows corresponding results for Fluency.

We ran a factorial multivariate ANOVA with Fluency and Clarity as the dependent variables. In the first version of the ANOVA, the fixed factors were System, Evaluator and Wikipedia_Side (indicating whether the Wikipedia text was shown on the left or right during evaluation). This showed no significant effect of Wikipedia_Side on either Fluency or Clarity, and no significant interaction between any of the factors. There was however a mild effect of Evaluator on both Fluency and Clarity. We ran the ANOVA again, this time with just System and Evaluator as fixed factors. The result for System on Fluency was $F_{(9,200)} = 37.925, p < .001$, and for System on Clarity it was $F_{(9,200)} = 35.439, p < .001$. Post-hoc Tukey's HSD tests revealed the significant pairwise differences indicated by the letter columns in Table 8.

Correlation between individual Clarity and Fluency ratings as estimated with Pearson's coefficient was $r = 696, p < .01$, indicating that the two criteria covary to some extent.

Apart from Base-name and WLV-STAND switching places, system ranks are the same for Fluency and Clarity. Moreover, system ranks are very similar to those produced by the string-similarity scores above. Perhaps the most striking result is that the ICSI-CRF system does succeed in improving Fluency compared to the original Wikipedia texts: it is preferred 9 times whereas the Wikipedia texts are preferred only 7 times.

System	(MUC+CEAF+B3)/3							M	C	B3
WLV-BIAS	62.64	A						57	62	69
ICSI-CRF	61.28	A	B					53	61	69
Base-name	61.11	A	B	C				55	61	68
Corpus	59.56	A	B	C				53	59	67
UDel-NEG-3	56.13		B	C	D			48	56	65
UDel-NEG-2	55.9		B	C	D			47	55	65
Base-freq	55.85		B	C	D			47	56	65
UDel-NEG-1	54.79			C	D			46	54	64
WLV-STAND	51.69				D			41	53	61
Base-rand	34.86					E		15	38	51
Base-1st	26.36						F	2	31	46

Table 9: MUC, CEAF and B-CUBED F-Scores for all systems; homogeneous subsets (Tukey HSD), alpha = .05, for mean of F-Scores.

6.4 Automatic extrinsic measures

We fed the outputs of all 11 systems through the two coreference resolvers, and computed mean MUC, CEAF and B-CUBED F-Scores as described in Section 4.4. The second column in Table 9 shows the mean of means of these three F-Scores, to give a single overall result for each of for this evaluation method. A univariate ANOVA with (text-level) mean F-Score as the dependent variable and System as the single fixed factor revealed a significant main effect of System on mean F-Score ($F_{(10,1089)} = 91.634, p < .001$). A post-hoc comparison of the means (Tukey HSD, alpha = .05) found the significant differences indicated by the homogeneous subsets in columns 3–8 (Table 9). The numbers in the last three columns are the separate MUC, CEAF and B-CUBED F-Scores for each system, averaged over the two resolver tools (and rounded for reasons of space.

7 Concluding Remarks

This was the first time the GREC-NEG Task was run. It is a new task not only for an NLG shared-task challenge, but also as a research task in general (post-processing extractive summaries in order to improve their quality seems to be just taking off as a research subfield). There was substantial interest in the GREC-NEG Task (as indicated by the nine teams that originally registered). However, only 3 teams were ultimately able to submit a system.

In particular because of the inclusion of plural references, multiple entities per text and embedded references, the GREC-NEG Task has a higher entrance level than the GREC-MSR Task. We are planning to run it again at Generation Challenges 2010 next year, and are considering the possibility of providing participants with a baseline system which would help e.g. with processing embedded references.

We are also planning to add a named entity recognition preprocessing task, so that this new task in combination with GREC-NEG can be used to perform end-to-end post-processing of extractive summaries (and other types of multiply edited texts) to improve the clarity and fluency of the referring expressions in them.

Acknowledgments

Many thanks to the members of the Corpora and SIGGEN mailing lists, and Brighton University colleagues who helped with the online MSRE selection experiments for GREC-NEG test set 1b. Thanks are also due to the Kings College London and University College London students who helped with the intrinsic evaluation experiment.

References

A. Bagga and B. Baldwin. 1998. Algorithms for scoring coreference chains. In *Proceedings of the Linguistic Coreference Workshop at LREC'98*, pages 563–566.

A. Belz and S. Varges. 2007. The GREC corpus: Main subject reference in context. Technical Report NLTG-07-01, University of Brighton.

A. Belz, 2009. *GREC Named Entity Generation Challenge 2009: Participants' Pack.*

R. Huddleston and G. Pullum. 2002. *The Cambridge Grammar of the English Language*. Cambridge University Press.

X. Luo. 2005. On coreference resolution performance metrics. *Proc. of HLT-EMNLP*, pages 25–32.

T. Morton. 2005. *Using Semantic Relations to Improve Information Retrieval*. Ph.D. thesis, University of Pensylvania.

M. Vilain, J. Burger, J. Aberdeen, D. Connolly, and L. Hirschman. 1995. A model-theoretic coreference scoring scheme. *Proceedings of MUC-6*, pages 45–52.

ICSI-CRF: The Generation of References to the Main Subject and Named Entities using Conditional Random Fields

Benoit Favre and **Bernd Bohnet**
International Computer Science Institute
1947 Center Street. Suite 600
Berkeley, CA 94704, USA
{favre|bohnet}@icsi.berkeley.edu

Abstract

In this paper, we describe our contribution to the Generation Challenge 2009 for the tasks of generating Referring Expressions to the Main Subject References (MSR) and Named Entities Generation (NEG). To generate the referring expressions, we employ the Conditional Random Fields (CRF) learning technique due to the fact that the selection of an expression depends on the selection of the previous references. CRFs fit very well to this task since they are designed for the labeling of sequences. For the MSR task, our system has a String Accuracy of 0.68 and a REG08-Type Accuracy of 0.76 and for the NEG task a String Accuracy of 0.79 and REG08-Type Accuracy of 0.83.

1 Introduction

The GREC Generation Challenge 2009 consists of two tasks. The first task is to generate appropriate references to an entity due to a given context which is longer than a sentence. In the GREC-MSR task, data sets are provided of possible referring expressions which have to be selected. In the first shared task on same topic (Belz and Varges, 2007), the main task was to select the referring expression type correctly. In the GREC-MSR 2009 task, the main task is to select the actual word string correctly, and the main evaluation criterion is String Accuracy.

The GREC-NEG task is about the generation of references to all person entities in a context longer than a sentence. The NEG data also provides sets of possible referring expressions to each entity ("he"), groups of multiple entities ("they") and nested references ("his father").

2 System Description

Our approach relies in mapping each input expression for a given reference to a class label. We use the attributes of the REFEX tags as basic labels so that, for instance, a REFEX with attributes REG08-TYPE="pronoun" CASE="nominative" is mapped to the label "nominative_pronoun". In order to decrease the number of potential textual units for a predicted label, we derive extra label information from the text itself. For instance a qualifier "first_name" or "family_name" is added to the expressions relative to a person. Similarly, types of pronouns (he, him, his, who, whose, whom, emphasis) are specified in the class label, which is very useful for the NEG task. Only the person labels have been refined this way. While we experimented with a few approaches to remove the remaining ambiguity (same label for different text), they generally did not perform better than a random selection. We opted for a deterministic generation with the last element in the list of possibilities given a class label.

For prediction of attributes, our system uses Conditional Random Fields, as proposed by (Lafferty et al., 2001). We use chain CRFs to estimate the probability of a sequence of labels ($Y = Y_1 \dots Y_n$) given a sequence of observations ($X = X_1 \dots X_m$).

$$P(Y|X) \propto exp\left(\sum_{j=1}^{n}\sum_{i=1}^{m}\lambda_i f_i(Y_{j-1}, Y_j, X)\right) \quad (1)$$

Here, $f_i(\cdot)$ are decision functions that depend on

Proceedings of the 2009 Workshop on Language Generation and Summarisation, ACL-IJCNLP 2009, pages 99–100,
Suntec, Singapore, 6 August 2009. ©2009 ACL and AFNLP

	MSR						NEG					
Evaluation Metric	**R1**	**R2**	**S1**	**S2**	**S2R**	**S2O**	**R1**	**R2**	**S1**	**S2**	**S2R**	**S2O**
REG08 Type Accuracy	0.36	1.00	0.74	**0.75**	0.75	0.75	0.40	1.00	0.83	**0.83**	0.83	0.83
String Accuracy	0.12	0.82	0.62	**0.67**	0.66	0.75	0.12	0.70	0.52	**0.79**	0.79	0.80
Mean Edit Distance	2.52	0.31	0.95	0.85	0.87	0.72	2.38	0.61	1.07	0.53	0.52	0.49
Mean Norm. Edit Dist.	0.79	0.09	0.31	0.28	0.28	0.24	0.84	0.22	0.43	0.19	0.20	0.19
BLEU 1	0.19	0.88	0.65	0.69	0.68	0.74	0.17	0.79	0.64	0.81	0.81	0.83
BLEU 2	0.14	0.76	0.55	0.60	0.59	0.71	0.18	0.75	0.69	0.83	0.83	0.85
BLEU 3	0.10	0.69	0.51	0.56	0.55	0.70	0.18	0.73	0.71	0.83	0.84	0.86

Table 1: Results for the GREC MSR and NEG tasks. Are displayed: a random[2] output (R1), a random output when the attributes are guessed correctly (R2), the CRF system predicting basic attributes (S1), the CRF system predicting refined attributes (S2), CRF-predicted attributes with random selection of text (S2R) and CRF-predicted attributes with oracle selection of text (S2O).

the examples and a clique of boundaries close to Y_j, and λ_i is the weight of f_i estimated on training data. For our experiments, we use the CRF++ toolkit,[1] which allows binary decision functions dependent on the current label and the previous label.

All features are used for both MSR and NEG tasks, where applicable:

- word unigram and bigram before and after the reference
- morphology of the previous and next words (-ed, -ing, -s)
- punctuation type, before and after (comma, parenthesis, period, nothing)
- SYNFUNC, SYNCAT and SEMCAT
- whether or not the previous reference is about the same entity as the current one
- number of occurrence of the entity since the beginning of the text (quantized 1,2,3,4+)
- number of occurrence of the entity since the last change of entity (quantized)
- beginning of paragraph indicator

In the MSR case, this list is augmented with the features of the two previous references. In the NEG case, we use the features of the previous reference and those of the previous occurrence of the same entity.

[1]http://crfpp.sourceforge.net/

3 Results and Conclusion

Table 1 shows the results for the GREC MSR and NEG tasks.[2] We observe that for both tasks, our system exceeds the performance of a random[3] selection (columns R1 vs. S2). In the MSR task, guessing correctly the attributes seems more important than in the NEG task, as suggested by the difference in string accuracy when randomly selecting the references with the right attributes (columns R2). Generating more specific attributes from the text is especially important for the NEG task (columns S1 vs. S2). This was expected because we only refined the attributes for person entities. We also observe that a deterministic disambiguation of the references with the same attributes is not distinguishable from a random selection (columns S2 vs. S2R). However it seems that selecting the right text, as in the oracle experiment, would hardly help in the NEG task while the gap is larger for the MSR task. This shows that refined classes work well for person entities but more refinements are needed for other types (city, mountain, river...).

References

J. Lafferty, A. McCallum, and F. Pereira. 2001. *Conditional Random Fields: Probabilistic Models for Segmenting and Labeling Sequence Data.* In Proc. of ICML, pages 282-289

A. Belz and S. Varges. 2007 *Generation of Repeated References to Discourse Entities.* In Proceedings of the 11th European Workshop on Natural Language Generation (ENLG07), pages 9-16.

[2]Our system is available http://www.icsi.berkeley.edu/~favre/grec/

[3]All random experiments are averaged over 100 runs.

UDel: Generating Referring Expressions Guided by Psycholinguistic Findings

Charles Greenbacker and Kathleen McCoy
Dept. of Computer and Information Sciences
University of Delaware
Newark, Delaware, USA
[charlieg|mccoy]@cis.udel.edu

Abstract

We present an approach to generating referring expressions in context utilizing feature selection informed by psycholinguistic research. Features suggested by studies on pronoun interpretation were used to train a classifier system which determined the most appropriate selection from a list of possible references. This application demonstrates one way to help bridge the gap between computational and empirical means of reference generation.

1 Introduction

This paper provides a system report on our submission for the GREC-MSR (Main Subject References) Task, one of the two shared task competitions for Generation Challenges 2009. The objective is to select the most appropriate reference to the main subject entity from a given list of alternatives. The corpus consists of introductory sections from approximately 2,000 Wikipedia articles in which references to the main subject have been annotated (Belz and Varges, 2007). The training set contains articles from the categories of cities, countries, mountains, people, and rivers. The overall purpose is to develop guidelines for natural language generation systems to determine what forms of referential expressions are most appropriate in a particular context.

2 Method

The first step of our approach was to perform a literature survey of psycholinguistic research related to the production of referring expressions by human beings. Our intuition was that findings in this field could be used to develop a useful set of features with which to train a classifier system to perform the GREC-MSR task. Several common factors governing the interpretation of pronouns were identified by multiple authors (Arnold, 1998; Gordon and Hendrick, 1998). These included Subjecthood, Parallelism, Recency, and Ambiguity. Following (McCoy and Strube, 1999), we selected Recency as our starting point and tracked the intervals between references measured in sentences. Referring expressions which were separated from the most recent reference by more than two sentences were marked as long-distance references. To cover the Subjecthood and Parallelism factors, we extracted the syntactic category of the current and three most recent references directly from the GREC data. This information also helped us determine if the entity was the subject of the sentence at hand, as well as the two previous sentences. Additionally, we tracked whether the entity was in subject position of the sentence where the previous reference appeared. Finally, we made a simple attempt at recognizing potential interfering antecedents (Siddharthan and Copestake, 2004) occurring in the current sentence and the text since that last reference.

Observing the performance of prototyping systems led us to include boolean features indicating whether the reference immediately followed the words "and," "but," or "then," or if it appeared between a comma and the word "and." We also found that non-annotated instances of the entity's name, which actually serve as references to the name itself rather than to the entity, factor into Recency. Figure 1 provides an example of such a "non-referential instance." We added a feature to measure distance to these items, similar to the distance between references. Sentence and reference counters rounded out

Proceedings of the 2009 Workshop on Language Generation and Summarisation, ACL-IJCNLP 2009, pages 101–102,
Suntec, Singapore, 6 August 2009. ©2009 ACL and AFNLP

the full set of features.

The municipality was abolished in 1928, and the name "Mexico City" can now refer to two things.

Figure 1: Example of non-referential instance. In this sentence, "Mexico City" is not a reference to the main entity (Mexico City), but rather to the name "Mexico City."

3 System Description

A series of C5.0 decision trees (RuleQuest Research Pty Ltd, 2008) were trained to determine the most appropriate reference type for each instance in the training set. Each tree used a slightly different subset of features. It was determined that one decision tree in particular performed the best on mountain and person articles, and another tree on the remaining categories. Both of these trees were incorporated into the submitted system.

Our system first performed some preprocessing for sentence segmentation and identified any non-referential instances as described in Section 2. Next, it marshalled all of the relevant data for the feature set. These data points were used to represent the context of the referring expression and were sent to the decision trees to determine the most appropriate reference type. Once the type had been selected, the list of alternative referring expressions were scanned using a few simple rules. For the first instance of a name in an article, the longest non-emphatic name was chosen. For subsequent instances, the shortest non-emphatic name was selected. For the other 3 types, the first matching option in the list was used, backing off to a pronoun or name if the preferred type was not available.

4 Results

The performance of our system, as tested on the development set and scored by the GREC evaluation software, is offered in Table 1.

5 Conclusions

We've shown that psycholinguistic research can be helpful in determining feature selection for generating referring expressions. We suspect the performance of our system could be improved by employing more sophisticated means of sentence segmentation and named entity recognition for identifying interfering antecedents.

Table 1: Scores from GREC evaluation software.

Component Score	Value
total pairs	656
reg08 type matches	461
reg08 type accuracy	0.702743902439024
reg08 type precision	0.702743902439024
reg08 type recall	0.702743902439024
string matches	417
string accuracy	0.635670731707317
mean edit distance	0.955792682926829
mean normalised edit distance	0.338262195121951
BLEU 1 score	0.6245
BLEU 2 score	0.6103
BLEU 3 score	0.6218
BLEU 4 score	0.6048

References

Jennifer E. Arnold. 1998. *Reference Form and Discourse Patterns*. Doctoral dissertation, Department of Linguistics, Stanford University, June.

Anja Belz and Sabastian Varges. 2007. Generation of repeated references to discourse entities. In *Proceedings of the 11th European Workshop on NLG*, pages 9–16, Schloss Dagstuhl, Germany.

Peter C. Gordon and Randall Hendrick. 1998. The representation and processing of coreference in discourse. *Cognitive Science*, 22(4):389–424.

Kathleen F. McCoy and Michael Strube. 1999. Generating anaphoric expressions: Pronoun or definite description. In *Proceedings of Workshop on The Relation of Discourse/Dialogue Structure and Reference, Held in Conjunction with the 38th Annual Meeting*, pages 63 – 71, College Park, Maryland. Association for Computational Linguistics.

RuleQuest Research Pty Ltd. 2008. Data mining tools See5 and C5.0. http://www.rulequest.com/see5-info.html.

Advaith Siddharthan and Ann Copestake. 2004. Generating referring expressions in open domains. In *Proceedings of the 42th Meeting of the Association for Computational Linguistics Annual Conference*, pages 408–415, Barcelona, Spain.

JUNLG-MSR: A Machine Learning Approach of Main Subject Reference Selection with Rule Based Improvement

Samir Gupta
Department of Computer Science and Engineering, Jadavpur University.
Kolkata-700032, India.
samir.ju@gmail.com

Sivaji Bandopadhyay
Department of Computer Science and Engineering, Jadavpur University.
Kolkata-700032, India.
sivaji_cse_ju@yahoo.com

Abstract

The GREC-MSR task is to generate appropriate references to an entity in the context of a piece of discourse longer than a sentence. In MSR '09 run of this task, the main aim is to select the actual main subject reference (MSR) from a list of given referential expressions that is appropriate in context. We used a machine learning approach augmented with some rules to select the most appropriate referential expression. Our approach uses the training set for learning and then combines some of the rules found by observation to improve the system.

1 Introduction

In this paper we provide a description of our system for the GREC MSR task of Generation Challenges 2009. GREC-2.0 Corpus of 2,000 Wikipedia introduction sections in which references to the main subject of the Wikipedia article have been annotated was provided to us by the organizers. The corpus was divided into five different domains like cities, countries, mountains, people and rivers.

The basic approach we used was to develop a baseline system first by training the system on the training set. This system then selects the most frequent referential expression based on a number of parameters of the corresponding reference. After evaluation on the development set we used the development set to deduce certain rules based on observation and iteratively added these rules to the system and evaluated resulting performance. Thus the system development can be divided into two phases which are discussed in sections 2 and 3.

2 Baseline System: Training and Classification

The machine learning approach we used for the baseline system was domain independent and hence was build by populating a single database with the training set data. First we parsed the contents of the XML files of the training sets using a Java DOM XML Parser. Then we inserted the training set data into the database named grec which had two tables: parsed_ref and possible_refex. There is a one to many mapping from possible_refex to parsed_ref. The possible_refex contains all possible REFEX elements i.e. referential expressions possible while parsed_ref contains all the parsed references of the training set with attributes such as syncat, semcat, paragraph number, reference number (with respect to a paragraph), sentence number and a foreign key refex id referring to the possible_refex table.

The prediction of the referential expression was done based on features such as the semantic category, syntactic category, paragraph number, reference number with respect to a paragraph and sentence number of the referent. One example from the database is, if the semcat of the reference is cities, syncat is np-subj, paragraph number is 2, ref number is 1 and sentence number equals 1 then in 74% of the cases of the training set the referential expression was with refex id=1 (i.e. type=common, emphatic=no, head=nominal and

Proceedings of the 2009 Workshop on Language Generation and Summarisation, ACL-IJCNLP 2009, pages 103–104,
Suntec, Singapore, 6 August 2009. ©2009 ACL and AFNLP

case= plain) and refex id = 4 (i.e. type=name, emphatic=no, head=nominal and case= plain) had the second highest count (19.6%). Thus we selected the most frequent refex from the possible referential expressions corresponding to the feature set of the reference, based on their count in the training set populated database. These decision rules with their associated probabilities are stored in a table which served as our model for classification. When a number of referential expressions from the alt_refex match from the list of the given refexes then we select the refex with the longest surface form. In certain case when the refex was not in the alt_refex element we select the second best case from our decision model. Results of this intermediate baseline system are given in Table 1.

Domain	String Acc.	Reg 08 type Acc.	Mean Edit Distance	Norm. mean edit distance
Cities	0.404	0.495	1.657	0.575
Countr.	0.468	0.576	1.467	0.471
Mount.	0.567	0.646	1.192	0.380
People	0.576	0.673	0.902	0.379
Rivers	0.6	0.6	1.06	0.36
Overall	0.532	0.62	1.205	0.421

Table 1: Baseline Results

3 Rule based Improvement

After the baseline system was evaluated on the development set we iteratively added some rules to optimize the system output. These rules are applied only when a reference matches the below stated condition, otherwise the result from the baseline system was used.
The different rules that we deduced are as follows:

- The referential expression is empty if its immediate preceding word is a conjunction and the referent's syncat is np-subj. Thus the surface form of the refex is null.
- In the people domain if the best case output from the baseline results in Reg-type = "name" and if earlier in the paragraph the person's full name has been referred to, then subsequent references will have a shorter version of the referential expression i.e. shorter surface form (example: Zinn's instead of Howard Zinn's)
- If the same sentence spans two or more references then generally a pronoun form is used if a noun has been used earlier.
- Generally common form of the noun is used instead of the baseline pronoun output if words like in, for, to, of, in precedes the reference (maximum distance 3 words). This rule is applied to all domains except people.

The first and the last rules had some effect to the system but the improvement from the other rules was very negligible. Final results are tabulated in Table 2.

4 Results

We provide final results of our system in Table 2 Script geval.pl was provided by the organizers for this purpose. We see that inclusion of the above rules in the system increased it's accuracy by almost 4-5%. More rules can be added to system by studying cases of the training set which do not get classified correctly by the best case baseline system. Overall reg08 accuracy, precision and recall were 66.4 %.

Domain	String Acc.	Reg 08 type Acc.	Mean Edit Dist.	Norm. mean edit Dist.
Cities	0.434	0.525	1.596	0.544
Countr.	0.5	0.619	1.381	0.431
Mount.	0.583	0.663	1.158	0.363
People	0.659	0.756	0.746	0.296
Rivers	0.65	0.65	0.95	0.31
Overall	0.575	0.664	1.12	0.377

Table 2: Final Results

References

Anja Belz and Albert Gatt. 2008. *Grec Main Subject Reference Generation Challenge 2009: Participants' Pack.* http://www.nltg.brighton.ac.uk/research/genchal09

Anja Belz, Eric Kow, Jette Viethen, Albert Gatt. 2008. The GREC Challenge 2008: Overview and Evaluation Results. *In Proceedings of the Fifth International Natural Language Generation Conference (INLG-2008)* pages 183-192.

UDel: Extending Reference Generation to Multiple Entities

Charles Greenbacker and Kathleen McCoy
Dept. of Computer and Information Sciences
University of Delaware
Newark, Delaware, USA
[charlieg|mccoy]@cis.udel.edu

Abstract

We report on an attempt to extend a reference generation system, originally designed only for main subjects, to generate references for multiple entities in a single document. This endeavor yielded three separate systems: one utilizing the original classifier, another with a retrained classifier, and a third taking advantage of new data to improve the identification of interfering antecedents. Each subsequent system improved upon the results of the previous iteration.

1 Introduction

This paper provides a system report on our submission for the GREC-NEG (Named Entity Generation) Task, one of the two shared task competitions for Generation Challenges 2009. The objective is to select the most appropriate reference to named entities from a given list of alternatives. The corpus consists of introductory sections from approximately 1,000 Wikipedia articles in which single and plural references to all people mentioned in the text have been annotated (Belz and Varges, 2007). The training set contains articles from the categories of Chefs, Composers, and Inventors. GREC-NEG differs from the other challenge task, GREC-MSR (Main Subject References), in that systems must now account for multiple entities rather than a single main subject, and the corpus includes only articles about persons rather than a variety of topics.

2 System Description

Our GREC-NEG systems build upon our work for the GREC-MSR task. Our original approach was to consult findings in psycholinguistic research for guidance regarding appropriate feature selection for the production of referring expressions. We relied upon several common factors recognized by multiple authors (Arnold, 1998; Gordon and Hendrick, 1998), including Subjecthood, Parallelism, Recency, and Ambiguity. We followed (McCoy and Strube, 1999) who stressed the importance of Recency in reference generation. Finally, we made a preliminary attempt at identifying potential interfering antecedents that could affect the Ambiguity of pronouns (Siddharthan and Copestake, 2004).

As an initial attempt (UDel-NEG-1), we simply extended our GREC-MSR submission. By adapting our system to account for multiple entities and the slightly different data format, we were able to use the existing classifier to generate references for GREC-NEG. We suspected that accuracy could be improved by retraining the classifier, so our next system (UDel-NEG-2) added entity and mention numbers as features to train on. Presumably, this could help distinguish between the main subject and secondary entities, as well as plural references. As all named entities are tagged in the GREC-NEG corpus, we leveraged this information to improve our recognition of other antecedents interfering with pronoun usage in a third new system (UDel-NEG-3). As in our GREC-MSR submission, all three of our GREC-NEG systems trained C5.0 decision trees (RuleQuest Research Pty Ltd, 2008) on our set of features informed by psycholinguistic research.

3 Results

System performance, as tested on the development set and scored by the GREC evaluation software,

Proceedings of the 2009 Workshop on Language Generation and Summarisation, ACL-IJCNLP 2009, pages 105–106,
Suntec, Singapore, 6 August 2009. ©2009 ACL and AFNLP

is offered in Tables 1, 2, and 3. Type accuracy for UDel-NEG-1 remained close to our GREC-MSR submission, and error rate was reduced by over 20% for UDel-NEG-2 and UDel-NEG-3. However, string accuracy was very low across all three systems, as compared to GREC-MSR results.

Table 1: GREC scores for UDel-NEG-1 (unmodified).

Component Score	Value
total pairs	907
reg08 type matches	628
reg08 type accuracy	0.69239250275634
reg08 type precision	0.688699360341151
reg08 type recall	0.688699360341151
string matches	286
string accuracy	0.315325248070562
mean edit distance	1.55126791620728
mean normalised edit dist.	0.657521668367265
BLEU 1 score	0.4609
BLEU 2 score	0.5779
BLEU 3 score	0.6331
BLEU 4 score	0.6678

Table 2: GREC scores for UDel-NEG-2 (retrained).

Component Score	Value
total pairs	907
reg08 type matches	692
reg08 type accuracy	0.762954796030871
reg08 type precision	0.749466950959488
reg08 type recall	0.749466950959488
string matches	293
string accuracy	0.323042998897464
mean edit distance	1.4773980154355
mean normalised edit dist.	0.64564100951858
BLEU 1 score	0.4747
BLEU 2 score	0.6085
BLEU 3 score	0.6631
BLEU 4 score	0.6917

4 Conclusions

The original classifier performed well when extended to multiple entities, and showed marked improvement when retrained to take advantage of new data. All three systems yielded poor scores for string accuracy as compared to GREC-MSR results, suggesting an area for improvement.

Table 3: GREC scores for UDel-NEG-3 (interference).

Component Score	Value
total pairs	907
reg08 type matches	694
reg08 type accuracy	0.7651598676957
reg08 type precision	0.752665245202559
reg08 type recall	0.752665245202559
string matches	302
string accuracy	0.332965821389195
mean edit distance	1.46306504961411
mean normalised edit dist.	0.636499985162561
BLEU 1 score	0.4821
BLEU 2 score	0.6113
BLEU 3 score	0.6614
BLEU 4 score	0.6874

References

Jennifer E. Arnold. 1998. *Reference Form and Discourse Patterns*. Doctoral dissertation, Department of Linguistics, Stanford University, June.

Anja Belz and Sabastian Varges. 2007. Generation of repeated references to discourse entities. In *Proceedings of the 11th European Workshop on NLG*, pages 9–16, Schloss Dagstuhl, Germany.

Peter C. Gordon and Randall Hendrick. 1998. The representation and processing of coreference in discourse. *Cognitive Science*, 22(4):389–424.

Kathleen F. McCoy and Michael Strube. 1999. Generating anaphoric expressions: Pronoun or definite description. In *Proceedings of Workshop on The Relation of Discourse/Dialogue Structure and Reference, Held in Conjunction with the 38th Annual Meeting*, pages 63 – 71, College Park, Maryland. Association for Computational Linguistics.

RuleQuest Research Pty Ltd. 2008. Data mining tools See5 and C5.0. http://www.rulequest.com/see5-info.html.

Advaith Siddharthan and Ann Copestake. 2004. Generating referring expressions in open domains. In *Proceedings of the 42th Meeting of the Association for Computational Linguistics Annual Conference*, pages 408–415, Barcelona, Spain.

WLV: A confidence-based machine learning method for the GREC-NEG'09 task

Constantin Orăsan
RIILP
University of Wolverhampton, UK
C.Orasan@wlv.ac.uk

Iustin Dornescu
RIILP
University of Wolverhampton, UK
I.Dornescu@wlv.ac.uk

Abstract

This article presents the machine learning approach used by the University of Wolverhampton in the GREC-NEG'09 task. A classifier based on J48 decision tree and a meta-classifier were used to produce two runs. Evaluation on the development set shows that the meta-classifier achieves a better performance.

1 Introduction

The solution adopted by the University of Wolverhampton to solve the GREC-NEG task relies on machine learning. To this end, we assumed that it is possible to learn which is the correct form for a referential expression given the context in which it appears. The remainder of the paper is structured as follows: Section 2 presents the method used in this paper. Section 3 presents the evaluation results on the development set. The paper finishes with conclusions.

2 Method

The method used to solve the GREC-NEG task was inspired by the machine learning approaches employed for coreference resolution. In these methods, pairs of entities are classified as coreferential or not on the basis of a set of features (Mitkov, 2002). In the same manner, each REF element from the text to be processed is paired with all the REFEX elements in its chain and machine learning is used to determine the lexical form of which candidate REFEX element can be used in the given context. To achieve this, a set of features was derived after a corpus investigation. As can be seen, some of these features are similar to those used by resolution algorithms (e.g. distance between entities), whilst others are specific for the task (e.g. empty markers). The features used for a (REF, REFEX) pair are:

- Whether the REF element is the first mention in the chain. We noticed that in most cases it corresponds to the longest REFEX element in the *plain* case.
- Whether the REFEX element is the longest string.
- Whether the REF element is the first word in the sentence as this word is very likely to be the subject (i.e. *nominative* or *plain* case).
- Whether the words before the REF element can signal a possible empty element. Example of such phrases are ", but" and "and then". These phrases were extracted after analysing the training corpus.
- The distance in sentences to the previous REF element in the chain. This feature was used because a pronoun is more likely to be used when several mentions are in the same sentence, whilst full noun phrases are normally used if the mentions are far away or in different paragraphs.
- The REG08-TYPE of the REFEX tags that were assigned by the program to the previous 2 REF elements in the chain. This information can prove useful in conjunction with the previous feature.
- The part-of-speech tags of the four words before and three words after the REF element as a way to indicate the context in which the element appears.
- A compatibility feature which indicates pairs of SYNFUNC and CASE that are highly correlated. This correlation was determined by extracting the most frequent SYNFUNC and CASE pairs from the training corpus.

Proceedings of the 2009 Workshop on Language Generation and Summarisation, ACL-IJCNLP 2009, pages 107–108,
Suntec, Singapore, 6 August 2009. ©2009 ACL and AFNLP

- The size of the chain in elements as longer chains are more likely to contain pronouns.

- The values of SEMCAT, SYNCAT and SYNFUNC attributes of REF element and REG08-TYPE and CASE of REFEX element.

- The number of words in the REFEX value.

- Whether REF is in the first chain of the document.

The last two features were introduced in order to discriminate between candidate REFEX values that have the same *type* and *case*. For example, the number of words proved very useful when selecting genitive case names and chi-squared statistic ranks it as one of the best features together with the compatibility feature, information about previous elements in the chain and the longest REFEX candidate.

Before the features are calculated, the text is split into sentences and enriched with part-of-speech information using the OpenNLP library. [1] The instances are fed into a binary classifier that indicates whether the (REF, REFEX) pair is *good* (i.e. the REFEX element is a good filler for the REF element). Since each pair is classified independently, it is possible to have zero, one or more *good* REFEX candidates for a given REF. Therefore, the system uses the confidence returned by the classifier to rank the candidates and selects the one that has the highest probability of being *good*, regardless of the class assigned by the classifier. In this way the system selects exactly one REFEX for each REF.

3 Evaluation

The method proposed in this paper was evaluated using two classifiers, both trained on the same set of features. The first classifier is the standard J48 decision tree algorithm implemented in Weka (Witten and Frank, 2005). The run that used this classifier is referred to in the rest of the paper as *standard* run. Given the large number of negative examples present in our training data, a meta-classifier that is cost-sensitive was used for the second run. In our case, the meta-classifier relies on J48 and reweights training instances according to the total cost assigned to each class. After experimenting with different cost matrices, we decided to assign a cost of 3 to false negatives and 1 to false positives, in this way biasing the classifier towards a higher recall for YES answers. The results obtained using this meta-classifier are referred to as *biased* run. Our results on the development set are presented in Table 1.

Measure	Standard	Biased
classification accuracy	94.40%	92.09%
total pairs	907	907
reg08 type matches	621	728
reg08 type accuracy	68.46%	80.26%
reg08 type precision	68.46%	80.26%
reg08 type recall	66.20%	77.61%
string matches	568	667
string accuracy	62.62%	73.53%
mean edit distance	0.845	0.613
mean normalised edit distance	0.351	0.239

Table 1: The evaluation results on the development set

The first row in the table presents the accuracy of the classifier on the training data using 10-fold cross-validation. The very high accuracy is due to the large number of negative instances in the training data: assigning all the instances to the class NO achieves a baseline accuracy of 88.96%. The rest of the table presents the accuracy of the system on the development set using the script provided by the GREC-NEG organisers. As can be seen, the best results are obtained by the biased classifier despite performing worse at the level of classification accuracy. This can be explained by the fact that we do not use the output of the classifier directly, instead using the classification confidence.

4 Conclusions

This paper has presented our participation in the GREC-NEG task with a machine learning system. Currently the system tries to predict whether a (REF, REFEX) pair is valid, but in the future we plan to approach the task by using machine learning methods to determine the values of REG08-TYPE and CASE attributes.

References

Ruslan Mitkov. 2002. *Anaphora resolution*. Longman.

Ian H. Witten and Eibe Frank. 2005. *Data Mining: Practical Machine Learning Tools and Techniques*. Morgan Kaufmann Publishers.

[1] http://opennlp.sourceforge.net/

Author Index